Diagram shows true north

BIRTHPLACE OF THE WEST

URAL MTS.

Dnieper R.

Don R.

Volga R.

Dniester R.

CAUCASUS MTS.

BLACK SEA

CASPIAN SEA

AEGEAN SEA

Tigris R.

Euphrates R.

Jordan R.

EAN SEA

RED SEA

Nile R.

THE EMERGENCE OF EUROPE

THE STORY OF WESTERN MAN

THE EMERGENCE OF EUROPE

EUROPE AND THE MODERN WORLD

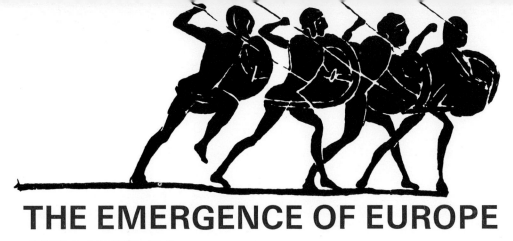

THE EMERGENCE OF EUROPE

JOHN C. RICKER, M.A., *Professor of History, The College of Education, University of Toronto*

JOHN T. SAYWELL, PH.D., *Professor of History, Dean of Arts and Science, York University, Toronto*

CLARKE, IRWIN  & COMPANY LIMITED Toronto, Vancouver

THE AUTHORS: In addition to his position as
Professor of History at The College of Education,
University of Toronto, John Ricker is the author and editor
of a number of history texts. John Saywell, Professor of
History and Dean of Arts and Science, York University, is
not only a distinguished academic figure, but also a well
known writer. The author of several full-length books,
he has been the editor of the *Canadian Annual Review*
since its inception in 1960. He is a frequent participant in
radio and television programmes dealing with history
and contemporary affairs.

Editor: RUTH BROUWER   Design: GENE ALIMAN
Special Assistance: Norma Pettit
Production director: ISOBEL WALKER

Photo research: Historical Services and Consultants Limited
                Nancy Leamen, chief researcher
Maps: Tony Bradshaw, Lewis Parker, Dudley Witney

THE COVER: *The Trojan Horse. Cerveteri: extended
Archaic vase painting. Bibliothèque Nationale, Paris. Photo
by Giraudon.*

ISBN 0-7720-0402-1

CONTENTS

PROLOGUE

3
THE ARRIVAL OF MAN

14
THE BIRTH OF CIVILIZATIONS
Civilization in the river valleys 15
The men of Han 34
Land of the pharaohs 56

78
GREECE: THE GREATNESS OF MAN
The epic of Greece 78
The glory of Greece 96

138
ROME: A STATE IN ARMS
From City-state to Empire 139
The Roman achievement 159
The City of God 184

195
THE BIRTH OF A NEW CIVILIZATION:
MEDIEVAL EUROPE
The Dark Ages: A.D. 400-1000 196
The medieval monarchies: the
emergence of England and France 211
The medieval Church 221
Moslem and Crusader 237
Village and town 250
Towards a new world: 1300-1450 270

ACKNOWLEDGEMENTS 280
PRONUNCIATION GUIDE 281
INDEX 282

MAPS

Birthplace of the West	Endpapers	Greek against Persian	116
River valley civilizations	15	The Pax Romana	148-9
The Fertile Crescent	17	The barbarian onslaught	198-9
The boundaries of empires	31	The Empire of Charlemagne	201
Land of the pharaohs	57	Europe besieged	202-3
Cradle of the West	85	The Hundred Years' War	210
Greeks overseas	88	The Unification of France	220
The conquests of Alexander	94	Highways of Commerce	260-61

Prologue

Modern Western civilization is like an iceberg. Only the tip shows. Just as the captain of a vessel in the North Atlantic must be aware of the mountain of ice beneath the iceberg's tip if he is to navigate successfully, so we must be aware of the past if we hope to understand the society in which we live. Without knowledge of the structure of an iceberg, the captain is likely to wreck his ship. Without understanding the structure upon which our civilization has been based, we are not likely to be able to preserve it.

Consider the condition of a person who was totally ignorant of the past, to whom the world and everything in it was new. He would not know how to switch on a television set, and if he were shown how to do so, the programme would have little meaning. He would know nothing of the earth on which he lived or of the differences between countries and peoples. He would have no knowledge of science and art, government, law and religion. He would be completely unaware of the achievements and ideas of men who had lived before him, of their successes and failures. Such common words as *family, property, war, democracy* and *nation* would have no meaning. He would not know what a book was, let alone how to read it. He would, in other words, be helpless as he attempted to live in the modern world.

The study of history is concerned with all of these areas of knowledge, for in the broadest sense it is the complete record of the past. It includes everything that man has done or thought or felt. Of course, our knowledge of the past can never be complete, for many of the things man has built and created have been destroyed or have decayed. Many of his thoughts and feelings were never recorded. In trying to reconstruct and explain the past, the historian must make the best use he can of the materials which remain. One of his most important sources of information is what man has written about himself and his society. But this written record contains only a fragmentary or partial account of the past, and this account has been influenced by the ideas, beliefs and experiences of the persons who wrote it. Other materials which help the historian to increase his knowledge of the past are physical objects which have survived. Often man's tools and weapons, buildings, art and sculpture tell us more about a society and the people who created it than do their written words.

Even if the historian could make use of all of the evidence which remains from the past, his account would still be incomplete. But he must, himself, select from these limited materials what he considers to be the most important in helping him to explain and make sense of the past. Furthermore, in making this selection he is likely to make mistakes, and he cannot help but be influenced by his own ideas, his likes and dislikes, and the values of the society in which he lives. And no matter how gifted he may be, he can be only partly successful in bringing to life a past in which he has played no part.

One of the surest ways to bring the past to life and to make it understandable is to let the people of the past speak for themselves. Throughout this book we have let them do just that; we have let them show us in stone and concrete, paint and glass how they saw and reacted to their world. Through the rich record of the works they created—their art, architecture and sculpture—they tell us about their gods and wars, their work and play, their government and laws, their hopes and fears.

This book, then, is theirs too, for we have let them speak with hammer and chisel, brush and pen, primitive pulley and potter's wheel.

THE EMERGENCE OF EUROPE

Scientists who study animal and plant fossils are called palaeontologists. Two of them are shown here excavating the remains of a giant prehistoric brontosaurus. Great care must be exercised by those who unearth fossil remains. Even shovels and picks are dangerous weapons, and as a result the scientists and workmen are usually more familiar with small trowels and brushes which enable them to remove earth without damaging the objects they uncover.

The arrival of man

When and how was the earth created? When did man first appear? What was he like? How did he live? We have all asked these questions. It seems likely that the very earliest men also asked them, for it is the nature of man to wonder about himself and his world.

Although we can now get to the moon, we still do not have complete or exact answers to the questions about the origin of man and his earth. Almost every day new information and evidence force scholars to change their previous opinions. Even as you read this book it may well be that fresh discoveries will have proved some of it to be wrong. This is most likely to be true of what is said about that very long period of man's existence on earth known as prehistory, the thousands of years before he left written records of his activities. But it may also be true of the period after men began to write, about 5000 to 6000 years ago, for their written accounts are often incomplete and inaccurate.

One reason that historians today know more about man's past than they did a century ago is that scholars in many different fields have provided them with a great deal of new evidence. *Archaeologists* have dug up the remains of skeletons of early man and some of his tools, weapons and pottery. These have told much about man's appearance and way of life. The examination of fossils, the remains of plants and animals embedded in rocks and earth, has made it possible to trace the development of all forms of life on earth.

Scientists have also discovered many new methods which enable them to date accurately objects over 30,000 years old. *Geologists,* through the study of rock formation, have increased our knowledge of the way in which the earth itself has changed. *Astronomers,* scanning the heavens through their telescopes, are constantly learning more about the workings of the universe of which the earth is merely a tiny speck.

One effect of these new discoveries has been to increase greatly the estimated age of the earth and the first appearance of man. We cannot say for sure either how or when the earth came into being. Scientists used to believe that it was flung off from the sun, perhaps four and a half to five billion years ago, and that for ages and ages it remained a fiery mass of boiling gases. At length, the surface cooled and became a lifeless ball of barren rocks and empty seas revolving in its orbit around the sun. Today the favourite theory is that the earth began as a small nucleus of gases that were once part of the sun. As time passed this nucleus first condensed and then was hit by other objects, and slowly grew in size.

THE WORLD BEFORE MAN

The first forms of life were apparently simple *cells* which developed in the seas perhaps two billion

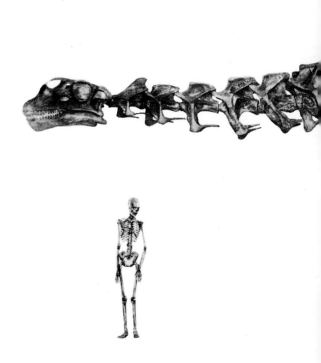

years ago. Over countless years these simple cells evolved into more complex forms of life. At first, life remained only in the seas, which teemed with all sorts of fish. For a very long time fish were the dominant form of animal life on earth. Then, about 350,000,000 years ago, plants began to appear on the land. It was now possible for animals to exist out of the water. From about 200 to 70 million B.C. various kinds of reptiles reigned supreme over the earth. Reconstructions in some museums reveal the fearsome appearance of these great, ugly creatures. Some, like huge crocodiles, crawled or walked on legs, sometimes on hind legs alone. There were enormous dinosaurs a hundred feet long whose heads towered twenty feet above the ground. Weirdest of all, perhaps, were the giant flying lizards known as *pterodactyls*. Because of their great size and strength these reptiles dominated the earth for millions of years. But when changes in climate produced new conditions to which they were not able to adjust, they eventually died out.

The next major stage in the development of life on earth took place about 60,000,000 years ago. At that time, volcanic changes began to shape the world's oceans and continents into something

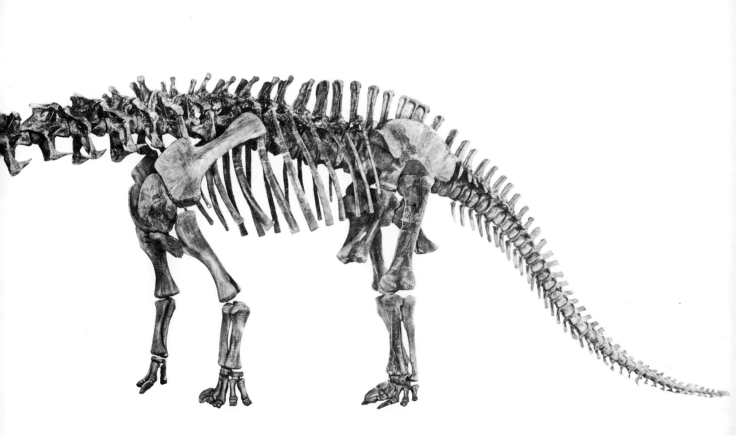

These monsters
inhabited the earth
over
one hundred million
years ago.

The skeleton of the brontosaurus, set beside that of a man, shows the immense size of these prehistoric reptiles. Up to eighty feet in length, the brontosaurus spent most of his life in the swamp, for his weight was too great to enable him to move easily on dry land. The largest "land" animal of all time, he is sometimes affectionately called the "swamp monster." His neighbour below is the allosaurus, a medium-sized dinosaur. The allosaurus, a flesh-eater, was usually over thirty-five feet in length.

like their present form. As the climate became warmer, there was increased vegetation. During this period mammals appeared, warm-blooded animals like ourselves who, unlike the reptiles, suckled their young and took care of them. Among the mammals were the earliest *primates,* the order of living creature from which man apparently developed. These included tree shrews, lemurs, tarsiers, monkeys and apes. All had hands and feet, some sense of smell, and an increased brain capacity.

A million or so years ago another great climatic change ushered in the so-called Ice Age. Four times or more, huge glaciers advanced across much of Europe, Canada and the northern United States, and Asia. These great changes in climate produced great changes in plant and animal life. As biting winds from the north swept over once-temperate regions, warm-blooded animals tried to survive by fleeing south. Some species could neither escape nor adjust to the new conditions and completely disappeared from the earth. Others, like the woolly mammoth and woolly rhinoceros, had warm, shaggy coats which protected them from the piercing cold. At the end of each glacial advance, the climate became very much warmer than it is today. As the glaciers melted, palm trees grew even in fairly northern areas. The hippopotamus wallowed in European rivers like the Thames and Rhine. The ocean levels, which had dropped as much as 300 feet, returned to their former levels. But by far the most important event of the Ice Age was the appearance of man.

No one can say for sure just when or how human beings began. All people living on the earth today belong to the species known as *homo sapiens.* Most scholars agree that homo sapiens, modern man, was not the first man-like creature on the earth. Most agree, too, although they are not sure about the details, that men evolved gradually from lower forms of life. Scientists no longer believe that man descended directly from apes, as has sometimes been claimed. They think, rather, that both men and apes had a common

ancestor. Perhaps we shall never discover the complete answer.

We do know, however, that long before men like us appeared on earth there were different kinds of man-like creatures known as *hominids.* Where or when the first hominids developed is still a mystery. Fossil skeletons have been discovered in Asia, Europe and Africa. Recent research suggests that man-like creatures possibly existed on earth 2,000,000 years ago. Not all hominids were the same in appearance or cultural development. Among the most advanced was the type known as Neanderthal man, named after a gorge in Germany where skeletal remains were first discovered. Neanderthal men have been portrayed imaginatively in comic strips and television programmes as delightful if rather odd-looking cave-men. There they wander about in animal skins and even play with pet dinosaurs—although these had been extinct for millions of years before they arrived.

We really cannot do much more than guess about their actual appearance, for fossils do not tell anything about hair, skin or colouring. However, the skeletons suggest that Neanderthal man was little more than five feet tall and had a slouching posture, a low, sloping forehead, deep-set eyes and a chinless jaw. Although he looked more like a modern man than an ape, he would certainly attract more than normal attention were he to stroll about in a modern town or city.

THE ARRIVAL OF MAN

It is impossible to state exactly when our own species of man, homo sapiens, appeared on earth. Estimates generally range from 20,000 to 50,000 years ago. The best known type of modern man is Cro-Magnon man, so-called from the cave in southern France where skeletons were found. He was a European, fairly tall and long-headed. Although there are probably no Cro-Magnons in the world today, they would not look very different from modern Europeans. At any rate, they and other races of homo sapiens spread rapidly over the earth and displaced all other species of men.

On December 18, 1912, Charles Dawson, on the left, claimed to have found the skull of a man 500,000 years old in this field at Piltdown in Sussex, England. Dawson was a lawyer, whose passionate hobby was archaeology. The top of the skull and the forehead were clearly similar to those of a modern man, but the jaw resembled that of an ape. Although some scientists doubted that the skull and jaw came from the same animal, most accepted the newly discovered Piltdown man as proof that man had evolved from the ape. The doubts, however, increased as other finds failed to support the man-ape relationship. Indeed, other discoveries showed that early man developed a jaw like that of modern man before he developed a similar forehead. Finally, in 1953, a group of British scientists decided to subject the Piltdown man to a series of exhaustive tests, none of which would have been possible in 1912. They were able to prove without any doubt that the cranium and jaw were not from the same animal; that the teeth had been filed down to make them look ancient; that the jaw must have belonged to an ape; and that the tools found with the skull were fake. Charles Dawson, or someone who was playing a trick on him, had carried out one of the greatest deceptions in history — a hoax which puzzled scientists for fifty years. The forgery shows how carefully one must examine the records of the past.

These three casts from The American Museum of Natural History reveal the main stages in man's development. The first is a model of Pithecanthropus Erectus, who lived over 300,000 years ago. His remains were first found by Eugène Dubois, a Dutchman, in Java late in the nineteenth century. The technical name reveals man's characteristics at this stage of development: an animal with an ape-like head (Pithekos is Greek for ape) who walked erect like a man (Anthropos is Greek for man). The second cast represents Neanderthal man, who lived into the last glacial age and is believed to be about 100,000 years old. He had a much greater brain capacity than the so-called Java man. The third represents Cro-Magnon man, whose skull is very similar to modern man's. Scientists estimate that he appeared in Europe about 35,000 years ago.

In a way, the very fact that man could survive and flourish is remarkable. At first sight he seems less well equipped to deal with his enemies than was a sabre-toothed tiger and less able to withstand cold than was a woolly mammoth. But, in fact, even primitive man had a number of definite advantages over all other creatures. The fact that he could walk erectly on his hind limbs meant that his hands and arms were freed for other activities than just moving himself from place to place. He was also more successful than other animals in coordinating the movements of his hands and eyes. His most important asset was a superior brain which greatly increased his ability to learn. This superior brain enabled man to remember and to develop language by which he could pass on the knowledge he had gained to his children. Some higher apes could invent an occasional tool, such as a stick used as a lever. But they lacked a language to pass on to others what they knew, and hence their inventions did not last. Since man alone has the ability to develop a language, he alone is able continually to invent and use tools. For all these reasons man was able to compete successfully against his enemies and to adjust to a changing world.

Even the most primitive man soon began to develop patterns of living or *cultures*. There are great gaps in our knowledge of man's cultural development. We know, however, that for the greatest part of human history, ninety-nine per cent of it, man lived in much the same way all over the earth. This early common culture has been given the name *Paleolithic*, which means Old Stone Age. The term arose because the tools and weapons which have survived from this period were made of stone. Actually, the term is somewhat misleading, for early man undoubtedly fashioned many things from wood and bones, but these no longer remain. At any rate, the most important feature of Paleolithic culture was not the fact that man's most important implements were made of stone. It is rather that man, during this very long period, lived as a food gatherer. He did not live as a farmer in a settled community pro-

ducing his food, but constantly roamed about, hunting and gathering it wherever it could be found.

Although man's progress seems to have been slow during the Old Stone Age, it was really remarkable. Remains of ash and charcoal show that sometime during this period he had learned how to use fire. By the end of the period he could produce fire when he wanted to by rubbing dry sticks together. This was a revolutionary achievement, for the discovery of fire was the basis for all later technological advances. Man's first tools of stone and quartz were designed to be held in the hand. They were shaped like a flattened pear with the larger end chipped so that it could be used for chopping or scraping. In time, man produced

The two imaginative reconstructions of life in the Old Stone Age are probably reasonably accurate. One group of hunters has trapped a mammoth in a pit and with their primitive weapons are attempting to kill it. Another family has seen some animals in the river below and is probably planning the best method of killing one of them.

People of the Old Stone Age had to spend much of their time just trying to stay alive in the face of such dangers as wild beasts, hunger, disease and an often harsh and changing climate. Most days were probably spent wandering through the forests in bands of fifty or sixty in search of food. It has been estimated that one person needed up to fifty square miles to find enough food with which to support himself. If this is true, then the entire population of Europe was probably fewer than 100,000 people — no more than that of a fair-sized town today.

much-improved tools for special tasks. Later discoveries reveal such tools as awls, needles and hatchets, as well as spearheads and arrowheads of flint. One of the greatest accomplishments of this era was man's gaining of the knowledge and skills to manufacture weapons from stone and wood, an achievement that made him an effective killer of animals.

About 10,000 years ago there occurred one of the most important advances in human history. For the first time man began to control his world by producing instead of gathering food. Two discoveries made this advance possible: men learned how to grow grain and how to domesticate animals. These two developments began a new era in man's cultural development, which is known as the *Neolithic* or New Stone Age.

Scholars still dispute where, when and how these changes came about. The world's first agricultural settlements appear, however, to have been those at Jericho in Palestine and Jarmo in Iraq. Scientific tests of remains date the settlements at about 7000 B.C. The first farmer was probably a woman who became interested in the fact that seeds she had dropped sprouted, for in early societies women usually gathered the grain. We can only guess, too, about how animals were first domesticated, but we do know that the earliest farm animals were cattle, goats, pigs and sheep, followed by donkeys, camels and horses. Early farmers gradually learned that raising grain and animals at the same time could be beneficial because the livestock could be fed on the stubble and grain husks and, at the same time, help to cultivate the fields. Evidence shows that early farmers had both fields and flocks.

More important than when and how it all came about were the revolutionary effects of the discovery of agriculture. Food producing made possible much greater economic and cultural growth. With an assured food supply, man could cease wandering and settle in much larger numbers in permanent villages. This greater security and leisure enabled food-producing man to increase the number, variety and quality of his material possessions. He produced new tools of ground and

Art of the hunt

We know very little about the way Paleolithic man thought. Despite their slow progress and great problems, older representatives of homo sapiens had the same physical and mental capacities as people living today. Certainly they produced remarkable art. Caves in Spain and France contain magnificent Old Stone Age paintings in vivid colours of a great variety of animals, and in some cases, of people such as the hunters in the Spanish cave (above). We cannot say for sure why these magnificent artists decorated their caves. Perhaps they were concerned mainly with the joy of creating works of lasting beauty. But since primitive man did not usually live in the caves he decorated, it seems likely that there was some other motive as well. Probably cave art had a religious purpose and was a kind of hunting magic. The artist painted the animal because he hoped to kill one and was appealing for supernatural assistance. There is some evidence to suggest that early man believed that spirits existed in all things and that his success and survival depended upon getting along with these spirits.

10

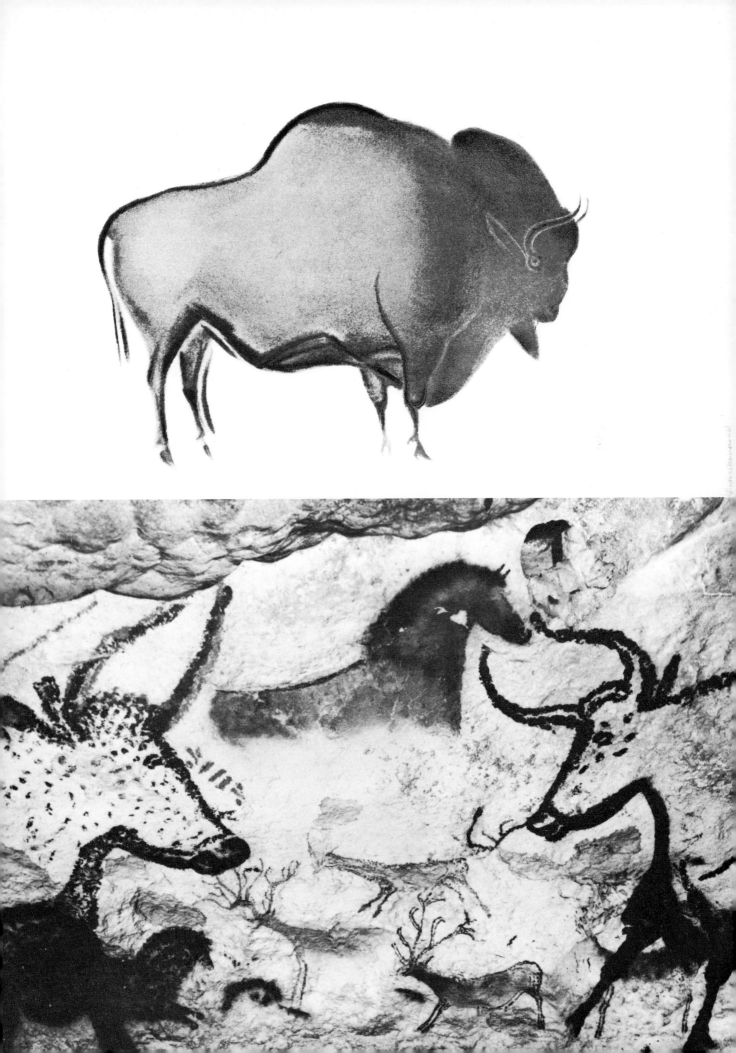

Neolithic villages were probably situated not only on fertile land, but also where they could be easily defended. The model shown above is a reconstruction of a village on a lake in Switzerland. Neolithic man used whatever building materials were at hand. In the Middle East and the Mediterranean areas, homes were built of pressed mud, which hardened with the heat of the sun, and had loose branches and a thin layer of clay for a roof. In Europe, where trees were plentiful, houses were built around a framework of poles.

polished stone such as axes, chisels, hoes and sickles. With the more efficient tools, carpenters built more comfortable houses of timber. Such domestic arts as weaving, basketwork and pottery-making developed rapidly.

The invention of the plow and the use of oxen to pull it enabled farmers to cultivate more land and thus raise more grain. This increased supply of food led to a great increase in population. From one of the most rare, homo sapiens became one of the most numerous mammals on earth. The surplus of food also made it possible for some men to specialize, to spend all of their time making special goods or providing special services for the community. And out of this specialization came the development of trade, for the new farmers often bartered or exchanged their food surpluses for other goods. These new activities broadened the economic base of society.

Other inventions appeared. Perhaps the most momentous was the discovery of the wheel, which not only caused a revolution in transportation but also greatly improved the making of pottery. In these days of rapid technological change, it is interesting to remember that man's most revolutionary achievements — the discovery of fire and the invention of the wheel — occurred very early in his development. Another discovery which quickened man's material progress was the use of metals. The first use of metals began as men found and hammered, in their natural state, lumps of gold, silver and copper which lay about on the ground. Between 3000 and 2000 B.C. man learned how to smelt, and how to extract pure copper from crude ore. He later discovered that by combining tin with copper he could produce bronze, an alloy that was much harder than copper. Bronze could also take a razor-sharp cutting edge. So valuable was it for the making of weapons and tools of all kinds that the name Bronze Age is sometimes given to this stage of man's cultural development.

The growth of population in village communities made possible by the new agriculture had great social and political effects. Since the problems of farmers were more complex than those of hunters, there was need for a more highly developed organization of society and government. The basic social unit appears to have been the family, usually combined into larger groups or clans to deal with the problems of the whole community. Co-operation was necessary to make common decisions about fields and crops, to settle legal disputes and to provide for defence. As society developed, clans united into larger family groups known as tribes. The centre of government during Neolithic times was probably the tribal chieftain. It is reasonable to suppose that he obtained his position because of his wealth or strength, his prowess as a fighter, or his ability to organize and direct the activities of the community. In time the position of chief often became hereditary, descending from father to son.

The settled life of Neolithic times also stimulated intellectual life. In the village communities legends grew up to explain the origin of the earth and man, to tell the story of man's history and to relate the deeds of great heroes. Although the legends were usually not true, men believed them and based their actions upon them. This folklore became an important part of village life and helped to create a heritage of common ideas. These ideas, along with common economic and political ties, helped to bind the community together.

Another unifying force was religion, which was a form of magic designed to explain and influence the forces of nature. Since spirits were thought to control everything from the weather and the fertility of the soil, to life and death itself, man developed elaborate ceremonies to appease them. Increasingly, the religion of Neolithic man centred around the forces of nature concerned with fertility. These were the forces that made a tiny seed spring from the earth and that added new animals to his herds. Thus, he came to place more and more faith in religious experts or priests who could see to it that the ceremonies to keep the gods and spirits happy were carried out properly. Often the priests became a special caste whose wealth and power made them the most influential group in the community. More than anyone else the priests bound the communities together by intellectual bonds as well as by economic and political ones.

The Neolithic peoples who developed the systems of agriculture, government, social institutions and religion that we have described laid the foundations for the first great civilizations. We must now turn to a study of why and how they developed in certain great river valleys. For it was in these valleys that history, the record and interpretation of civilization, was about to begin.

Using the best evidence available an artist has re-created this Neolithic field on a mural in The American Museum of Natural History. The picture suggests that while Neolithic man had settled on the land, men continued to hunt some of their food much as North American Indians did when first encountered by the white man. This is a model of a Neolithic settlement in Denmark about 2700 B.C. As will be seen, men in other parts of the world had moved well beyond the Neolithic stage of development by that time.

THE BIRTH OF CIVILIZATIONS

Civilization in the river valleys

The men of Han

Land of the pharaohs

About twenty-five miles southwest of Jerusalem lay the biblical city of Lachish. The city, with its walls and fortifications, was supposed to be impregnable to attack. But in 701 B.C. Sennacherib, King of Assyria, easily captured it and forty-five other cities in Palestine. In a scene repeated countless times in the early history of peoples in the eastern Mediterranean and the Fertile Crescent men, women and children were taken into captivity by the victors to serve as slaves. The less fortunate were executed.

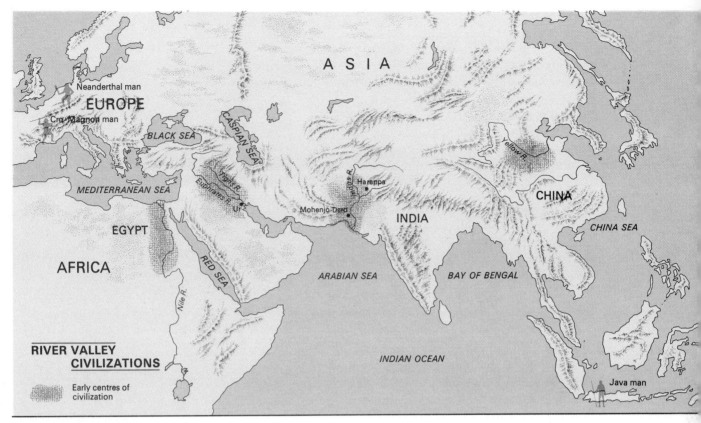

RIVER VALLEY CIVILIZATIONS

Early centres of civilization

Civilization in the river valleys

Throughout much of the world people remained in the Neolithic stage until modern times, living in small villages, weaving cloth and making pots, and using only oxen and primitive plows to gain their livelihood. In Africa, Asia and Australia one may still see such Neolithic communities inhabited by people who have a language but not writing. About five or six thousand years ago, some peoples advanced beyond the Neolithic or prehistoric period and began the first true civilizations. The word civilization comes from the Latin word for citizen, *civis*. Historians use the word to describe societies that share many common features: city life, as opposed to village communities of peasants; a government that controls a territory that can be marked off on a map; and a society with many classes—peasants, workmen, craftsmen, merchants, nobles, priests and rulers — each performing a specialized task.

We do not know exactly when and why some people moved from the Neolithic stage to create the first civilizations. What we do know is that about 4000 B.C. civilizations had developed in the fertile valley between the Tigris and Euphrates rivers in Mesopotamia, the land "between the rivers" as the Greeks named it, and on the Nile in Egypt. Soon afterwards other great civilizations emerged in the Indus Valley in India and in the valley of the Yellow River in China. The first civilizations then seem to have grown out of needs and problems that man first experienced in the river valleys. Why might there be a connection between the rise of a civilization and the river valley?

Neolithic farmers at first avoided the hot river valleys in Mesopotamia, preferring to farm the grassy uplands. Yet they must have known that if they could control the life-giving water of the river in flood-time and use it to irrigate the desert lands of the valley, they could produce much more food than on the hillsides. At some point they must have decided or they must have been forced to move into the valley. Some historians argue that changes in climate may have made the hillsides too dry for farming. Others suggest that the growth of population forced settlers to open up new lands. Still others maintain that improved farming methods gave them the confidence to try to control and use the river. Whatever the reason, by 5000 B.C. Neolithic farmers were moving into the valleys of the Tigris-Euphrates and the Nile. In doing so they were stepping boldly onto the pages of Western history and beginning one of the greatest revolutions in the story of man.

To live successfully in the valley required many more people and much greater organization than did life in the village. The settlers had to drain the stagnant pools and swamps that lay in the lower sections, build dams and dikes to control flooding, and construct a network of canals to irrigate the dry areas of the valley floor. These were not tasks for a small village community. They were projects that could only be accomplished with the wealth and organization of a city. To carry out the work, men had to create a form of government much more elaborate and powerful than the simple tribal government that had served to meet the needs of a few dozen farmers in a small village.

There had to be some ruler or central authority powerful enough to command the army of workers and officials, and to levy taxes on the people in order to finance the building of dams, dikes and canals. Moreover, the simple rules and regulations, or laws, of the village were quite in-

adequate in a city of many thousands of people. There had to be a more elaborate network of laws as well as police, courts and soldiers to see that they were obeyed.

Such a system of government and the planning and executing of great public projects could not have been achieved without some kind of written records and a number system more efficient than one which indicated *1000* simply by one thousand marks scratched on a rock. Perhaps, more than any other invention, writing had made civilization possible. Like the city, writing also developed in the river valley civilizations. The invention of writing made it possible for man to pass on his learning, inventions and thought from one gen-

These Babylonian clay tablets provide a good illustration of the early form of writing in the Fertile Crescent. This script was called cuneiform, *from the Latin word* cuneus *meaning wedge. The writing consisted of wedge-shaped marks made on tablets of wet clay with a special type of stilus or pen. Like Chinese writing, it is a difficult system to master, for it contains hundreds of characters.*

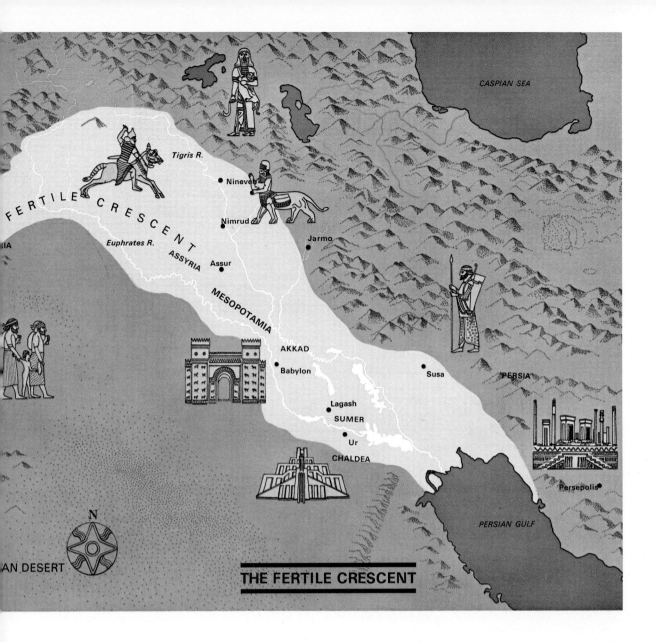

THE FERTILE CRESCENT

eration to the next. It enabled him to take great forward strides in mathematics, science, literature and law. Finally, it provides the historian with the most important evidence he needs to reconstruct the past. History properly begins with the invention of writing in these first civilizations.

WAR AND PEACE IN THE FERTILE CRESCENT

From the Persian Gulf to the southeastern shore of the Mediterranean stretches an arc of good land known as the Fertile Crescent, one of the cradle lands of Western civilization. The eastern part of the arc, which runs between the Tigris and Euphrates rivers, is usually called Mesopotamia. In the south of this valley, where the rivers begin

the last two hundred miles of their race to the sea, began one of the earliest civilizations.

More and more, as men moved into the valley, villages grew into cities, each with its surrounding farmland. The population grew and the city expanded to become a city-state. Continued expansion brought the city-states into conflict with one another, and their wars led to the creation of kingdoms. In the same way, wars between kingdoms led to the creation of giant empires. Sometimes the kingdoms and empires in the valley fell before new conquerors from outside, who, though less civilized, were usually tougher, more aggressive and more highly skilled in warfare than the valley farmers. For over 2500 years all of Mesopotamia

17

This diorama shows a typical street scene in the working class area of Ur, capital city of Sumeria, about 2000 B.C. Like most other cities in the Fertile Crescent, Ur was surrounded by a moat and a wall of baked brick. Inside the gates soldiers policed the streets. Behind the streets stretched small pathways and alleys along which the great mass of people lived in small, flat-roofed huts such as these. From these huts the farmers walked to the fields outside the city every day. Many of them kept some animals in their mud-brick homes in the city. Looming over the city were the temples. Each city had its god and built a temple for him on an elevated mound called a ziggurat.

was a battleground as one people after another fought for control.

Despite the centuries of conflict, men throughout the valley lived and worked, governed and worshipped in much the same way. The government was usually headed by a powerful king or emperor, who acted as war leader, judge and high priest, and who was often regarded as a representative of the gods. Assisting him was a large civil service of military, civilian and religious officials, all of whom enjoyed great power and privilege in the state. The mass of the people, heavily taxed to support the king and his officials, had no voice in the government or state.

Among the Assyrians, hunting was regarded not only as the sport of kings, but as the best training for the battlefield. The most famous hunting scenes show Asurbanipal, King of Assyria from 668-631 B.C., armed with a bow and arrow either on horseback or in a chariot. The detailed and forceful relief (left) of Asurbanipal at the lion hunt shows something of the Assyrians' skill as marksmen. Lion hunting was not exactly a fair sport, for the lions were first captured and then let loose as the king arrived for the hunt. However, destruction of the lions seems also to have been a necessity. As Asurbanipal apparently said, the lions "kept bringing down the cattle of the plain, they kept shedding the blood of men." The same emphasis on the Assyrians' prowess is shown in the reliefs dealing with war. The relief (right) shows Asurbanipal leading an assault on a city. The decapitated bodies of the enemy reveal the bloodthirstiness of Assyrian warriors.

Each new civilization of the region rapidly developed a rigid system of classes. At the top was the king and his family, followed by his host of officials. Among these the priests were extremely important, for their temples were the main religious centres. They also owned much of the farmland, which they either rented to peasants or farmed with gangs of hired men under a foreman. Acting in the name of the gods, the priests often controlled markets, banks, fleets of ships, caravans and a wide variety of manufacturing shops.

Manufacturing and trade were carried on by a small class of artisans and merchants. The latter developed a considerable trade in luxury goods — precious stones, metals and spices — to serve the demands of the upper class. Some traded along the rivers and the Mediterranean coast, but most of the trade moved in the caravan trains across the hills and deserts to central Asia, India, Syria and Egypt. But probably nine out of ten people worked on the land. These were illiterate peasants who lived in mud huts in the city slums or in small villages outside the walls. Although their lives were fairly secure, they shared in few other benefits of civilization. They had to pay heavy taxes in produce or silver to the king or temples.

They were forced to build and maintain the dikes, the canals and the city walls. In time of war they were drafted to serve in the army.

Even worse off were most of the slaves, the lowest class in society. Some men were forced to sell themselves and their families into slavery to repay their debts. Prisoners of war were another source of slaves. Once a person became a slave he lost all rights and could be treated like any other piece of property. Temples and palaces were often built with slave labour, and slaves were the servants in the homes of the wealthy.

One of the earliest peoples to develop this pattern of Near Eastern civilization were the Sumerians. Sometime before 3000 B.C. they had established cities such as Ur and Lagash near the mouth of the Tigris-Euphrates. Among the achievements of the brilliant Sumerians was the invention of a calendar by which they could regulate their sowing and reaping. They also learned how to make copper tools, and bricks for buildings. Within their cities, literature, the arts and trade flourished. It was probably the need to keep business records that led to the development of writing, one of their greatest accomplishments. The Sumerians also revealed their genius in the

creation of a number system based on 60. The Western world still uses this system to divide the hour into 60 minutes, the minute into 60 seconds, and the circle into 360 degrees.

About 2400 B.C. the Sumerians were overthrown by the Akkadians, a people who lived to the north of Sumer. Under their great leader, Sargon, the Akkadians founded the world's first empire extending from the Persian Gulf to the Mediterranean. Further conquests followed as successive waves of barbarians fought for the choice settled land. About 1900 B.C. the Amorites from the west gained control of Mesopotamia. They established their capital at Babylon, which became the most magnificent city of the ancient world. Eventually, under their young king, Hammurabi, they brought all of lower Mesopotamia within a new empire.

Shortly after Hammurabi's death a new wave of invading people, the Hittites, swept in from their mountain home land in Asia Minor and toppled his empire. Between 1700 and 1200 B.C. they extended their rule over Mesopotamia, Syria and much of Asia Minor. One reason for their success was their possession of iron weapons, which were far more effective than the bronze ones of their enemies. The Hittites were probably the first people in the world to master the art of producing good quality iron in large amounts. They guarded the secret of iron smelting for many years, but after their empire also collapsed, the use of iron spread throughout the Near East.

The collapse of the Hittites paved the way for the rise of a new power, Assyria. The Assyrians came originally from northern Mesopotamia and began their expansion in the ninth century. They were warriors and empire builders, the most savage of all the conquerors of the Fertile Crescent. Under them, warfare developed into an exact science. Led by outstanding rulers they established the largest empire yet known in the world. At its height, it included most of the Near East as well as Egypt.

The Assyrians, however, made more positive contributions to civilization than the arts of war. Their system of governing their empire served as a model to later empire builders. Their splendid capital city, Ninevah, boasted what was probably the world's first aqueduct to bring water into the city. They were also brilliant artists; their relief carvings of animals have never been surpassed. But at length, the Assyrians found their sprawling empire too large to control, and they too fell before an alliance of the peoples they had conquered. With the destruction of Ninevah in 612 B.C., the Assyrians vanish from history.

For a brief period the Chaldeans gained control of the Fertile Crescent and established a second Babylonian Empire. Their most famous ruler, Nebuchadnezzar, restored the ancient city of Babylon to its former glory and built the mag-

Grandeur in stone

The magnificent capital built by the Persians at Persepolis was under construction from 520 to 460 B.C. Only quiet ruins now are witness to the striking events that took place there 2500 years ago. Everything in the Persian capital was designed to stimulate a sense of pride and nationality and to portray the greatness of the emperor and the Empire. The greatest ceremony of all was on New Year's Day when the great men of the Empire and the delegations of subject peoples arrived to pay their respects and to bring tribute. The scenes (top and bottom) pictured on the walls of the giant stairways leading to the King of Kings gave the guests a preview of the scene about to unfold, and tell the historian what it must have been like. A relief from the throne room (centre) shows lines of Persians and Medes (the Medes were the second dominant people in the empire), dignitaries marching in the solemn New Year's procession. Some of the Medes, in their round bonnets, are in knee-length tunics and tight-fitting trousers, the uniform of the royal horse guards. Others wear a cloak over their shoulders. The Persians have either a short sword in their belt or a sheath for arrows.

"Let any oppressed man who has a cause come into the presence of the statute of me, the king of justice, and then read carefully my inscribed stele [a pillar of stone] . . . .may he understand his cause; may he set his mind at ease!" So wrote Hammurabi on the giant pillar recording his code of laws. The pillar contains 3600 lines, at the top of which is a relief eight feet tall showing Hammurabi being ordered by Shamash, the sun god, to write down the law. The young ruler did not make new laws, but rather revised and improved existing ones. Their importance lies in the fact that they were written down; thus, they were always the same and everyone could know what the law was. Although the code was based on the principle of revenge — "an eye for an eye and a tooth for a tooth" — it was a great advance, for it was applied uniformly throughout the whole Babylonian Empire. Hammurabi prided himself on his treatment of the subject peoples in his empire. As he had written: "I sought out peaceful regions for them; I overcame grievous difficulties, I caused light to rise on them . . . I made an end of war."

nificent hanging gardens, known in ancient times as one of the seven wonders of the world. Nebuchadnezzar is best remembered, however, for the sack of Jerusalem and the deportation of many Hebrews to Babylonia — the so-called Babylonian Captivity described in the Bible. Shortly after this, in 538 B.C., the Chaldeans themselves went down to defeat before the invading Persians under their great king, Cyrus.

The Persians created the last and greatest of the Near Eastern empires. The Persian Empire lasted for two hundred years and at its greatest extent, stretched from northwest India to the shores of the Mediterranean. Only the Greeks were able to withstand the Persian advance and ultimately to defeat them. But the Persians were more than conquerors. They were brilliant rulers and administrators who organized their territories into well-governed provinces linked by a magnificent system of highways. Probably the greatest, and certainly the most lasting, of the Persians' contributions to civilization was their religion. Unlike most ancient religions, the Persian faith stressed that man was responsible for his actions. It taught that all life was a struggle between good and evil. Man was free to choose either. If he chose the side of right against evil, he would enjoy an after-life in heaven following a last judgement. Persian religious ideas and practices had a tremendous influence on the development of three other great religions: Judaism, Christianity and Islam.

Not all of the people of the Near East who contributed to Western civilization were great empire builders like the Persians and Assyrians. A small group known as Phoenicians formed an independent state, after the collapse of the Hittite Empire, in what is now Lebanon. The Phoenicians were adventurous sailors and traders whose ships ranged throughout the Mediterranean, reached Britain, and may even have sailed around Africa. In addition to trading, they also established many colonies, among them Carthage in North Africa, which one day would rule a great empire of its own. Through their trade and colonization the Phoenicians spread Near Eastern civilization throughout the Mediterranean world. Their most important and lasting achievement was a simplified alphabet of twenty-two letters which later became the basis of Latin writing and eventually of the writing of the West today.

THE MIRACLE OF SINAI

Looking back on the troubled history of the Fertile Crescent today, however, it is clear that the most important people were not the Sumerians, the Assyrians or the Phoenicians. They were not people who built empires or left giant monuments in stone. They were a people who made the names David, Solomon, Abraham and Moses part of the lasting inheritance of the Western world. They were the people who created one of the world's most enduring and influential religions. They were the Hebrews.

From the Old Testament and a wide variety of other sources, historians have been able to piece together the long and involved history of the early Hebrews. About two thousand years before Christ, the Jews left Mesopotamia for the western hill country and the Negev desert, led by their tribal leader, Abraham. For centuries they wandered as nomads, following their flocks through the for-

This mosaic from the ancient synagogue of Beth Alpha in Israel illustrates one of the most famous stories in the Old Testament. In the scene shown here, Abraham, who is considered the ancestor of all the Hebrews, is about to sacrifice his beloved son, Isaac, in response to God's command. But God spoke to Abraham once again, saying, "Lay not thy hand upon the lad." Abraham's faith had stood even this supreme test, and at the final moment, Isaac was saved. A ram was substituted for the human sacrifice.

bidding deserts and highlands. One group apparently settled in Egypt, but about 1300 B.C., when conditions became too harsh, they followed Moses from "the land of bondage." Gradually they crossed the Jordan River into the land of Canaan or Palestine and lived alongside the Canaanites.

Before long, however, they were threatened by the Philistines, another group of invaders who had settled along the Mediterranean coast. Faced with disaster, the Hebrew tribes united under Saul, and later under David and Solomon, to check the advance of the Philistines. The result was the creation of a powerful kingdom under David and Solomon with a magnificent capital at Jerusalem.

With the death of Solomon in 925 B.C. the kingdom split into two parts: Israel in the north and Judah in the south. But the two kingdoms were too small and weak to defend themselves against the mighty Near Eastern empires. Between 733 and 721 B.C. the Assyrians conquered Israel; Judah fell to the Babylonian king, Nebuchadnezzar in 586 B.C. During the next 600 years Persia, Macedon and Rome in turn became the ruling power in Jerusalem. Finally in A.D. 70 Roman soldiers punished a Jewish revolution by destroying the temple and killing or enslaving thousands of the inhabitants of Jerusalem. The remaining Hebrews were scattered throughout the ancient world in what is called the "great dispersion." Not until modern times was there to be another state of Israel. Yet for almost 2000 years the Jewish people throughout the world have remained united by their devotion to the religion and law of Judaism.

Like most other peoples in the Fertile Crescent, the Hebrews at first believed in many gods. Among these was Yahweh, or Jehovah, sometimes thought of as the god of war and storms. During their exodus from Egypt, however, the followers of Moses had a dramatic religious experience. According to the Old Testament, when they reached the foot of Mount Sinai Jehovah revealed himself to Moses from the clouds surrounding the mountain peak. A covenant or contract was made. Through Moses, the Hebrews promised to wor-

The Bible as history

The fall of Israel came at a time when the kingdom was enjoying great prosperity. According to the prophets Amos and Hosea the moral decay in Israel was certain to result in catastrophe. As they thundered against the luxury and injustice they saw about them, Tiglathpileser III (745-727 B.C.), the King of Assyria, was preparing to march against Israel. With a huge army of infantry, chariots and cavalry he fell upon the northern kingdom. The Assyrian relief (right) from his palace at Nimrud shows the troops scaling the walls of a city, which they soon would destroy and plunder. Although this description from Ezekiel (26:9) refers to a Babylonian attack on another city, it seems strikingly apt here: "And he shall set engines of war against thy walls, and with his axes he shall break down thy towers."

"In the third month, when the children of Israel were gone forth out of the land of Egypt, the same day they came into the wilderness of Sinai . . . and there Israel camped before the mount. And Moses went up unto God, and the Lord called unto him out of the mountain, saying, Thus shalt thou say to the house of Jacob . . . Now, therefore, if ye will obey my voice indeed, and keep my covenant, then ye shall be a peculiar treasure unto me above all people: for all the earth is mine: And ye shall be unto me a kingdom of priests, and a holy nation. These are the words which thou shalt speak unto the children of Israel."

In these words the book of Exodus (19: 1-6) tells of the miracle at Sinai, the red granite mountain (above) that thrusts out of the desert. Nomads, like those pictured here beneath its peaks, were to carry this message first to their people and then to transmit it throughout the earth. According to Exodus, it was at Mount Sinai that Moses received the Ten Commandments: "And God spake all these words, saying, I am the Lord thy God . . . Thou shalt have no other gods before me. Thou shalt not make unto thee any graven image . . . Thou shalt not bow down thyself to them, nor serve them: for I the Lord thy God am a jealous God . . . Thou shalt not take the name of the Lord thy God in vain . . . Remember the sabbath day, to keep it holy . . . Honour thy father and thy mother . . . Thou shalt not kill. Thou shalt not commit adultery. Thou shalt not steal. Thou shalt not bear false witness against thy neighbour. Thou shalt not covet . . . ."

The invasion of Israel by Tiglathpileser III (called Pul in the Bible) in 733 B.C. resulted also in the conquest of most of Galilee and what is now Transjordan. Ten years later his successor completed the conquest. Tiglathpileser carried many Hebrews to exile in Assyria. His successor, Sargon II, drove large numbers of the remaining inhabitants, chiefly the upper classes, from the kingdom and scattered them throughout his empire. The tribes of the northern kingdom were no more, and are known to history as the Lost Ten Tribes. Probably they were absorbed by other peoples in the Fertile Crescent. "I beseiged and captured Samaria, and carried off 27,290 of its inhabitants as booty," reads Sargon II's victory statement. The Book of Kings recounts: "Then the king of Assyria came up throughout all the land. . . . In the ninth year of [King] Hoshea the king of Assyria took Samaria, and carried Israel away into Assyria . . . ."

With the final capture of Jerusalem by Nebuchadnezzar in 586 B.C. many of the inhabitants were sent to exile in Babylon. The event is described in II Kings:
"And he carried away all Jerusalem, and all the princes, and all the mighty men of valour, even ten thousand captives, and all the craftsmen and smiths: none remained save the poorest sort of the people of the land." This relief (right) showing captives being driven into exile is Assyrian, but from it one can probably get a fairly good idea of the kind of scene the writer was describing in II Kings.

ship only Jehovah and to obey his laws, including the Ten Commandments which Moses received at Mount Sinai. Jehovah undertook to care for the Hebrews in the future as he had during the flight from Egypt.

These early Hebrews did not believe that Jehovah was the only god in the universe or that he was the god of all peoples. The first commandment states only that "thou shalt have no other gods before me." They did think of him as a personal god, not in the sense that he was a physical being, but in the sense that he was present and played an important part in the lives of all men. In the biblical account he appears first as a stern and jealous god who would wrathfully punish those who disobeyed his commands.

Although an increasing number of Hebrews gradually became followers of Yahweh, it was not until the reigns of Saul, David and Solomon that almost all accepted him. Jerusalem, with its great temple built by Solomon, became the centre for his worship. Yet strangely enough, it was during the centuries after their power began to decline that the Hebrews developed their deepest and most influential religious ideas. The suffering caused by the division of their kingdom into the two rival states of Israel and Judah, and foreign invasion led the Hebrews to re-examine their religious ideas and life. Leading the movement were a group of great religious leaders known as the prophets. These men were preachers who believed that because they were in direct contact with God, their words expressed the divine will. They condemned social evils and bitterly attacked those Hebrews who had forsaken simple virtues to live in luxury and corruption. They particularly denounced those who had given up Yahweh to wor-

ship other gods. Although they were often treated harshly, the prophets refused to remain silent.

The teaching of the prophets changed the course of world history, for it was their ideas that formed the main part of Hebrew religion and influenced other great religions throughout many parts of the world. The prophets were the first to insist that Yahweh was the only god, not just the god of the Hebrews but a universal god of all peoples.

The prophets also preached new ideas about the nature of Yahweh. According to their teaching, he was not just an all-powerful heavenly judge who was angry in his treatment of sinners. He came to be looked upon also as a kind and gentle father full of love for all mankind.

The prophets taught that men should treat each other with the justice and decency with which Yahweh treated them. Men would be judged, they said, by their moral conduct and not by their wealth or power, or their observance of religious practices. There was no mystery about the way men should behave on earth, for Yahweh had made his will known in a code of law known as the Torah. The Torah means "law of teaching," and is generally taken to include the first five books of the Old Testament.

By the fourth century B.C. when Alexander the Great of Macedon had conquered all the Near East, the Hebrews had won few converts to their religion or their god. Yet both the Hebrews and their faith survived and their religious ideas became the base upon which Christians and Mohammedans developed their religions. The influence of Judaism has been so great that it has often been said that "Western civilization walks on two legs, one of which is Greek and the other Hebrew."

An Egyptian wall relief shows Ramses, a New Kingdom Pharaoh, on his battle chariot. The horse had been unknown in Egypt before the Hyksos invasion, but the Egyptians soon mastered the art of fighting with horse and chariot. Their horses apparently were not strong, for the artist here reveals that two were harnessed to the chariot. The chariots themselves were light and provided no protection for the occupant. The relief also shows clearly the nature of Egyptian writing. The hieroglyphics above probably tell the story of Ramses' great triumphs over the enemy.

THE VALLEY OF THE NILE

While empires rose and fell in the lands of the Fertile Crescent, Egyptians in the valley of the Nile were creating a brilliant and stable civilization. At first sight, Egypt seems an unlikely place for such a development. More than nine-tenths of the country is desert and there is almost no rain. Only the miraculous flooding of the Nile made civilization possible. As a Greek historian remarked, Egypt is "the gift of the Nile."

Once a year the Nile overflows its banks and deposits a thin layer of life-giving topsoil which makes the land fertile and productive. The river is a gift in another way, for it serves as Egypt's main artery of trade and communication. Since the Nile is the only source of water, Egypt's habitable area is limited to the narrow ribbon of land on either bank of the river which the flood waters can reach. This area stretches for about 800 miles southward from the delta on the Mediterranean Sea, and is never more than fourteen miles in

Almost in the shadow of the pyramids a present-day Egyptian farmer cultivates his field with the same type of primitive plough and skinny oxen that his ancestors used thousands of years before.

width. On either side of the narrow, fertile strip stretch miles of forbidding desert scorched by the relentless sun. Though useless for settlement, the deserts discouraged invading armies from east and west. The Mediterranean Sea also served as a protecting shield, for only a strong naval power could hope to invade Egypt successfully from the north. Behind their natural defences, the desert and the sea, the Egyptians were able to develop a more stable society than was possible for the peoples of the unprotected Fertile Crescent.

The beginnings of Egyptian civilization go back beyond 3000 B.C. when Neolithic farmers moved from their drying lands into the well-watered Nile Valley. Here they faced difficult problems, for to farm successfully they had to control the annual floods. To ensure that the water would bring life and not disaster, they had to build dams, dikes and canals. They had to guard against flood damage and at the same time store up the water so that it could be used for irrigation. Such great engineering projects could not be done by individuals

in a haphazard way. To complete them successfully able leadership was required as well as the co-operative effort of thousands of people. This need stimulated the creation of large organized communities or states with strong governments. About 3000 B.C., according to tradition, a king named Menes united all the city-states of Egypt into a single kingdom. This early achievement of political unity was important. It lessened conflict within the country and made possible the rapid development of Egyptian civilization.

Following unification, Egypt went through three periods of growth and decline: the Old (c. 2700 - 2200 B.C.), Middle (c. 2100 - 2000 B.C.), and New (1580 - 1090 B.C.) Kingdoms. There were fairly long periods of strong government, prosperity and expansion interspersed with periods of political unrest. But despite these ups and downs, Egyptian culture and society remained remarkably unchanged.

During the period of the Old Kingdom a number of able kings or *pharaohs* ruled Egypt from their capital city, Memphis, near the head of the Nile Delta. The years were peaceful and prosperous with a flourishing agriculture and increasing trade. It was during this period that the Egyptians established the basic forms of their art, architecture and government. They developed writing and built most of the great limestone pyramids which were to serve as tombs for their rulers. But after about five centuries of order and progress, the Old Kingdom began to decline and the pharaoh lost much of his power to nobles and priests. There is no agreement about the reasons for this decline, but historians have suggested a number of possible causes. The cost of pyramid building may have been too great a strain on the royal treasury. Possibly the high taxes necessary to finance such projects led to widespread unrest and revolt. Some kings may simply have lacked the ability to rule effectively. Whatever the reasons, the decline of the Old Kingdom was followed by a hundred years of weak government and social unrest.

Strong kings gradually restored order and established the Middle Kingdom with a new capital further up the Nile at Thebes. Although it lasted for only a century, the period was one of great accomplishment. But eventually weak rule paved the way for invasion by barbarians from Asia Minor, known as Hyksos. Equipped with horses and war chariots, they easily conquered the Egyptians. The Hyksos, or "Shepherd Kings" ruled until 1580 B.C. when they in turn were overthrown by a new line of Egyptian warrior-pharaohs. Under these new rulers Egypt entered upon the last great era of her history, the New Kingdom or Empire.

During the Empire period, Egypt expanded east and north into Palestine and Syria and southward to Nubia and Sudan. The conquest of new territories led to increased trade. Thebes became for a time the greatest city in the western world with wealth pouring in from subject territories. The colossal temples and monuments at Karnak and Luxor are among the most dramatic signs of the

A modern Egyptian peasant is shown here working irrigation equipment similar to that used four thousand years ago. Water is still as precious to the Egyptian farmer as it was when this system was first introduced. In the distance the great pyramids stand silhouetted against the sky.

wealth and splendour of the New Kingdom. But finally, the high costs of maintaining her sprawling empire weakened Egypt's economy. By the fourteenth century the Empire had begun to crumble. During a long period of decline, Egypt fell under the control of a succession of foreign powers which included Assyria and Persia. Egyptian attempts to regain control were unsuccessful. When Alexander the Great added Egypt to his vast empire in 332 B.C., he had finally brought an end to thirty Egyptian dynasties which had governed Egypt for 3000 years.

Throughout the thousands of years of Egyptian history there were few changes in the way most Egyptians lived. There were few sudden breaks with the past. For the most part government was carried on by the pharaohs and their officials. When times were peaceful and prosperous, the pharaohs usually had enormous personal power. In periods of unrest they sometimes had to share power with groups of nobles and priests. At no time, however, did the common people have any control over Egyptian affairs. Everything was planned and regulated from above.

Few ancient civilizations have had a greater influence on the modern world than the Egyptian. This is not surprising, for the Egyptians were among the first people to develop a great civilization. Important elements of government, law, science, mathematics, engineering and art had their beginnings in Egypt. From Egypt came one of the world's earliest organized systems of government and law, and one of the earliest forms of writing. The ideas and practices of Egyptian architects and engineers, craftsmen and farmers were widely used by later peoples. Egyptian scientists invented a solar calendar which the modern world still uses in a modified form. The Egyptians also developed a useful system of mathematics. They were the first people to develop a religion based on a belief in one god who was the father of all men, and they were among the first to teach that all men could win everlasting life. Finally, Egyptian artists have left works of such warmth and skill that they have inspired artists ever since.

THE EMERGENCE OF CHINA

About 4000 years ago Chinese civilization began to develop in the fertile and protected valley of the Yellow River which flows across the great plain of Northern China. By the time of the birth of Christ, Chinese civilization had spread over much of North China. Later, a second major centre of Chinese society developed in the valley of the Yangtze River, which today is the most densely populated part of China.

Throughout these long centuries China's story is one of conflict, change and achievement. Time and again the rich river valleys echoed with the clash of battle, as waves of invading armies tried to conquer them. Often the invaders were successful because they had better weapons and techniques of warfare. Sometimes the victorious peoples grew weak and soft and fell before other invaders. Within China one powerful family after another tried to gain political power and extend its control over the whole country. Some families or dynasties were successful and ruled for several centuries. Others were short-lived and were overthrown by hardier and more energetic peoples under more capable rulers. The pattern of invasion was repeated many times. One dynasty followed another until 1911 when a successful revolution finally destroyed China's last great ruling family. Yet despite the centuries of warfare and invasion, the ancient Chinese developed a brilliant and flourishing civilization which has remained a vital force in the lives of the people until the present day.

The Shang dynasty which lasted from 1523 to 1027 B.C. is the first for which we have historical proof. The discovery in 1928 of the ancient capital revealed a highly developed civilization. In the well-planned city were great palaces and impressive public buildings. Burial sites were filled with weapons, pottery, implements and beautiful bronze vessels. Most exciting was the discovery of a number of flat animal bones on which ancient Chinese had written. From these *oracle* bones, as they are called, historians have been able to piece together much of the history of China 3500 years ago.

After five centuries of rule the Shang kings were overthrown by a strong and warlike people known as the Chou (Joe). Since the Chou kings could not personally control the vast area they had con-

These "oracle" bones are so named because they were used by ancient Chinese to find answers to questions. Shang priests carved a small groove on one side of the bone and then heated it. From the cracks that appeared they believed they could tell whether the answer to the question they had asked the spirits was yes or no. Many of the bones have the questions written on them, and some have the answers as well. It is from these questions and answers, concerning crops, the weather, war, hunting, travelling and relatives, that we can find out a good deal about Shang society. This bone is about four inches long.

quered from their capital city, they divided the country into sections. To govern each section for them they appointed a number of officials, usually relatives or friends. In theory, the Chou king ruled all of China, but in time real power passed into the hands of the local officials. Many of these local rulers became as powerful as the king himself and dreamed of replacing him and ruling over all China. Their ambition led to such constant warfare among the states that the last two centuries of the Chou period is known as the age of the "Warring States." By 300 B.C. only a handful of the stronger states had survived.

In 221 B.C. the wars came to an end when the powerful state of Ch'in triumphed over the rest. The new rulers came from the western frontier where they had been hardened by constant warfare against barbarians beyond their borders. The Ch'in ruler was also able to profit from the mistakes of the Chou. He divided the country into provinces and districts but controlled them through a host of officials sent out from the national capital. These officials were responsible to

him for keeping law and order, collecting taxes and supervising the building of highways and other great public works. One of the greatest of these was the Great Wall of China, which eventually ran 1400 miles across Northern China.

The centralization of government under the Ch'in ruler helped to unify the entire country. Even more important was the unification of the written language. The Ch'in ruler adopted one written language from a number of different scripts which had developed over the years. This one written language was to be used throughout the land. Thus, although China has always had a great many different spoken languages, there was for all Chinese who could read, a common script. Ever since the Ch'in ruler established a common written language, it has been the greatest source of unity in Chinese society.

The Ch'in ruler had boasted that his empire would last for 10,000 years. However, within a year of his death his subjects revolted against the harsh conditions which had made their lives miserable. In 206 B.C. one of the rebel leaders, Liu

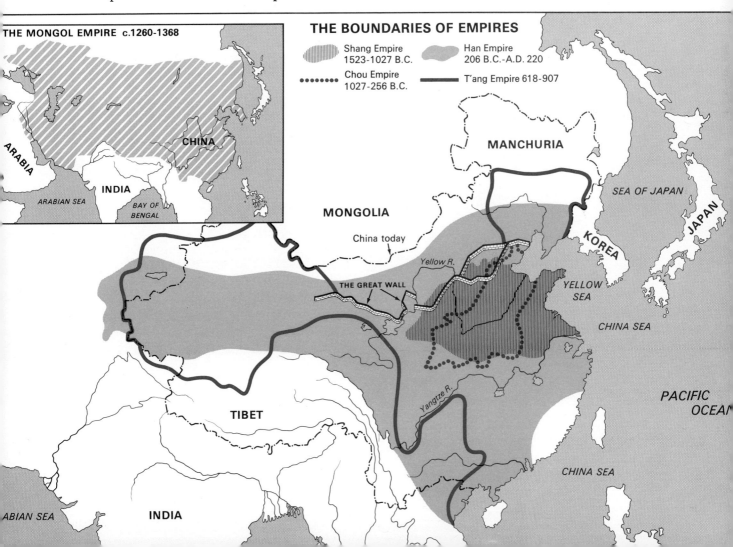

THE MONGOL EMPIRE c.1260-1368

ARABIA

CHINA

INDIA

ARABIAN SEA

BAY OF BENGAL

THE BOUNDARIES OF EMPIRES

Shang Empire 1523-1027 B.C.

Chou Empire 1027-256 B.C.

Han Empire 206 B.C.-A.D. 220

T'ang Empire 618-907

MANCHURIA

MONGOLIA

China today

Yellow R.

THE GREAT WALL

Yangtze R.

TIBET

INDIA

ABIAN SEA

SEA OF JAPAN

JAPAN

KOREA

YELLOW SEA

CHINA SEA

PACIFIC OCEAN

CHINA SEA

Pang, ascended the Dragon Throne and established the mighty Han Empire.

The Empire lasted approximately 400 years and became so powerful and famous that to this day the Chinese refer to themselves as Men of Han. During this period China made tremendous material and cultural progress. The invention of paper was one of the most important factors in stimulating an increased interest in the arts, literature and history. Even in distant lands the Han Empire became famous for its wealth, power and learning. In these years Chinese soldiers and traders expanded into northern India and Korea. From Korea Chinese ideas and customs filtered across to the islands of Japan where they had an important influence upon the development of Japanese society. Traders from China also moved across central Asia carrying their beautiful goods as far westward as the Roman Empire. But eventually the pattern of invasion and conquest reappeared. In 220 A.D. the Han Empire, weakened internally, collapsed in the face of foreign invasion.

During the next 400 years China once again was split into many states. But finally the country was reunited, and under the brilliant T'ang and Sung dynasties enjoyed a long period of peace and prosperity which lasted until 1279. During these years there was increased contact between China and foreign lands. Traders, missionaries and entertainers found their way to China from India, Persia and Byzantium. Contact with these foreigners convinced the Chinese that they had little to learn from the outside world. When they compared their system of government, their immense wealth, their poetry and art with the achievements of all other peoples, they had no doubt that the Chinese way of life was superior.

In the thirteenth century new conquerors swept into China. These were the fierce Mongol warriors of Genghis and Kublai Khan. "Man's highest joy," said Genghis Khan, "is in victory: to conquer one's enemies, to pursue them, to deprive them of their possessions, to make their beloved weep." In a short time his terrifying horsemen had conquered most of Asia, including China. But in

For almost four hundred years after the fall of the Han dynasty Northern China was constantly overrun or menaced by semi-nomadic invaders from the north and west. In the south, one short-lived dynasty after another tried and failed to re-establish a united empire. The period was one of war, unrest and insecurity. Many men gladly became what amounted to the slaves of wealthy and powerful landowners in return for protection. The great families had their own armies and built their own fortresses. Trade, commerce and cities declined, and coinage almost disappeared. Chinese art in this period often deals with military subjects, as can be seen in the clay figures of the infantryman and the mounted warrior. At this time, the sixth century A.D., the stirrup, seen here, was not yet used in western Europe.

China the Mongols soon discovered that the country could be conquered from the saddle but not ruled from it. It was not long before they were happy to listen to the advice of the Chinese officials and adopt Chinese methods of government. Mongol rule of China produced remarkably few changes, for Chinese society had matured so fully that even foreign conquest could do little to alter it.

During the Mongol period a number of travellers and missionaries from western Europe reached China. The most famous was Marco Polo, the Venetian trader who remained at the court of Kublai Khan for many years. On his return to the West he wrote of the wonders he had seen in China, or Cathay, as it was then known. Europeans refused to believe his tales of the fantastic riches and incredible inventions that he had seen while a guest at the court of the great Khan.

But as had happened so often in the past, the combination of weak rulers and economic problems soon undermined the Mongol dynasty. In 1368 a new group of Chinese leaders overthrew the Mongols and established the Ming dynasty, which lasted until 1644. China was then conquered by the Manchus, a non-Chinese people from Manchuria who ruled until a revolution in 1911 toppled the last Chinese empire. During these later centuries there was little change in the general pattern of Chinese civilization. The foundation of that great and enduring civilization had been laid in the time of the Han dynasty. At that time the most characteristic features of Chinese life were already clearly emerging.

While cities flourished in the valleys of the Tigris-Euphrates, the Nile and the Yellow rivers, another civilization was developing in India. The first centres of Indian civilization were the cities of Harappa and Mohenjo-Daro which arose along the valley of the Indus River about 2800 B.C. The ruins of these cities, as well as later examples of Indian literature, reveal a highly cultured people who had mastered engineering techniques and developed an effective system of government. Like the river valleys of the Near East, the fertile Indus was also a magnet which attracted an endless succession of invading peoples. Each new conqueror tried to unify and govern large parts of the country. But all early attempts failed. Not until a little more than a century ago were the British able to impose their rule over the entire continent. When they finally left in 1947 after ruling India for more than a century, the civilization which the Indians had created over the centuries remained in many ways unchanged.

The Emperor Wen-Ti, despite his shrewd
and thoughtful appearance, remained on
the throne of the Ch'en dynasty only from
A.D. 559-566. History is silent as to his
accomplishments, and as a result he is
known to us only through this magnificent
portrait by Yen Li-pen.

The men of Han

The foundations of Chinese civilization were firmly established during the Han dynasty (206 B.C. - A.D. 220), a period that corresponds roughly to that of the Roman Empire in the West. The Empire built by the Han rulers was the mightiest in East Asia. Its riches and glories were known as far away as the Roman world. For the Chinese its brilliance has survived, and to this day the Chinese refer to themselves as the "Men of Han."

Between the seventh and third centuries B.C. China had been disunited and torn by almost constant war. Educated men had asked why men could not live with each other in peace and harmony. While many different solutions to the problem were suggested, most scholars had agreed that there was little point in appealing to gods or spirits. The answer would be found only through a discussion of the ideal ways in which men should live with each other in *this* world. Therefore, a main characteristic of most Chinese thought came to be its humanism — that is, its concern for man and the relations between men, rather than for other-worldly things.

THE CONFUCIAN VIEW OF LIFE

The most famous Chinese thinker or philosopher

Although Confucius never achieved his ambition of becoming a great statesman, he became one of the world's greatest teachers. Much more than any single politician or ruler, he has influenced the lives of millions of Chinese. On the surface he seemed to be a failure during his own lifetime, but for more than 2000 years he has been revered as the perfect man. Like other good teachers, Confucius demanded honesty of his pupils. "When you know," he said, "say you know; when you do not know, say that you do not know. This is the secret of knowledge." Some of his other teachings also have a familiar ring: "Never do to others what you would not like them to do to you."

This "Son of Heaven" was Emperor Hsüan Ti of the Ch'en dynasty. The Ch'en was one of the many dynasties that attempted to re-establish the Han Empire. The dynasty was founded in A.D. 557 in the lower Yangtze Valley, but collapsed thirty-two years later when attacked by invaders from the north.

Although he did not create a powerful empire, Hsüan Ti was made famous in this painting by Yen Li-pen, who lived during the seventh century. Experts regard it as one of the great portraits in early Chinese painting. Comparing it with earlier portrait painting, one of them wrote: "It is in the figure of Hsüan Ti of the Ch'en dynasty, though, that facial characterization has reached the highest degree of individualism. The emperor is by no means attractive, but there is a gleam of thoughtfulness in his sharply slit eyes which imparts life to the bloated face."

was Confucius (551-479 B.C.). Confucius travelled widely throughout China offering advice to the rulers of various states. He died a disappointed man, for no ruler at the time accepted his ideas. Yet he became China's greatest teacher and gathered about him a large number of disciples and followers.

Although he taught how man should live, Confucius was not a religious leader like Jesus. He was mainly interested in finding a way to restore peace and order in China. When a disciple asked about spirits, he answered, "If we are not yet able to serve man, how can we serve spiritual beings?" When the disciple went on to ask him about death, the Master replied, "If we do not yet know about life, how can we know about death?" Confucius believed that society and government should rest on five basic relationships, and that if these were obeyed man could live in peace and happiness. The five basic relationships were those between ruler and subject, father and son, husband and wife, older brother and younger brother, and older friend and younger friend. The ruler must be kindly, and the subject loyal; the father must show love, and the son respect and obedience; the husband must be kind, and the wife obedient; and the older brother or friend must be gentle and patient, and the younger respectful. The true gentleman must be loyal, co-operative, well-behaved and humane in his treatment of others. If all men developed these virtues and accepted the proper relationship to others, said Confucius, China's problems would be solved.

Not all thinkers agreed with Confucius. One group of men known as the Taoists (pronounced dowist) said that man could never be happy if he lived in a man-made society. They thought that men should live as close to nature as possible. War, crime, and suffering, they argued, were caused by men who were too much concerned with material things. If man had not made laws, would there be crime, they asked. Without wealth, could there be stealing? The ideal for many Taoists was the hermit, living alone amid the beauties of nature doing nothing.

The third major school of thought was called Legalism or Realism. These thinkers accused the Taoists of trying to escape from society. They maintained that such escape was impossible. They also ridiculed the ideas of Confucius, for they believed that man was essentially bad and could not be expected to lead a good life unless forced to do so. Peace and order could be secured only when a strong ruler had total power. Such a ruler would have to regulate man's conduct with laws which would provide rewards for those who obeyed them and harsh penalties for those who did not.

In the third century B.C. the Ch'in dynasty adopted Legalist ideas; as a result their rule was harsh and intolerable. When the Han replaced them, the ideas of Confucianism became the official state belief. This did not mean that all rulers and individuals observed the Confucian ideal. But Confucianism did establish a society based on the rights and duties of each of the five relationships. Confucianism remained the theory of government and society for China until 1911.

GOVERNMENT

Confucianism compared the state to a large family in which the emperor was the father and the subjects his children. The father was to be respected and obeyed, but he was expected to rule for the benefit of his children. He was to rely on setting a good example rather than using force in running the state. The Chinese believed that the emperor, the Son of Heaven, was responsible for keeping the affairs of heaven, earth and man in some kind of harmony. Indeed, the word for king was made up of a figure which showed three horizontal lines representing heaven, earth and man, with the vertical line joining them representing the king.

In practice, of course, all Chinese emperors were not good rulers. Many of them were harsh and mean, and far more concerned about their own wealth and power than with the well-being of their subjects. In that case the emperor eventually lost the Mandate of Heaven, or the right to rule, and the people had the right to rebel and overthrow him. Moreover, natural calamities such as earthquakes or floods, or omens like the appear-

The Chinese official shown here was painted during the T'ang dynasty (618-906), which is one of the great periods for early Chinese painting, music and poetry. The official, or what we would call the civil servant, was an essential figure in government from the time of the vast Han Empire.

There were almost 60,000,000 people in the Empire, so that China, then as now, was the most populous state in the world. The civil service numbered about 130,000 in the first century B.C. These officials were placed in one of eighteen grades, with each grade entitling them to certain privileges such as reduced sentences for crimes and, for the highest grade, exemption from taxation.

ance of comets or strange animals could be taken as a sign that heaven was showing its displeasure with the emperor and withdrawing his right to rule. Here again was the justification for overthrowing an unpopular emperor.

Confucianism also required that the emperor must rule with the assistance of the best educated and most virtuous officials. Early in the Han dynasty the emperor issued orders to have the most honest and talented men sent to the capital to become officials in the government. He particularly demanded young men who were filial, that is, who were loyal and obedient to their parents. This method of filling government positions was the beginning of China's famous "merit civil service," which is based on the idea that the government should hire its employees on the basis of ability rather than rank or wealth. Men who wished to become government officials had to be learned as well as virtuous, and their knowledge was tested before they were given a government position. As the centuries passed, more and more of China's officials were selected by examinations and fewer and fewer men were given positions just because of their wealth or their aristocratic birth. Western countries began to adopt this merit system only about a century ago or less, but the Chinese have had it for 2000 years!

When the merit system was fully developed, an applicant would normally have to pass three sets of examinations before he was given a government post. There were exams first at the district level, then at the provincial capital, and finally in the national capital. Usually only one or two out of a hundred passed, but those who failed might try again and again. Sometimes a father, son and even grandfather would all be attempting the same examination together! For the successful, the rewards were great. The exams not only gave men the chance of public office but also put them into the highest social class — the gentry or degree holders.

The government examinations were mainly tests on China's history, literature and philosophy, particularly the ideas of Confucianism. Often the knowledge expected had little to do with actual problems of government. Frequently the candidate's handwriting, or calligraphy, and his ability to write poetry or memorize long passages of writing were more important than anything else. It took young Chinese students years to learn enough to pass these examinations. In fact the average age at which Chinese passed the national examination and received a government job was thirty-five. Although anyone could sit for the exams, only the wealthy could usually afford the long period of preparation. Sometimes poor families pooled their savings so that one relative could be educated and perhaps someday become an important government official who could then help his family in return.

These officials rather than the Son of Heaven were responsible for the day-to-day governing of China. A small group of leading advisers helped the Emperor to make major decisions. But these decisions were carried out by a number of separate ministries or departments. Each ministry was responsible for one area of activity such as public works, war, taxation, law and so on. Each ministry employed thousands of officials, clerks, secretaries and messengers.

Orders from the national capital were sent to the governors of the various provinces. The governors in turn passed the orders to local magistrates, the only government officials with whom the people had any real contact. The magistrate's main task was to keep peace and order in his area and to make sure that enough taxes and tribute in grain were sent to the central capital. Often, these local officials were dishonest and corrupt. They would squeeze as much money and grain from the peasants as possible to line their own pockets. The central government tried to prevent such corruption by moving the officials at least every third year before they had time to learn how to take advantage of local conditions for their personal benefit. Officials were also forbidden from taking government posts in their own provinces where they might possibly favour friend and family. A group of men known as censors periodically checked their efficiency and honesty. These investigators, appropriately called the "eyes and ears" of the emperor, could criticize and punish wayward officials.

The central government had to ensure the loyalty of the people as well as that of the local officials. One way in which this was done was called the *pao-chia* (bow jeeah) system. Households were grouped into units of ten and then one hundred. In each group of one hundred, one family served as the leader and represented the group's interest to the government. But all the families within a unit were responsible for each other's conduct. Therefore, if one family broke the law or failed to pay its share of the taxes the other families were equally responsible.

Chinese government did not always work as smoothly in practice as it might appear on paper. Often the emperor was an arrogant and haughty man who ignored the advice of his officials. If he were a weak-willed and pleasure-loving man, he would often be controlled by court favourites. Scheming servants and relatives often won the upper hand at court and directed the affairs of state for their own benefit and enrichment. But on the whole, the Han government was a relatively efficient one. Later conquerors like the Mongols and Manchus did not destroy it but ruled in much the same way as had the Chinese emperors.

SOCIETY

Chinese society was divided into three major classes. At the top was the group of scholars and officials known as the gentry. Although this class included many of the great landowners, its prestige was based not on land but on having passed the government exams. Every parent hoped to have his sons become scholar-officials. The long-robed scholar was the ideal Chinese. He was specially favoured in many ways. People had to address him with respect; only he could wear certain types of clothing. He was exempt from physical labour and certain laws. In their own districts, the gentry families were often responsible for charity, keeping the dikes and roads repaired and settling disputes. No group in China had as much honour and prestige as the gentry.

The great respect for the scholar in China can be seen in the inscription placed on this portrait of Four Scholars: "There are many scholars in the State of Lu whom I have seen, among them my teacher of whom I always dream, whose ways I follow as an example, scholars who were very learned and well-known during their lifetime but now they have passed away and I feel very sad. Mr. Ning Chü-chung showed me the four portraits . . . and for a moment I saw my dear teacher in my mind's eye and felt very sad, so I wrote this to express my sorrow, fourteenth year of Chih Cheng, eleventh month, first day [1354] signed Su Ta Nien. Bowed twice and written (in deep humility)."

The second class was that of the farmers. Most farmers were poor peasants who faced a constant struggle merely to survive. At best a peasant could only hope to keep his family housed, clothed and fed. If he were very thrifty and lucky, he might manage to save a little and purchase more land so that when he died the division of the land amongst his sons would provide each with a decent-sized plot. Usually he was not so fortunate. Flood, drought or pests might at any time wipe out his crops; roving bandits might seize his grain, or campaigning armies tramp through his fields. Robbing or begging then was the only alternative to starvation. A peasant might also be ruined by high taxes. Often he would have to borrow money at high interest rates to pay his taxes. He seldom found it possible to repay his debt without selling his land and becoming the tenant or worker of a large landowner.

The artisans, merchants and soldiers were lowest on the social ladder. The artisans and craftsmen in China's towns and cities often joined together in societies or guilds to assist each other. Merchants, no matter how wealthy or powerful, were looked down upon, for according to Confucian teaching they were parasites living off the hard-earned money of others. Consequently, whenever they accumulated a surplus of money, the merchants usually purchased land. As land-

41

lords they won greater respect, and their sons could then try the government exams and perhaps become scholar-officials and members of the gentry. This practice of investing profits in land continued into modern times and was one of the reasons China did not become an industrial nation. Industrialization depends upon businessmen using their profits to keep building larger and larger enterprises. But in China these profits went into the purchase of land.

The family probably played a more important role in China than in any other society. It was the basic social group. The ideal family consisted of as many relatives living together as possible. It included everyone from the great-great-grandparents to the great-great-grandchildren and outward to third cousins. In the wealthiest families, many of these relatives often lived in a single great household which was divided into sections by beautiful courtyards. The poor peasant family normally consisted only of parents, children and possibly grandparents.

The respect and devotion of children and the closeness of family ties are a frequent subject in Chinese art. These sixth century A.D. engravings on stone slabs tell two such stories. (Top left) The orphan Wang Lin offers himself bound to a group of bandits who are about to eat his small brother for supper. (Bottom right) Yüan Ku, forced to help his father carry his aged grandfather into the woods to die, shames his father into carrying the old man home again.

The most important relationship in the Chinese family was that between the parents and children. Whether they were young or even adults with their own families, children were expected to be completely respectful and obedient to their elders. A person was expected to show more respect for his father than for his brother, and more for an older than a younger brother. Chinese law upheld this ideal by providing for harsher penalties for a crime when committed against an older or close relative than when the same crime had been com-

42

mitted against a younger or more distantly related person.

Within the family, the individual always had to place his own interests below those of the group. Disobedience to the head of the family could be punished by the state. There were even rigid regulations concerning how long one must mourn for his parents or other close relatives when they died.

In Chinese society, women had far less authority and freedom than men. A woman's supreme duty was to serve her husband and rear his children. Women were seldom educated. Difficult times might force poor families to sell their daughters or even kill female babies. A woman was not allowed to remarry after her husband's death, though men could have second wives. It was said that a woman obeyed her father when young, her husband in middle age and her sons in old age. This was often more the ideal than the practice. In peasant households where women often joined their husbands in the fields they had more responsibility and equality. And among the

wealthy, the beautiful woman often controlled the men around her.

When a son married, his bride would come to live in his mother's home. Then, often the mother-in-law would act like a tyrant over the young bride. Marriage itself was a family concern in which the young people had no choice. Parents of both families arranged the marriages and were concerned primarily with whether the union would improve their own position or fortune. Sometimes these arrangements were made even before the birth of the couple. During the marriage arrangements, "go-betweens" settled the gifts that would be given. Frequently, fortune-tellers were consulted. Their task was to interpret the stars and other signs to determine whether it would be a lucky marriage.

RELIGION

The family was also the most important religious unit in China. From earliest times the Chinese worshipped the spirits of their dead ancestors

who, it was believed, might come to harm if not properly honoured. Thus, Chinese families regularly prayed and offered sacrifices before the ancestral tablets and graves. Since ancestor worship was mainly the duty of the male members of the family, fathers were very anxious to have sons who would make sure that their spirits were properly cared for in the next world.

Like most early peoples the Chinese worshipped a great variety of gods and spirits. Since they were mainly a farming people, most of these were nature gods. There were gods of the wind and water, of heaven and earth. There were also a great number of household gods that had to be worshipped, and evil spirits or demons that had to be kept away.

But when people today refer to the religions of China, they are usually thinking about Confucianism, Taoism (dowism) and Buddhism. Confucianism, as we have seen, was not really a religion. It was neither an organized church nor was it concerned with life after death or a supreme being. It taught that men should live moral lives and behave properly towards each other and the state. But the practical wisdom of Confucius made little appeal to the great mass of Chinese people, who could neither read nor write. What they wanted was some kind of spiritual comfort, some assurance that there was a life after death to make up for the miseries of this world.

This desire became particularly strong as human misery increased with the breakup of the Han dynasty and with the centuries of strife and turmoil that followed. Moreover, since the Han dynasty had been based on the ideas of Confucius, its collapse seemed to discredit these ideas. As a result many Chinese turned to Taoism, which during the late Han dynasty took on some of the aspects of an organized religion. Taoism as a religion taught that the world was full of spirits who lived in the mountains, rivers and forests. Since these spirits could bring disaster or prosperity to a community, it was necessary to win their favour. Only Taoist priests knew how to perform the ceremonies necessary to obtain the help of the spirits. Some Taoist priests also claimed that they were able to foretell the future and also to cure diseases through the use of magic charms and spells. Taoism as a religion was less concerned with man's behaviour in this world than with his personal salvation in the after-life. Since salvation did not depend upon good conduct, Taoism did not greatly affect the kind of lives men lived. Nevertheless, for many Chinese people Taoism filled a deep spiritual need by offering the hope of a pleasant life after death.

An even more influential religion was Buddhism which came from India during the Han period. Buddhism is based on the teachings of Buddha (the Enlightened One), who was born in India about 563 B.C. As a young man Buddha was distressed with the suffering he saw about him and determined to find out why people suffered so much. He concluded that life was an endless process of suffering. Man went through an endless cycle of births and rebirths as his soul went from one life to another in this world. To escape from this cycle one had to be free from worldly desires, for desire was the basic cause of all pain and suffering. The way to get rid of desire, he maintained, was to live according to the Noble Eightfold Path. The steps in the Eightfold Path included right knowledge, thought, speech, conduct, livelihood, effort, mindfulness and meditation. This Path was the Middle Way that led men to love all

The gentle religion of Buddhism, one of the world's most influential faiths, is based on the teachings of a man named Siddhartha Gautama. As a boy and young man Gautama lived in luxury enjoying all the pleasures money could buy. However, after he became aware of the misery and suffering in the world, he gave up his pleasant existence and became a penniless monk, determined to solve the riddle of life. Only after six years of searching and meditation was he convinced that he had found the meaning of life in the so-called middle way. As he said in his first sermon, "I have gained the knowledge of the Middle Path which leads to insight, which leads to wisdom, which conduces to calm, to knowledge and to Supreme Enlightenment. . . . It is the Noble Eightfold Path."

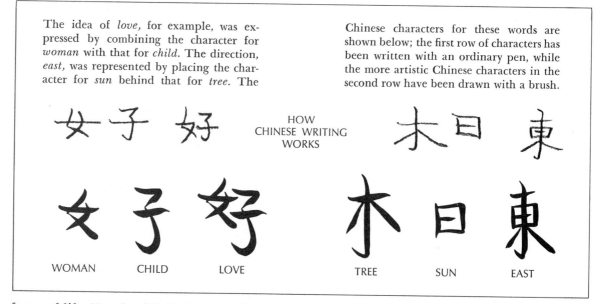

The idea of *love*, for example, was expressed by combining the character for *woman* with that for *child*. The direction, *east*, was represented by placing the character for *sun* behind that for *tree*. The

Chinese characters for these words are shown below; the first row of characters has been written with an ordinary pen, while the more artistic Chinese characters in the second row have been drawn with a brush.

HOW CHINESE WRITING WORKS

WOMAN   CHILD   LOVE   TREE   SUN   EAST

forms of life. He who did his best to follow the Path in his many lives would eventually be freed from the endless cycle of rebirths. He would then reach a condition of perfect peace known as *nirvana*.

Buddhism was the closest thing China had to an organized church as we know it in the West. It attracted a large following only after the Han dynasty, and reached its height in the ninth century A.D. From that time on it began to decline, although it remained an important force in Chinese life until the twentieth century.

Perhaps the most unusual feature of Chinese religious practices was their great tolerance. The Chinese believed in many different spirits and gods at the same time. The Emperor T'ai Tsung declared on one occasion "religion has many names; there have been many wise men, and even if their teachings differ, they can be a blessing to mankind." As a result the Emperor was tolerant of all the religions of the foreigners who flocked to China during his regime. When later Christian missionaries went to China and spoke of their religion being the only true one, the Chinese quite naturally felt that such a claim was outrageous and ridiculous.

CULTURE

Since the scholar was the most respected man in

China, it was natural that learning and literature were very important. But Chinese literature affected relatively few people because the Chinese written language is very difficult and takes a long time to learn. It does not have an alphabet. Each word is represented by a completely different *ideograph* or character. Originally these symbols looked very much like the objects they represented. With the passage of time the characters or symbols became more streamlined and less pictorial. The Chinese quickly learned how to use characters to express abstract things like ideas, colours and directions. This was usually done by combining two or more characters, each of which had a separate meaning by itself but which, when combined, meant something entirely different. (See above.) The Chinese language has about 40,000 different characters. The bare minimum necessary for reading is between 3000 and 5000. Since each character has to be individually memorized, it is obvious that learning to read and write in Chinese is a long and tedious task. Chinese characters are traditionally written in vertical columns, and are read from top to bottom and from right to left.

We do not know when the first Chinese literature was written because it was done on materials like wood and bamboo which have long since perished. Only the records written on bone and bronze have survived. The earliest examples of

46

books and poems that we have are as much as 2500 years old. These books, written before and during the Han dynasty, are particularly concerned with history and philosophy. Together they are known as the Classics. Educated Chinese, especially those trying the civil service exams, had to learn them thoroughly, and often commit long passages to memory. History and poetry were especially important in China. Indeed, no other people have been as conscious of their history as the Chinese.

One of China's greatest contributions to the world was the invention of paper. The Chinese made paper in the first century A.D. This early paper was made from the inner bark of the mul-

This remarkable painting, "Poet at ease," was done by Liu Kuan-tao about 1300. The poet is resting on a couch in front of a large screen which is decorated with a picture of another poet or scholar. The poet and scholar are often included in Chinese art, for few peoples have ever had such admiration for the intellectual class in society. All prominent Chinese, for example, were expected to be able to write poetry. Many of China's most famous rulers, including Mao Tse-tung, the leader of Communist China, have been noted poets. Ts'ao Ts'ao and his two sons, the family that brought about the final downfall of the brilliant Han dynasty, were men of action who did not hesitate to murder the Emperor's family and use any means to secure power, but who, at the same time, wrote brilliant and imaginative poetry.

berry tree, which was beaten into a pasty sub-
stance, mixed with water and poured into a
mould. When dry it was ripped off in sheets and
rubbed until smooth and thin. In the tenth century A.D. the Chinese invented printing. The use
of paper and later, printing, gave a great stimulus
to the growth of Chinese literature. Perhaps in no
other civilization has the written word had such a
great influence upon the development of its
people.

The ability to paint, like the writing of poetry,
was expected of all educated men. Chinese painting was based on Chinese handwriting or calligraphy, which was done with a brush. The best
calligraphy, beautifully painted on long narrow
scrolls, is as attractive as any other form of art.
Perhaps the best known Chinese art form is the
landscape painting which developed mainly after
the Han period.

The earliest forms of Chinese art that have survived are engravings on pottery and bronze. Since
the magnificent bronze vessels of the Shang dynasty were normally used for sacrifices and other religious occasions, their designs tend to suggest deep
mystical and spiritual forces. By Han times these
designs had become more purely decorative and
less magical and mysterious. In Han China the
best bronze work was that done to decorate the

An art to capture the spirit of nature

*The great period of Chinese landscape
painting came after the end of the Han
dynasty, and reached its perfection under
the Sung dynasty (960-1276). In their
approach to nature the artists were strongly
influenced by Taoism. Nature is overwhelming. The tiny figure of a man (usually
seen in the landscape as two of them are
here in the lower left corner) is insignificant compared to the surrounding
mountains, trees and clouds. The landscape
paintings, done with Indian ink and light
colour on either silk or paper, were also
mysterious, for the artists attempted to
capture the spirit of nature. Clear Weather
in the Valley was painted by Tung Yuan,
a Buddhist monk, and shows two people on
their way to the Buddhist Temple which
is faintly visible in the misty gorge.*

backs of mirrors. Often these were inlaid with gold, silver and precious gems. Later, bronze was also used in sculpture. But sculpture only became an important art form in China with the introduction of Buddhism around the third century A.D. The Buddhists wanted idols and images carved for use in their temples.

The making of various kinds of vessels, other than bronze, dates back to prehistoric times. Even then some objects were shaped by a wheel. As time passed, the Chinese perfected the art of ceramics and made this one of their greatest contributions to the world's art treasures. They had discovered the secret of making porcelain hundreds of years

This grey pottery model of a house was made during the first century A.D. The Chinese often left models in the tombs of the dead; the subjects were not only houses but servants, guards and animals. These figurines provide us with an important source of information about daily life in Han China.

before Westerners did. Their porcelain became so widely known and cherished in other parts of the world that most people call all similar porcelain "china" or "china-ware."

The Chinese also became famous for their jade and lacquer. Even before the Shang dynasty, the Chinese seem to have loved jade. Beautiful objects carved out of jade were used on ceremonial swords and daggers, and as jewelry. Lacquering, a shellacing process, using the sap of a tree, became an important industry in Han times. Coat after coat of lacquer (often of a cinnabar-red colour) was applied to things like drinking cups and cosmetic boxes, which were exquisitely carved.

By Han times, China was abreast of, or ahead of, the rest of the world in its scientific knowledge

49

and inventions. At a very early stage in their history, the Chinese knew how to date eclipses, and they had developed an excellent calendar. A kind of seismograph for recording earthquakes had even been invented. Later, they developed the water-powered mill and invented the shoulder-collar, which made the work of draft animals far more efficient. From this early period as well, the Chinese techniques of casting iron spread to the West.

From Han China, Chinese silk flowed out across the caravan routes of Central Asia to the Western world. In Rome it was one of the import products most in demand, and China reaped the rewards of a great trade in it. From Han times, until about the seventeenth or eighteenth centuries, the West learned more and imported more from China than the Chinese did from the West.

Court ladies at work preparing silk. Above, a woman is rolling up her sleeves before joining the others in pounding the silk. To the right, one woman draws out the thread; another sews, and a servant fans the charcoal burner. Finally, a little girl inspects the ironing by peering underneath the long roll of silk cloth.

THE CHINESE VIEW OF THE WORLD

The Chinese view of the rest of the world is clear in the very name of their country. In Chinese it is "Chung Kuo" (Joong gwo) which means the "Middle Kingdom" or the "Middle Country." The Chinese believed that they were at the centre of the world. They thought of themselves as the only civilized people surrounded on all sides by "barbarians." The Chinese emperor was referred

50

This painting, done in gold and green, shows the first Han Emperor entering the Ch'in capital. The Emperor is visible amid some of his troops in the lower right-hand corner. Farther along the road he is travelling, some men, who appear to be enemy dignitaries, wait on their knees for the conqueror to pass. Behind Liu Pang, or Han Kao Tsu as he is sometimes called, stretch the banners of his army.

to as the "Son of Heaven" and his empire was "T'ion Hsia" or "that beneath Heaven."

The Chinese permitted foreigners to come to their land, but it had to be on China's terms. The system of foreign relations that developed from this requirement was known as the tributary system. Foreigners who wished to trade with China brought tribute or gifts to the Chinese emperor. At court, the foreign envoy recognized the supremacy of the Chinese emperor by going through an elaborate ceremony known as the "kowtow." The envoy kneeled in front of the throne three times, and after each kneeling completely prostrated himself and knocked his forehead on the floor three times.

In ancient China, diplomats from neighbouring Asian states were quite prepared to recognize China's superior position in return for the benefits they would receive. Once in China they were well cared for, could engage in trade, and might even win other favours like military assistance from the Chinese. Often, emperors who had just ascended the throne went to great trouble and expense to have foreign states send tribute missions to their court, for when they came it made the emperor appear more powerful and awesome in the eyes of his Chinese subjects.

While the Chinese thought of themselves as the only truly civilized people in the world, they were well aware of the military strength of others.

"A Lady Before Her Mirror" was painted early in the twelfth century A.D. by Su Han-Ch'en. Delicately coloured in the original, it is a magnificent example of Chinese painting. The scene is a garden terrace, and the artist has included the branch of a blossoming plum tree to capture the spirit of spring. The lady sits on a low bench in front of a beautifully lacquered table with a high screen-like back. The table, the vases and the other objects set out before her are all exquisite pieces of art themselves. An obedient servant stands behind the lady, no doubt agreeing that her ladyship is the most beautiful woman in all China.

54

They knew that when their country was weak, northern tribes might sweep down into China to raid, and even conquer. From Han times on, the Chinese used a variety of devices to defend themselves. The Great Wall and military garrisons in the north provided some protection. But the Chinese recognized that their safety was threatened most when these small wandering tribes united into a strong league. As a result, the Chinese tried to prevent this unity by keeping the barbarians divided. They befriended some tribes while fighting others. Sometimes they made payments of money or arranged marriage alliances.

Despite 4000 miles of seacoast, the Chinese never became a great sea-faring people eager to explore or conquer distant lands. As early as Han times, foreign ships from India and Southeast Asia had reached Chinese ports. But for a number of reasons the Chinese always looked more inland than outward to the sea. The birthplace of Chinese civilization was in the north. For the most part of her history, her capitals were there. And of course it was from the north that the threat of foreign invasion usually came. Therefore China remained more interested in the continent of Asia than in the islands of the Pacific or the lands beyond.

China had a good deal of contact with other peoples, but she never felt it necessary actually to control distant lands. Most of the products, food and goods she needed could be found within her own borders. Besides, it was felt that China was the very centre of civilization and that there was nothing to be gained from other societies. China was proud of her own great achievements and confident of her own supremacy.

This feeling of superiority was strengthened later during the centuries when the Mongols and Manchus ruled China. Although the Chinese were then a conquered people, their foreign rulers found that they had to rule the land as the Chinese themselves had done. Once in China, these barbarian rulers often adopted Chinese customs and ideas. The longer they remained, the more they became like the Chinese. Thus, they did not destroy any of the main features of Chinese civilization. For these reasons, China continued to develop a distinctive Chinese civilization. That development remained unbroken for close to 4000 years. Not until the nineteenth and twentieth centuries was Chinese civilization strongly influenced by the customs and ideas of the barbarians.

This painting of a Chinese courtyard was done about 1100. It is part of a series which tells the story of the Lady Wen-chi, who was captured by nomads from Mongolia in A.D. 195. Later, the lady was ransomed and returned to China. This scene shows her arriving home. The painting provides a good illustration of a courtyard in a wealthy Chinese home a thousand years ago. At the same time, this style of entrance gate and inner courtyard is very similar to Chinese architecture today.

A bas-relief from the famous temple at Karnak, built between 1550 and 1350 B.C. shows a temple priest making an offering of food to the pharoah.

Land of the pharaohs

On the west bank of the Nile in northern Egypt stands the city of Gizeh. Modern bridges link it to the capital city of Cairo of which it is now a part. About six miles from Gizeh to the west and south, near the edge of the Sahara Desert, stands the Great Pyramid. Built as a tomb for the Pharaoh Khufu, it was completed about 2600 B.C. Long regarded as the greatest of the seven wonders of the ancient world, it is still the largest stone building in existence. The Great Pyramid is only the largest monument to a brilliant civilization that flourished in the Nile Valley while our skin-clad ancestors struggled to keep alive in the forests and caves of Europe.

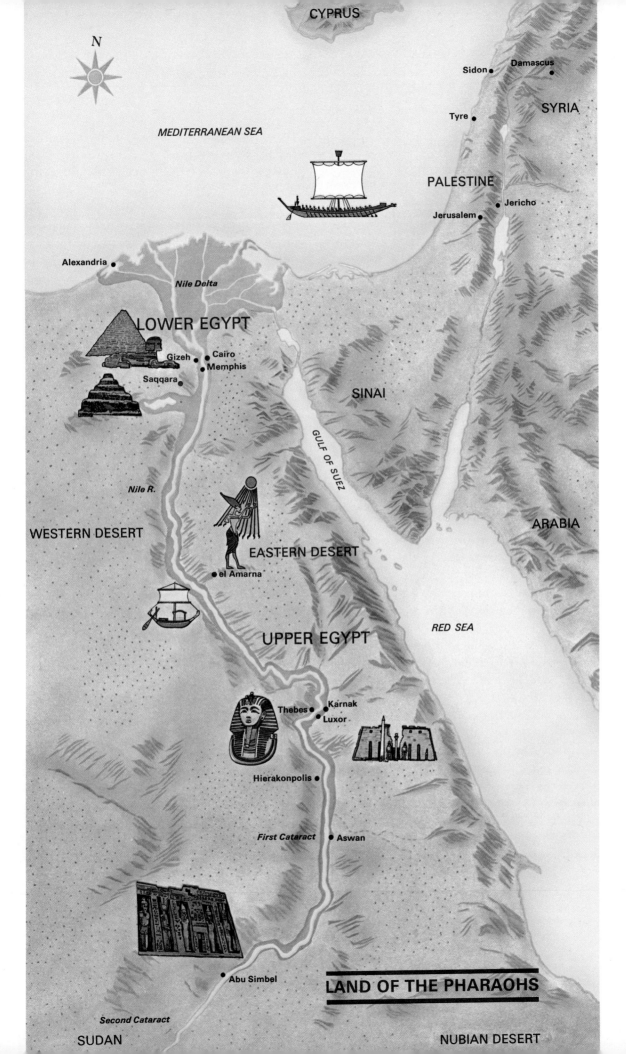

CYPRUS

N

MEDITERRANEAN SEA

SYRIA

Sidon •   • Damascus

Tyre •

PALESTINE

Jericho •
Jerusalem •

Alexandria •

Nile Delta

LOWER EGYPT

Gizeh •   • Cairo
Saqqara •   • Memphis

SINAI

GULF OF SUEZ

Nile R.

WESTERN DESERT

EASTERN DESERT

ARABIA

• el Amarna

UPPER EGYPT

RED SEA

Thebes •   • Karnak
• Luxor

Hierakonpolis •

First Cataract   • Aswan

LAND OF THE PHARAOHS

• Abu Simbel

Second Cataract

SUDAN

NUBIAN DESERT

GOVERNMENT BY THE PHARAOH

Egypt developed a system of government designed to meet her two main needs — to keep the country strong and unified. The king or pharaoh ruled as an absolute monarch whose every wish or word was law. He owned all the land and controlled every aspect of the country's life. He supervised the irrigation system, the great building projects, trade and commerce, the army and the administration of justice. The king was also accepted as a god, and it was customary to refer to him not by name but as Per-o (a term which survives in the Hebrew as Pharaoh) or Great House, the temple in which the god lived. Since the ruler was a god, it was natural for him to supervise the religion of the country. As a result, in Egypt the pharaoh controlled all political, civil and religious matters.

To assist him the pharaoh needed a large number of deputies or officials. Among the most important of the higher officials was the pharaoh's chief assistant, known as the *vizier*. The vizier must have been the busiest man in Egypt, for his duties seemed endless. He was the chief magistrate, and supervised the highest court of justice. He was directly responsible for agriculture, building programmes, policing the country, the conduct of war and the collection of taxes. The position of vizier was usually hereditary, that is, it was passed on to members of a particular family. Another influential representative of the pharaoh was the governor of each of Egypt's forty provinces. If the pharaoh was weak, the governor ruled over his province almost as an independent prince.

Since religion was a tremendously powerful force in Egypt, it was natural for a strong class of priests to arise. Egyptians expressed their gratitude to the gods for good harvests and victories over their enemies by giving gifts to the priests whose role it was to serve and placate the gods. As the wealth and power of the priests increased, the pharaohs tried to ensure their support by excusing them from the payment of taxes. During the New Kingdom, the influence of the priestly class reached its highest point. As foreign conquests brought new lands and wealth to Egypt's empire, a grateful people showered the priests with yet more gifts. And since the gods (it was reasoned) must have been responsible for all the good fortune, it was natural for their spokesmen on earth to gain more authority in running the affairs of the country. Thus, during the last years of the New Kingdom the priests became almost partners in government with the pharaoh. It has been estimated that at this time they controlled about thirty per cent of all the land.

The imperial expansion of the New Kingdom also stimulated the development of another group in Egyptian society, the army. Previously, the Egyptian army had been made up mainly of peasants who were drafted to meet an emergency. When the emergency passed, they went back to the fields. But empire-building required a permanent army of professional soldiers, either Egyptians trained from boyhood, or foreigners who either served for pay or had been captured. The need for highly skilled officers paved the way for men of ability to gain great influence in running the affairs of the country. Thus, throughout this period the army joined nobles and priests in sharing the power of the pharaoh.

As the business of the government, the army and the temples became bigger and more complex, there was an increasing need for officials to keep everything running smoothly. Just as modern governments today depend upon large bodies of civil servants, so it was in ancient Egypt. The backbone of the Egyptian bureaucracy or civil service was the scribe. Drawn from every class in society (except probably the peasants) on the basis of ability, the scribes looked after the multitude of details, including the keeping of records, by which a highly civilized society functions. Their close contact with the pharaoh, nobles, priests and army officers made them an influential group in Egyptian society.

The life of the people

Egypt was an agricultural country, and most of the people were peasants who toiled in the fields. Leaving their mud huts at dawn, the peasants worked in the fields of the wealthy until dusk. Their life was an endless round of cultivating the fresh silt, ploughing and planting, cutting and threshing, and tending the livestock. Even the annual flood brought little relief, for during the period when he could not work the land the peasant was likely to be summoned to work on one of the great public works projects, such as a pharaoh's temple or a pyramid. And always he was watched over by the scribes and overseers of the pharaoh, the nobles or the priests.

One such scribe was Menna, a field scribe for the pharaoh. It was Menna's job to supervise the work of the labourers, and of the other scribes who kept a record of the harvest. Not surprisingly, Menna's tomb contained a huge wall painting which showed the many aspects of his work and gives us a glimpse of the life of the peasant. The section reproduced here shows the wheat being cut and then carried in a rope basket on the shoulders of two men. A foreman watches as two labourers spread the piles of wheat on the ground, preparing it for the oxen to trample the kernels out of the husks. The next peasant is winnowing the wheat, scooping it into the air so that the wind will blow the chaff away. Finally, the wheat is loaded on board ship for its journey down or up the Nile, or away to ports across the Mediterranean.

Menna himself appears often in the original painting. In this section he was shown standing

just to the left of the top section watching his overseer beat a peasant for not doing his work or, perhaps, for not paying his taxes to the pharaoh. Another wrongdoer seems to be pleading for mercy, while a second overseer musters more of the guilty for their punishment. But it was not all work and punishment. The artist has shown two peasants under a tree, one sleeping and the other playing a flute. The foreman leaning on his stick is probably being told by the two peasants, "Why bother us; look at those two loafing right behind you." Agriculture has changed since the days of ancient Egypt, but it would seem that men have not.

The produce of the land supported an army of workers and craftsmen without whom the brilliant civilization of Egypt could not have flourished. Labourers were needed to perform the backbreaking work of building the pyramids and temples. Highly skilled craftsmen completed and beautified the great buildings. The army demanded a steady stream of weapons and equipment—bows and arrows, swords and daggers, war chariots and warships. The wealthy provided a ready market for jewelery, fine furniture and clothing, wine and perfume, art and sculpture.

The tomb of Rekhmire, Vizier, and Governor of Thebes, contains a huge wall painting showing many illustrations of the Vizier's greatness. A number of workers and craftsmen are shown at their tasks. At the bottom of the painting bricklayers are at work, making bricks from the Nile mud, setting them out to bake, and carrying them off to be used. As always, they are working under the careful eye of an overseer. Above them are some metal-workers. Two men on the left are grasping a tong holding a crucible of hot metal, while above them two other men are taking turns with the foot bellows to keep the charcoal glowing properly. The molten metal is then poured through the funnels into what appears to be a mould for a large door. Other men are bringing supplies. Above the metal-workers can be seen wood-workers, a cabinet-maker, carvers, and men apparently working on some pottery.

These craftsmen were better off than the peasants. Since the Egyptians did not have money, everyone was paid in food products. Nevertheless, the craftsman was able to live in a brick house and often could earn enough to buy a few luxuries and even a fairly elaborate tomb.

60

An economy based on men, not machines

A flourishing economic life needed merchants and sailors to carry and distribute the products of the fields and shops. As early as 2600 B.C. Egyptian merchants were developing a vigorous trade. Caravans moved overland across the desert. Egyptian trading ships, loaded with grain, wine and other products plied the Nile and the coasts of the eastern Mediterranean and the Red Sea. The merchants returned with such treasures as copper and bronze, gold and silver, ivory and timber, spices and perfumes. The merchants and traders were not independent. Like everyone else they worked for the pharaoh or rich nobles.

This interesting picture of a ship arriving in port gives some idea of the type of vessel Egyptian traders used. Power came both from sails and from banks of oarsmen. The detail of the stern of this ship shows that rudder and sail were moved by the same lever.

At the bottom of the social order were the slaves, usually foreigners who had been captured in war or purchased on the Mediterranean slave market. Their numbers increased during the New Kingdom when frequent wars increased the number of prisoners. The most unfortunate slaves were those assigned to the gold and copper mines, where their only hope was that a shortage of water or the unendurable heat and harsh conditions would quickly bring life to an end. The workers shown in the relief above may well have been slaves. Far more fortunate were the slaves (shown on page 65) assigned to work in the great homes of the nobility. Here their sole task was to wait on and entertain their masters. Sometimes a very talented slave could hope for rewards which could lead him to an important position in the government of the country.

Sharp contrasts between rich and poor

The life of the Egyptian upper classes contrasted sharply with that of the peasant and slave. Their large and gracious homes were set in beautiful gardens and were filled with fine furniture and paintings. A host of servants (like the slave girls on the right) catered to their every need. Banquet scenes like this show fashionably dressed ladies with elaborate hair styles. The perfumed cones on their heads melted during the party while they watched the musicians and dancing girls, filling the air with exotic scents. The banquet table groaned under a rich assortment of foods and wines.

But even the people who made such a luxurious life possible, like the farm workers (below) who are making wine and catching and cleaning water-birds, do not seem to have been too unhappy. Apart from the labourers who went on strike—the first recorded in history—because they had not been paid for two months and were hungry, there seem to have been no

revolts. (Of course, the pharaoh's army and the host of overseers would have made a successful revolt unlikely.) Moreover, although the paintings were done for the rich, they suggest that while life was dull and hard, it was not without its lighter moments. Portions of Egyptian songs also suggested a good-natured and reasonably contented people. Despite hard work and high taxes, the Egyptians enjoyed much greater security than was usual in the ancient world.

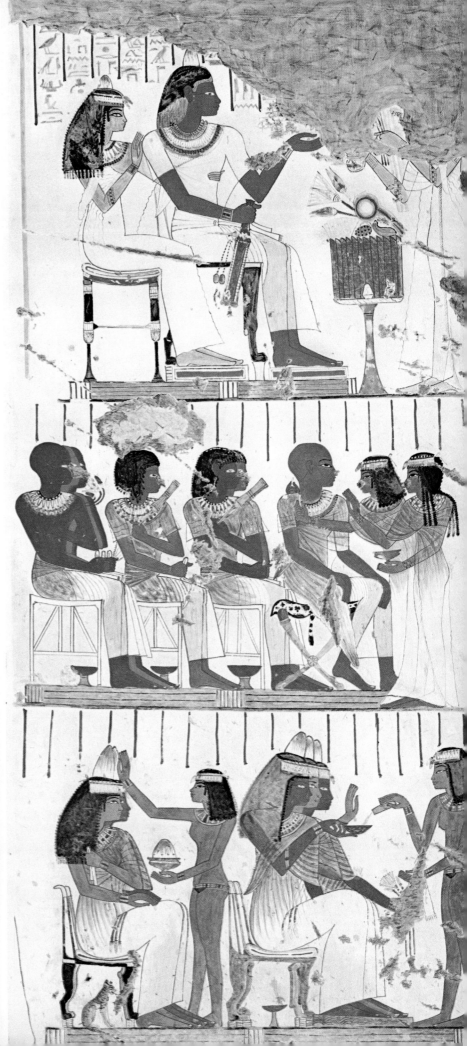

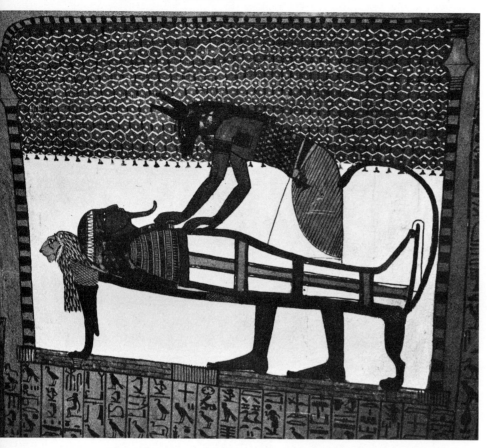

The gods of the Egyptians

No people have been more influenced by religion than the ancient Egyptians. Religion dominated everything—the political system, for the pharaoh was supposed to be a god; art and architecture, for the pyramids were built to house the bodies of the dead in their after-life; and the everyday life of the people, who believed that the gods caused the rain to fall, the River to flood and the crops to grow. The Egyptians believed in a great many gods, who lived everywhere on earth and in heaven and who might appear at any time. As is quite common among a people living close to nature, many of their gods were given an animal form, such as a ram, a bull, a crocodile or a jackal. The jackal god was Anubis, the funeral god. Anubis was an important god, for he watched over the body as the dead man prepared for and then entered into his after-life.

The cheerful Egyptians loved life on the Nile far too much to believe that it could ever end. Many other peoples have also believed in an after-life, but no other people has ever taken such elaborate steps to ensure it. The Egyptians believed that man had a soul which would survive and return to the body after death. As a result, they went to great lengths to preserve the body from decay to provide a home for the soul. Techniques of preservation were developed to a high degree. Embalmers worked for weeks on the bodies of nobles and for months on those of the pharaohs. In the final stage the body was wrapped in layer after layer of linen strips. The *mummy,* as we call it, was then placed in a coffin ready for its earthly resting place.

In 1922 the mummy of Pharaoh Tutankhamen was discovered. The mummy lay in the innermost of three coffins, each shaped like the king, and the last of solid gold. Within this final coffin the face of the mummy was covered by the gold mask reproduced here.

For company in the after-life, and to make certain that his soul would recognize him, models of the dead man's possessions—boats and animals, weapons, and paintings of friends and relatives—were placed in the tomb. In Tut's tomb there was everything he might need in the after-life: vases, knives, two war chariots in case he should go on a military campaign, chairs, chests and a host of other objects. There were also statues of gods and goddesses as well as some likenesses of the dead man himself to provide a home for the soul if his body should not obey the funeral priest's prayer, "O flesh decay not, perish not, let not thy odor be evil."

The day of judgement: trial before Osiris

Although the Egyptians continued to worship many gods, two of them became by far the most important. The first was Re, the sun god (seen below to the right of Anubis), who perished at dusk but rose again in the morning to sail his ship across the earth. The importance of Re is easy to understand because he represented the cycle of birth, death and renewal with which the Egyptians were familiar through their work in the fields. Furthermore, without mountains or clouds to cut off the sun, Re was always present in the Egyptian sky. When Thebes became the capital of the Empire, Re was united with Amon, the Theban god of the wind, to form the all powerful Amon-Re, king of the gods uniting the air and the sun. The pharaoh was the son of Re, and joined the god in his kingdom after death. But Re was the guardian god of the pharaoh and the country; he was not concerned with the life of individuals.

Osiris (seated on the throne below) was a more important god in the everyday life of the people. An Egyptian myth told how Osiris, a good ruler, was treacherously killed by his brother Seth, who cut up the body and scattered the parts throughout Egypt. But Isis, Osiris' faithful wife, collected the parts and with the help of Anubis, put the body back together and restored Osiris to life. Osiris then descended to the underworld to become the judge of the dead. When his son Horus grew up, he avenged his father by killing Seth.

The death and resurrection of Osiris corresponded to the flooding and recession of the Nile, on which the Egyptian's life on earth depended.

More important was the belief that just as the god had triumphed over death, so might those individuals who followed him inherit everlasting life. There were also in the myth a number of ideas that made a direct appeal to ordinary Egyptians: the faithful wife and son, the concern of Osiris for his subjects, the punishment of treacherous enemies. For the mass of the people, such factors made the worship of Osiris much more satisfying than the worship of the remote god, Re.

The Egyptians came to believe that the dead appeared before Osiris for judgement. Their trial had three stages. First, they had to declare their innocence of forty-two sins, including murder, falsehood, dishonesty, greed and pride. Egyptian paintings show forty-two figures, each representing one of the deities passing judgement. Next, the dead man had to assert his virtues. Finally, Anubis weighed the dead man's heart in the balance against an object representing truth. Thoth, god of the moon and patron of writing and the sciences, recorded the result as Osiris watched the proceedings from his throne. A heavy heart would outweigh truth, and the dead would be judged guilty. His soul would then be devoured by the combination crocodile and lion

shown in the painting above. But most, if not all men, seem to have passed the test and entered a realm of everlasting delight and pleasures in beautiful gardens and orchards inhabited by beautiful singing birds and gentle animals. The knowledge that they would appear before Osiris helped to guide Egyptians in their daily living. Each hoped to be able to say on judgement day, "I did no evil thing," "I did not report evil of a servant to his master," "I allowed no one to hunger," "I did not decrease the offerings to the gods," "I did not dam the running water."

The painting, showing the trial before Osiris and the other gods, is taken from one of a number of books which together are known as the Book of the Dead. Placed in the tomb of the dead to ensure his survival, these books tell how the priests developed the worship of Osiris. The priests persuaded the people that they could ensure life after death. Then they sold magic charms which would prevent the heart of the deceased from betraying the truth. They also sold a collection of spells and inscriptions, which prevented the dead from making any mistake, proclaimed his innocence of all wrong-doing and even threatened the gods with punishment if they did not grant eternal life.

69

Amenhotep IV was a brilliant pharaoh who disapproved of the corruption of religion by the priests. He also believed that there was only one god, not the hundreds which Egyptians worshipped. The one god, he declared, was Aton, the name for the visible disc of the sun. (Here he is shown with his wife, Nefertiti, and their children, basking in the rays of Aton.) Changing his name to Ikhnaton, he ordered all his subjects to worship Aton as the creator of the world and the father of all men. Priests were driven from the temples and the old gods were destroyed. Ikhnaton's belief in one god is the first recorded monotheism in history, but it was doomed to failure and did not reappear again until the time of the Hebrews six hundred years later. Yet it is possible that Ikhnaton's religion influenced later Hebrew prophets, for Psalm 104 of the Hebrew Bible is similar to the Egyptian *Hymn to the Sun* which glorifies Aton:

How manifold are thy works!
They are hidden from the face of
    man, O sole God
Like unto whom there is no other.
Thou madest the earth at thy will
    when thou wast alone:
Men, cattle, all animals, everything
    on earth that goes on its feet,
Everything that is on high that flies
    with its wings,
The foreign lands, Syria, Kush, and
    the land of Egypt.

Since the priests and the people were opposed to Ikhnaton's religious revolution, the pharaohs who succeeded him returned to the old ways. Under his successor and son-in-law, Tutankhamen, the priests were allowed to return to the temples and soon the old ways were re-established. Among some of the better educated Egyptians, the belief in one god persisted and they endowed Amon-Re with the qualities of the sole god. But for the mass of the people, the power of the priests to ensure salvation through their charms and books became increasingly important. Religion became less a code of good conduct or an explanation of life and more and more the magic of the priest.

The art of the Egyptians

Almost everyone is aware of the grandeur and massiveness of the Egyptian pyramids. But the three great pyramids at Gizeh, and the dozens of others that dot the landscape, were only one example of the genius of the ancient Egyptians. Like all other forms of Egyptian art they show the importance of religion in Egyptian life.

The pyramids were the indestructible tombs of the pharaohs of the Old Kingdom. Safely preserved in their depths the pharaoh would live forever. Moreover, the pyramids were ideal objects for the worship of the god Re, for the first light of the sun would strike the peak and slant downwards into the valley below.

The largest pyramid, that built by the Pharaoh Khufu, is shown on the extreme right. Completed about 2600 B.C., it has a base covering thirteen acres and was originally 484 feet high. It took twenty-three years for an army of workmen to fashion the pyramid out of 2,300,000 blocks of limestone weighing over two tons each. Yet so capable were the Egyptian builders that the pieces have

joints of about one-fiftieth of an inch, and the southeast corner stands only half an inch higher than the northwest corner 755 feet away.

The Egyptians did not use slaves for building the pyramids. They were to be the supreme monuments to the glory of the pharaoh and the country, and all Egyptians were forced to work on them a few months each year, much as they might be expected to serve in the army. (The pictures on pp. 72-73 show stages in pyramid-building.)

The large blocks of limestone were cut out of the cliffs with chisels and saws, while granite blocks were secured by using chisels and wedges. Once cut away and chipped to size, the massive blocks were skidded on rollers to the river bank where they were loaded on barges which carried them down-river. Unloaded from the barge, the blocks were dragged by workers and rolled to the site.

The blocks were next moved to the exact section of the pyramid for which they had been cut. Sloping ramps enabled the workmen to move blocks weighing several tons to the very top. Others went into the long passageways

Pyramid building, Hollywood style:
scenes from THE EGYPTIAN

and tomb rooms in the depths of the pyramid. Each block fitted with the next almost perfectly. When the rough work was finished, artists and sculptors moved inside to decorate the walls of the tomb with pictures representing the pharaoh and his life on earth.

At length, the time came for the pharaoh to reach his earthly resting place. After months had been spent embalming his corpse, the funeral procession moved off. The whole nation mourned for the pharaoh, but for many Egyptians the ranks of genuine mourners made up of friends and relatives were swelled by professional mourners. Surrounded by objects he loved and needed, the pharaoh finally reached the tomb, where his body would rest and his soul would return from time to time. When the mummy had been put in its place, the priests and others departed. A slab of stone was removed and massive blocks of granite fell into place to seal forever, it was hoped, the entrance to the tomb. Yet in later years the tombs of the pharaohs were found and the treasures removed. The one tomb that survived almost intact, mummy and all, was not in a pyramid at all, but in an underground burial chamber. But from that tomb of the ruler, Tutankhamen, known to history mainly because he was the son-in-law of Nefertiti and because his tomb was found in 1922 by a British archaeologist, we can tell something about the treasures that accompanied the pharaohs to their tombs in the pyramids.

pharaohs added to it in gratitude to the god of empire. The most spectacular addition was the great hall, which contained 134 columns, like those standing here, glorifying Amon. On the top of the capital of each column there is room for one hundred men. The massive and solid construction is typical of Egyptian architecture. It reflects the confidence of the pharaoh and the people that they were building for all time. Like the Nile, the Egyptians felt, the world would remain unchanged forever.

Equally massive were the statues that adorned the exterior of many Egyptian temples. Usually of the pharaohs, the giant sculptures seemed to indicate the desire to recognize or foster national pride, the glory of the empire, and the magnificence and power of the pharaoh and his people. Among the most famous are the four giant statues (above right) of Ramses II seated outside one of the two temples he had built at Abu Simbel. Over sixty-five feet high, the statues are carved, like the temple itself, out of the cliff. Impressive, too, are the six huge figures, four of Ramses and two of his wife, Nofretari, standing outside the Queen's temple at Abu Simbel.

While not all Egyptian sculpture was this massive, it was usually just as lifeless and rigid. Although the faces on masks or statues may have been accurate, they tend to be impersonal. No face in Egyptian art ever betrays the suggestion of sadness or gaiety, fear or anxiety. The Egyptians did not attempt to picture reality—the pharaoh was always larger than other men, for example—but to tell a story or make a point.

Although Egyptian painting seems almost equally lifeless to the modern eye, it is far more natural or realistic than the sculpture. While much of the painting was done to decorate tombs and temples, it was not religious art. In his paintings of agricultural workers, or artisans, a banquet or mourners, the artist was able to capture some of the spirit of Egyptian life. Pharaohs and high officials were always treated in a formal way, as in sculpture, but ordinary people were always alive with movement and vigour.

In praise of the gods

During the Middle Kingdom the pharaohs stopped erecting pyramids and spent much of their energy building temples and palaces. Most of these structures have been destroyed, but the magnificent ruins of the temples built during the New Kingdom remain. The largest is the Temple of Amon at Karnak, near Thebes. The temple began as a small shrine. As the empire expanded through victories outside Egypt, the

Literature and learning

Among the most important achievements of any people is the creation of a system of writing by which they can record their ideas. The invention of writing seems to have occurred at about the same time in Mesopotamia and Egypt. Probably the Egyptians followed the example of the Mesopotamians. In any case, both peoples developed a form of picture writing. The Mesopotamians, as we have seen, gradually changed the pictures into wedge-shaped marks to develop their distinctive cuneiform writing. The ancient Egyptians never gave up their form of picture writing, known as *hieroglyphic,* examples of which can be seen in many of their paintings. The name "hieroglyph" comes from the Greek and means *sacred carving,* no doubt because the Greeks first saw the writing on the walls of temples.

At first each hieroglyph or sign represented a single object or idea. In time most of the signs came to stand for sounds. By putting such signs together, the Egyptians could spell out words. The Egyptians were never able to develop a true alphabet because their hieroglyphs never reached the point where vowels and consonants had a

single fixed symbol. They represented only consonant sounds. Lacking vowel sounds, they had to combine hieroglyphs that stood for sounds with those that stood for ideas. Hieroglyphs were fine for making formal records on stone. But they were time-consuming and difficult to make on wood, or on the papyrus paper widely used in business transactions. As a result there developed simplified forms of hieroglyphic writing for everyday use.

Most of our knowledge of Egyptian literature

comes from papyrus rolls. Thanks to Egypt's dry climate, some of these have survived sufficiently well that the lampblack ink is still readable. All the writing carved on stone walls or pillars has, of course, endured, but much of this was not "literature" but was concerned with biographical details and historical records. At any rate, from the samples which remain it is clear that the Egyptians produced a varied and extensive literature. Much of it was serious, in the form of religious writing, prayers and hymns. There was also a good deal of political writing, usually in praise of a ruler but occasionally to protest some injustice. Some protests suggest that at times there must have been considerable freedom of speech. More interesting are the folk songs and adventure stories which combine romance with vivid and colourful description. Like adults of all times the Egyptians enjoyed giving advice to the young. Some of this is tedious and boring, but on occasion "wisdom literature" reached heights of excellence. The *Instruction of Amenemope* is an interesting example because of its similarity to parts of the Book of Proverbs in the Bible.

Give thy ears, hear what is said,
Give thy heart to understand them.
To put them in thy heart is worth while . . .
Let them rest in the casket of thy belly . . .
They shall be a mooring-stake for thy tongue.

The similar lines in Proverbs are these:

Incline thy ear and hear my words,
And apply thy heart to apprehend.
For it is pleasant if thou keep them in thy belly,
That they may be fixed like a peg upon thy lips.

From many other examples of such similarities, scholars have concluded that Egyptian writing had a considerable influence on parts of the Old Testament.

The Egyptians also made great advances in science and technology. It is a bit strange that a people so much concerned with life after death could have been so much at home in this world. The Egyptians were an extremely practical people, however, and most of their intellectual achievements grew from their need to solve defi-

nite problems. They were not, for example, interested in the theory of mathematics. To Egyptians, mathematics was simply a useful and necessary tool that would enable them to build pyramids, lay out fields, control the River and estimate supplies for the army. Once they had developed a system of mathematics that enabled them to meet the problems of everyday living in the Nile Valley, the Egyptians were content.

The most important achievement of Egyptian scientists was the creation of a solar calendar of 365 days. This was a brilliant achievement based on years of observations and records by many astronomers. The breakthrough came when they realized that the bright star Sirius appeared once a year, just before dawn, on the eastern horizon. Since the Nile floods began at about the same time, the Egyptians began their year with the appearance of Sirius. In this way, they worked out for the first time in history a calendar based on the sun. There were twelve months of thirty days each, with an additional five days which they added at the end of the year. Although the Babylonians were more advanced than the Egyptians in other areas of astronomy, they retained a calendar based on the moon. They then had to put up with the inconvenience caused by the fact that the number of days in a moon month is not always the same.

Another field in which the practical nature of the Egyptians led them to great achievements was medicine. No doubt they had learned a good deal about the organs and working of the human body in their search for the best ways of mummification. Yet there remained much superstition and magic in the practice of medicine in Egypt. Most diseases could only be explained in terms of evil spirits and were treated with a combination of foul tasting concoctions and witch doctor mumbo jumbo. It was different with physical injuries like broken arms, legs and noses. In these cases the cause and nature of the trouble was clear, and Egyptian doctors diagnosed and treated such cases in a completely scientific and modern manner. For this reason, Egypt can claim to have produced the first real doctors in the world.

The epic of Greece

Wherever we turn we become aware of our debt to Greece. Greek thinkers laid the foundations for much modern thought. Greek scientists, mathematicians, doctors and architects pointed the way for their modern counterparts. The works of Greek artists and sculptors and playwrights have always inspired Western man. If there were no other reasons, these would be sufficient to justify a study of Greece.

GREECE: THE GREATNESS OF MAN

The epic of Greece
The glory of Greece

The Parthenon standing boldly on the hill overlooking Athens embodies the grace, dignity and majesty of ancient Greece.

But there is one other reason which outweighs all the others in importance. The Greeks contributed to Western civilization a new idea. It was simply a belief in man as a free and worthy individual. As the dramatist Sophocles wrote, "The world is full of wonders, but nothing is more wonderful than man." This belief is all the more remarkable because throughout most of the world of that day individual men were not free. For the most part, men were dominated by kings or pharaohs. Their lives were often controlled by superstitious beliefs. To the Greeks, however, it was neither king, nor God, but man who was at the centre of things. The Greeks insisted that man was the most important thing in the world. They were the first to believe that the individual man was responsible for his own actions and that all men were free and equal. They were the first to believe in freedom. They had a deep respect for the law. But they made and enforced the laws themselves so that no man's freedom would interfere with another's. As a result of these beliefs, the Greeks became the first people in history to develop a democratic system of government. In this system of government and in their ideas lie the foundation and spirit of Western civilization.

FROM LEGEND TO FACT

A hundred years ago many people were familiar with the tales told by Homer, the blind Greek poet who is supposed to have lived about 800 B.C. These legends told of men and gods who roamed about performing great and heroic deeds. In one of his best-known stories Homer told how the Greeks were able to capture the city of Troy by hiding soldiers in a huge, wooden horse that the Trojans foolishly pulled inside the walls of their city. Homer also wrote about a large and wealthy civilization on the island of Crete.

> There is a land amid the wine-dark sea
> Called Crete; rich, fruitful, girded by the waves,
> She boasts unnumbered men and ninety towns . . .
> One city in extent the rest exceeds
> Knossos, the city in which Minos reigned.

Ancient legends said that King Minos owned a ferocious beast, called the Minotaur, with a bull's head and a man's body. He kept the Minotaur in a confusing network of passageways, called a labyrinth, or maze. As punishment for the killing of

When the ancient ruins of Crete were at last uncovered, the doors to the secrets of the brilliant civilization unlocked, vivid wall paintings like this greeted the discoverers. This painting, done about 1500 B.C., illustrates a favourite sport of Cretan youths, bull-vaulting. The boy grasped the horns of a charging bull and did a handspring over his back.

his son, King Minos demanded that every ninth year the Greek city of Athens send a tribute of seven boys and seven girls to Knossos to be devoured by the Minotaur. One year Theseus, son of the King of Athens, volunteered to go. But Aphrodite, the goddess of love, made King Minos' daughter Ariadne fall in love with Theseus. Ariadne gave Theseus a sword and a ball of string. With the sword he killed the Minotaur, and having attached the string to the door of the labyrinth, he rewound it and found his way out.

A century ago Homer's stories of the Trojan War, Knossos and King Minos, as well as many other tales from ancient times, were regarded as myths and legends. No one knew for sure whether such a place as Troy had ever really existed. Few believed in the existence of King Minos or the fabulous city of Knossos.

One German schoolboy, Heinrich Schliemann, was fascinated by the tales and refused to believe that they were not true. Beginning life as an errand boy, he gradually earned a great fortune which made it possible for him to travel and investigate the truth of the Homeric legends. In 1870 he stood on a hilltop in Asia Minor near the Dardanelles Strait, where he believed Troy had once stood. Before long the shovels and picks of his workmen began to uncover the walls of a city, and later a temple filled with vases and cups of gold and silver. The experts who had laughed at Schliemann were amazed. The schoolboy was right. Other archaeologists continued Schliemann's work and proved not only that Homer's Troy had existed but that many other cities had stood on the same site.

Schliemann also uncovered the fabled Greek city of Mycenae where King Agamemnon, the conqueror of Troy, had lived. Here were graves crammed with a fortune in gold vessels, masks and weapons, as well as the bones of royal children wrapped in thin sheets of gold. Near one of the royal graves lay a golden rattle. Ten years later Schliemann stood on a mound on the island of Crete. He insisted that beneath his feet lay the legendary city, Knossos, and the palace of King Minos. Although Schliemann died before he was able to complete the excavation, others continued the work. Homer's stories had not been mere fairy tales. Troy, Mycenae and Knossos *had* existed. Homer's gods and goddesses were imaginary, but Schliemann and the other archaeologists proved that the *Iliad* has much to tell us of ancient history. Their excavations enabled man for the first time to reconstruct the history of ancient Greece.

THE ORIGINS OF GREEK CIVILIZATION

Thanks to the archaeologists and historians we now know that we must look to Crete for the first Western or European civilization comparable to those of the Near East of Asia. Between 3000 and 2500 B.C., during part of what is known as the Neolithic period, Cretans fished and farmed, working mainly with implements made of stone. Gradually the Bronze Age emerged in Crete and the Aegean area, as Cretans learned to make weapons, tools and vessels of bronze.

While the surrounding sea discouraged invasion of Crete, it served as a trading highway which led the island merchants to the rich cities and markets of Egypt and the eastern Mediterranean.

The throne room at Knossos was only one of the magnificent rooms in the palace. The vast palace contained large halls for ceremonies, private living quarters, storerooms and workshops. The walls were decorated with frescoes, like the one which shows bull-vaulting. Wide staircases and sweeping corridors lined with tall, coloured columns gave the palace a grand and spacious appearance that impresses even modern visitors.

81

The Lion's Gate at Mycenae starkly reveals the massiveness of the ancient capital and the walls surrounding it. Through this gate may have marched the Greeks who went off to fight the Trojans more than 3000 years ago. The two lionesses over the gate were the guardians of the city and its inhabitants.

Rich in agriculture and energetic in trade, Crete flourished. One sign of progress was the growth of such prosperous cities as Knossos. Here kings, nobles and wealthy traders invested their profits in luxurious palaces and houses which are a source of wonder even to modern eyes. Many dwellings were decorated with gay wall paintings. They also boasted terraces and a system of plumbing that included flush toilets not matched until a century ago.

Situated in the Aegean Sea at the crossroads of Europe and Asia, Crete was the bridge over which passed the Near Eastern culture that enriched Western civilization. Cretan traders naturally in-

fluenced development on the mainland of Greece. There, about 2000 B.C., invaders from the north had overrun and conquered the earliest settlers. The civilization they established was called Mycenaean, after the city which soon became the largest and most powerful in the Greek peninsula.

The warlike Mycenaeans were organized for a time in independent kingdoms. Their paintings show large, bearded men obviously proud of their physical strength. Other evidence has revealed buildings with walls ten feet thick, built more for protection than for looks. Struggles for power among the kingdoms were frequent, if not constant. After a few hundred years, however, the city of Mycenae with its massive fortifications dominated Greece.

Like all ancient peoples the Mycenaeans had to depend largely on the land for a livelihood. They also relied heavily on war and booty. They quickly learned the art of navigation and began to take to the sea as pirates. Then, as often happens, the pirates became honest traders. They soon came into contact with Crete and apparently adopted or imitated many of the finest aspects of Cretan culture. Many historians believe that about 1450 B.C. the Mycenaeans conquered Crete. At any rate, after the conquest of the island, leadership in the Aegean world, in war and peace, lay with the Greek mainland.

Over the next two hundred years Mycenaean traders, pirates and warriors ranged far and wide across the Mediterranean. Greek products were sold throughout the Mediterranean, and Mycenaean colonies were established along the coast of Asia Minor. Textiles, gold and silver, ivory and spices flowed back to the Greek mainland to adorn kings, nobles and wealthy merchants in life and death. Inscriptions on clay tablets found only a few years ago show that the Mycenaeans had a complex system of government, including a king and court, military leaders, mayors of villages surrounding the city, tax collectors and other officials. The tablets also reveal over one hundred occupations. There were goldsmiths, shipwrights, farmers, woodcutters, winemakers, potters, cooks,

oarsmen, carpenters, bath attendants, doctors and many others. Mycenaean art shows that gradually the people became more refined. But they always admired grandeur and power, courage and physical strength.

This Mycenaean period was the Age of the Heroes that Homer tells us about in his famous *Iliad* and *Odyssey*. The life pictured by Homer was filled with banquets and battles, men and gods, huge armies and personal combats, and the launching of a thousand ships. It was a life in which men tried, above all, to be courageous and heroic. The war of the Greeks against Troy was the high point of this exciting age.

Although the Greeks won the Trojan war, they may have lost more than they won, for the long war sapped their strength just at the time when they badly needed it. When Troy fell, supposedly about 1184 B.C., new waves of migrating peoples were disturbing the whole eastern Mediterranean world. With trade no longer safe, the wealth of the Mycenaeans declined. They then had to rely on the produce of their own farms. As it became more difficult to make a living from the overworked land, the Mycenaean kingdoms apparently struggled among themselves for territory. At the same time, another group of Greeks from the north, called Dorians, threatened the whole Greek peninsula.

The Dorians were at a less advanced stage of development, but their iron weapons were superior to the weapons of the Mycenaeans. The invasions continued for about a hundred years. The Dorians destroyed Mycenaean cities and moved on from Greece to Crete and Rhodes and neighbouring colonies. Records show how the Mycenaeans moved women and children to safety, how they gathered supplies of weapons, and how they mo-

A Mycenaean warrior is waved farewell by his wife as he leaves for a war. This painting from a Mycenaean vase gives a good picture of the appearance and dress of the Mycenaean men and women in the great age of the Homeric heroes.

bilized troops at key points. Then the record is silent, for the Dorians had triumphed. A period known as the Dark Ages (because we know so little about it) descended on Greece. The Dorians had conquered all of Greece except the barren region of Attica. Refugees flocked to the hilltop city of Athens in Attica. From there, many crossed the Aegean Sea to Asia Minor, where they established new colonies in Ionia, so-called after the dialect spoken in Athens. These Ionians preserved much of the Mycenaean civilization. Later they returned and greatly influenced Greek culture.

RISE OF THE CITY-STATES

While it is impossible to tell exactly what did happen during the Dark Ages, the general outline seems clear. Much of the old Mycenaean civilization was destroyed by the Dorian invasions. As trade declined, the rich cities disappeared. The basic social unit was the family, or groups of families, organized into tribes or clans. At the head of the clan was the king, whose task was to lead the people in war. The king ruled with the aid of a council or group composed of the heads of leading families.

The geography of Greece played a very large part in determining its history during the Dark Ages. Greece is a land of mountains and valleys. Every district is separated from its neighbour by lofty mountains or rocky gulfs and bays. As a result Greece was made up of a number of isolated settlements. Usually the centre of each settlement was a small town huddled around a fortified hilltop, or *acropolis*. Here the surrounding farmers and artisans who lived below the walls of the acropolis could withdraw in time of danger. And times of danger were frequent as the settlements fought for more territory. Their borders gradually became fixed, usually at some natural boundary. Each geographical unit that could be defended then tended to become a separate political unit, known as the *polis* or the city-state.

These city-states were not large. Most covered only a few square miles and had a population of only one or two thousand male citizens. Even Athens, which became the most populous, had only 40,000 citizens. The centre of the polis was the acropolis, on which was located the temple and the market place or *agora* as the Greeks called it. The agora was the centre of everyday life. Here men gathered to discuss politics, conduct their affairs, shop, argue and gossip. Beneath the acropolis were the homes of the artisans and traders, and beyond, on the valley floor, stretched the lands of the farmers. The city-states were so small and compact that their citizens developed a fierce pride and loyalty and a sense of comradeship. This was a source of greatness for ancient Greece. Yet this same civic pride was also one of its weaknesses. For that same loyalty often prevented the many Greek states from co-operating to protect themselves against a common enemy. Finally it led to a tragic civil war among the city-states, which left Greece an easy prey to foreign conquest.

The city-states had another serious weakness. Very few of them had enough good land. Thus, as their populations grew, there were too many people for the available food. One attempted solution was to make war against a neighbouring state and gain land at its expense. But while warring against one's neighbours satisfied the fighting instincts of the people, it did not solve the problem of over-population, for the conquered people also had to be fed.

By 750 B.C. many Greek city-states had hit upon a more effective solution — colonization. Land hungry city-states sent abroad groups of citizens to set up new colonies in fertile lands. Such colonies not only relieved the pressure on the food supply at home, but led to the development of new sources of food supplies abroad. Moreover, a rich trade could develop between the mother state and the colonies. Since many city-states existed on or near the sea, their inhabitants had mastered the art of seafaring. Thus, overseas colonization was not a difficult task. But economic reasons alone do not explain why the Greeks founded colonies. Then, as now, there were many people who thirsted for adventure and found an exciting challenge in the thought of exploring and settling new lands.

MACEDONIA

RHODOPE MTS.

THRACE

HELLESPONT
(DARDANELLES)

CHALCIDICE

MT. OLYMPUS

ILLYRIA

Troy

PINDUS MTS.

THESSALY

LESBOS

ASIA MINOR

AEGEAN SEA

DORIS

EUBOEA

MT. PARNASSUS

Delphi

Chalcis

BOEOTIA

Marathon

ATTICA

IONIA

Eleusis

Athens

GULF OF
CORINTH

The Piraeus

SAMOS

Corinth

SALAMIS

Olympia

ARCADIA

Mycenae

Argos

Epidaurus

Tiryns

Miletus

ARGOLIS

DELOS

PELOPONNESUS

MESSENIA

SPARTA

NAXOS

Eurotas R.

MELOS

TAYGETUS MTS.

RHODES

MEDITERRANEAN SEA

Knossos

CRETE

CRADLE OF THE WEST

The sea and its god

The ruins of the shrine at Lindos (below) on the island of Rhodes, where the Greeks founded a colony, or of the temple of Sounion (right) reveal better than words the closeness of the Greeks and the sea. One of the great gods was Poseidon, brother of Zeus and god of the sea. Poseidon's wrath caused the sudden Aegean storms so feared by Greek sailors. Before leaving shore the Greeks prayed to the awesome god with the trident to "be kindly in heart and help those who do voyage in ships."

The great age of Greek colonization lasted for more than 200 years. Although most city-states and the best harbours were in the east, the Greeks first looked westward. They soon established flourishing colonies all over the toe and heel of the Italian peninsula. Southern Italy became known as Greater Greece. Other colonies, including the great city of Syracuse, soon followed on the island of Sicily. Pressing farther westward the Greeks reached the coast of what is now southern France; there they established a number of colonies, including one at what is now the French port of Marseilles. They then moved on to the Mediterranean shore of Spain. Meanwhile, in the east, Greek colonies had begun to dot the shores of the Aegean Sea, the Dardanelles and the farthest reaches of the Black Sea.

Colonization and the rich trade that followed from it helped for a time to ease the pressure of land hunger and poverty in the Greek city-states at home. But the solution was only temporary. As the population grew, these economic pressures returned to create tension and conflict within the polis and among the city-states.

By this time large landowners or aristocrats had generally replaced kings as the rulers of the city-states. Since these aristocrats had most of the land and the wealth of the polis, they alone could afford the equipment necessary to defend the polis. The ordinary farmers were usually deeply in debt and often on the verge of starvation. Hence they often turned against the landowners and demanded a fairer distribution of the land. Other classes also became more important because of changes in the military tactics. Single-combat between nobles was being replaced by battles between armies of infantrymen, or hoplites, heavily armed and carrying spears, swords and shields.

GREEKS OVERSEAS

⬚ Areas of colonization

Although the purchase of a suit of armour and weapons was beyond the means of the peasants, they could be afforded by the yeomen of the farms, or by traders in the towns. These town merchants also resented the political power of the aristocracy. Naturally, as these various classes became more important, they demanded from the aristocracy more voice in running the polis.

As a result of these developments there was violent unrest and revolution in most Greek city-states between 600 B.C. and 500 B.C. Well-meaning or ambitious men often appealed for support to the discontented middle class or lower class. Usually such men were successful and were able to overthrow the aristocrats. These men were called tyrants, and the century, the Age of Tyrants. Today we think of a tyrant as an unjust and cruel person who relies on violence and terror to gain his ends. Some Greek tyrants were just that, but others were genuine reformers. In some states the tyrants broke up the large estates and divided the land among the peasants. To retain support of the merchants they encouraged the development of industry and commerce, the building of harbours and other public works. They erected magnificent public buildings and temples to adorn the city and at the same time to provide work for

the poor. Some made their city a haven for poets, artists, philosophers and scientists.

Some Greek states remained under the rule of tyrants throughout the rest of their history. Others fell under the control of a small group of men who generally ruled in their own interests. Such a system was known as *oligarchy*. Still others followed a different path, to achieve government by the mass of the people, or democracy. Two states stand out as representatives of the two extremes. Sparta remained a tightly controlled military community governed by a few. Athens, on the other hand, became the world's first true democracy. Each in its own way made an enormous contribution to the history and greatness of ancient Greece.

SURVIVAL AND DECLINE

The political turmoil within the city-states and the constant wars among them caused serious weaknesses. Such weaknesses could be fatal if a strong power threatened Greece. By 500 B.C. Darius, King of the Persians, proved to be such an enemy. Darius was the despotic ruler of a vast empire ranging from Egypt to India and from the Persian Gulf to the Black Sea.

88

This small bronze statue provides an excellent picture of a hoplite. The right hand is in a position for hurling a spear. A metal helmet and visor protect his head and face, while a stout shield protects his body from spear or sword. His body is covered with a decorated cuirass, and metal greaves cover his lower legs.

The conquest of the small Greek city-states, he must have felt, would be a simple matter of marching. First he sent an army to conquer Thrace and Macedonia in northern Greece. Then he sent messengers to demand that the city-states surrender and send him earth and water in token of submission. According to Herodotus, a contemporary historian, the Athenians threw the messengers into a pit and told them to dig their own earth, while the Spartans threw them into a well and urged them to get their own water. But apart from this show of bravado the Greeks did little to prepare for an attack. They were much too involved in their own internal problems and much too suspicious of their neighbours.

In 490 B.C. Darius attacked. A huge fleet moved by sea across the Aegean and landed a great army at Marathon in Attica. Finally aware of their danger, the Athenians sent a small army under Miltiades to meet the Persian host. Ordering his hoplites to assemble in close order, Miltiades charged the astounded Persians. The Persian ranks broke before the onslaught and fell back to their ships. Athens had survived the first contest.

Ten years later, Xerxes, son of Darius, renewed the attack. The Greeks first stood at the narrow pass of Thermopylae, where King Leonidas and his 300 Spartans fought to the death. The Persians then moved south and captured Athens, but were lured into a naval battle off the islands of Salamis. Here the Greeks won a decisive victory and routed the Persian navy. Xerxes went home, leaving a large army in Greece. A short while later, however, the Greeks defeated this army at Plataea. On the same day a Greek fleet destroyed remnants of the Persian fleet at Mycale on the coast of Asia Minor. The defeat of mighty Persia by a league of small Greek states has never ceased to astound mankind. It is one of the great epics of human history.

Much of the credit for the victory went to Sparta, whose generals and admirals commanded the Greeks. But the Athenians, who had been responsible for Marathon and Salamis, were convinced that the survival of Greece owed much to their efforts. They became more self-confident, more

The battered helmet of Miltiades is mute testimony today to the great events on the plains of Marathon almost 2500 years ago.

convinced that their democratic system, in which all citizens ruled, was the best form of government. They felt certain that Athens was born to be the leader of the Greek city-states. This glorious self-confidence could also be seen in the brilliant flowering of Athenian culture in the century which followed the Persian Wars. That century, the fifth century before Christ, is known as the great or classical period of Athens.

After the defeat of the Persians the Spartans retired to their gloomy fortress. The Athenians, however, organized a league of Greek states to guard against further Persian attacks. The Delian League, as it was called, included the Greek states on the coast of Asia Minor, most of the Aegean islands, and most of the city-states on the mainland. In all, between 250 and 300 states belonged to the League. Each state agreed to contribute ships or, if too poor, money for the Athenians to build ships. All members in theory had an equal voice, but in practice Athens soon dominated the League.

The value of the League was seen in 468 B.C. when Xerxes mustered another giant fleet for a new invasion of Greece. Led by the Athenians, the League not only destroyed the fleet but liberated several provinces outside Greece that had been conquered by the Persians. So convinced were the Athenians of the League's value that they regarded as treachery any attempt to withdraw from it. States which tried to leave were forced by arms to stay and pay tribute. States which did not wish to join were conquered and

forced to belong. As time passed, the League ceased to be a free organization of voluntary members and, in fact, became an empire under the control of Athens. Member states often found themselves governed by Athenian officials, "defended" or garrisoned by Athenian troops, and forced to provide money and men for the Athenian army. The Athenians were so sure of the value of their democracy that they even imposed the same system on many members of the League.

Athens was no longer concerned only about the welfare of Greece and the danger of the Persians. She had become an expanding military power, campaigning for land and riches all over the Mediterranean world. As the Athenian Empire expanded, many Greek states became alarmed at the growth of Athenian might. In some states aristocrats who had lost their power when Athenian democracy was introduced were anxious to see the defeat of Athens and the restoration of their power. Gradually, the Greek states were drawn into two armed camps, with Sparta assuming the leadership of the anti-Athenian states. War was inevitable. It came in 431 B.C.

The Peloponnesian War, as it is called, of Greek against Greek, was more than a war to curb Athenian aggression. It was also a war between two sets of ideas. Sparta and many of her allies were conservatives. Athens was radical and was determined to spread Athenian democracy and culture everywhere. This kind of war fought both for ideas and for power is common throughout Western history.

90

The war raged for almost thirty years. Athenian money and the Athenian fleet were pitted against the tough, disciplined army of the Spartans. Spartans harassed the Athenians on land, besieging cities and burning crops. Athenian fleets destroyed enemy cities along the coast and cut off their trade. The war became a record of atrocities that darken the pages of Greek history. Slowly Athens was worn down. Led at first by the brilliant general and statesman, Pericles, she suffered when he and a quarter of the population were killed by a plague which swept through the city. The Athenians discovered that in time of crisis their democratic system was perhaps not the best to make rapid decisions and execute them efficiently.

The end came when the great land power, Sparta, became a sea power as well. Persian money helped Sparta build a navy. In 405 B.C. the Spartan fleet surprised the Athenian navy while the crews were ashore eating, and destroyed it. A few months later, in 404 B.C., the Athenians surrendered. By the treaty of peace Athens gave up all her foreign possessions, surrendered her fleet, and agreed to become an ally of Sparta.

Athens was never again to be the dominant power in Greece. But despite her defeat, her rich cultural life continued to flourish and she remained the centre of Greek civilization.

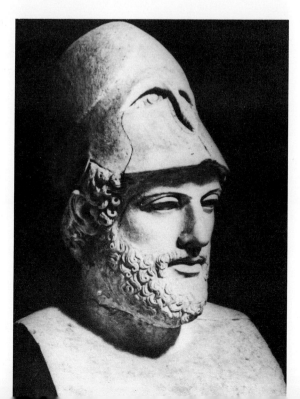

Pericles is perhaps the most famous statesman in the history of Athens. Born about 490 B.C., the son of Xanthippus who in 479 won the battle of Mycale, he was the leader of Athens from 461 until his death in 429. In foreign affairs he worked continuously to achieve the supremacy of Athens in Greece. At home he had two policies: to extend democracy in Athens and to make the city the cultural and artistic centre of the Greek world. It was under Pericles, for example, that the magnificent Parthenon and many other buildings on the Acropolis were built. As an orator he had no equal.

As Alexander passed through Asia Minor and entered Syria in 333 B.C. his army accidentally met the mighty forces of King Darius at Issus. Alexander roused the enthusiasm of his troops, who attacked and routed the enemy. This mosaic, found in the ruins of the Roman city of Pompeii, shows Alexander and Darius in the midst of the battle. The Persian leader seems terrified as he sees Alexander fighting his way towards him.

THE EMPIRE OF ALEXANDER THE GREAT

The triumph of Sparta did not bring peace to Greece. Spartan attempts to control her allies led to the same resentment and unrest as had the Athenian. Once again Greece became a number of armed camps with state fighting state. It seemed clear that the Greek city-states would never find the common bond of unity that would hold them together.

To the north, however, there was a man who believed he could conquer all Greece and unite it under his leadership. That man was Philip, King of Macedon, who inherited the throne in 359 B.C. at the age of twenty-two. Philip soon transformed his peasant foot soldiers and aristocratic warriors into a superb fighting force. He conquered Thrace, whose rich silver mines brought about 8,000,000 dollars a year into his treasury. This wealth enabled him to enlarge his army and extend his power into northern Greece. Through bribery, diplomacy and marriage alliances he attracted a number of Greek states to his side.

Athens and other states realized that Philip intended to conquer them but they seemed unable to form a strong alliance against him. Their preparations came too late, and in 338 B.C. Philip easily routed the combined Greek forces. He then summoned all representatives of the Greek city-states to a meeting at Corinth. There he formed the League of Corinth under his leadership. For the first time in history Greece was united. But the states had of course lost their independence, for in fact they were part of the military empire of Philip of Macedon.

Two years later Philip was murdered. He was succeeded by his twenty-year-old son who has become famous in history as Alexander the Great, the greatest empire builder of the ancient world. Alexander was strong, tough-minded and ambitious. Unlike his patient and cautious father he was headstrong, and liked to make quick decisions and take great risks. Dashing and brave, Alexander is one of history's most romantic figures, a man with the appearance and personality of the

perfect warrior-king. More than a warrior, he was intelligent and cultured. Under his tutor, the famous Aristotle, he learned to understand and enjoy Greek culture. In his camp, wherever he travelled, were men of learning: engineers, doctors, botanists, poets, historians, geographers. Wherever he went, he spread Greek ideas.

Alexander took up his father's plans to lead the Greeks against Persia. In 334 B.C., with only 35,000 troops and a month's supplies, he moved boldly against the giant Persian Empire. Quickly and decisively he routed the Persian armies that were sent against him. He then freed the Ionian Greek states along the coast of Asia Minor, and captured Persian naval bases on the Mediterranean coast. In Egypt at the mouth of the Nile he founded the city of Alexandria, which was to become a great centre of learning.

In the fall of 331 B.C. he entered Babylon, winter capital of the Persians; and in December

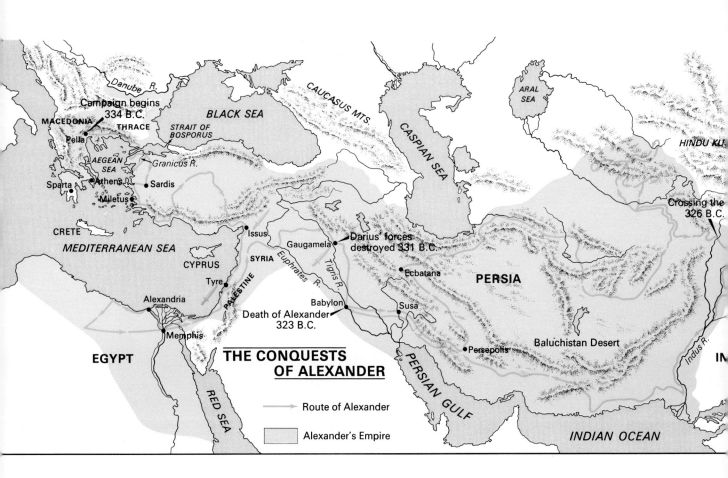

The following map labels appear:

Danube R.
MACEDONIA
Campaign begins 334 B.C.
THRACE
BLACK SEA
STRAIT OF BOSPORUS
CAUCASUS MTS.
CASPIAN SEA
ARAL SEA
HINDU KU
Pella
AEGEAN SEA
Granicus R.
Sparta
Athens
Sardis
Miletus
CRETE
MEDITERRANEAN SEA
CYPRUS
Issus
SYRIA
Euphrates R.
Tigris R.
Gaugamela
Darius' forces destroyed 331 B.C.
Ecbatana
PERSIA
Crossing the 326 B.C.
Tyre
PALESTINE
Babylon
Death of Alexander 323 B.C.
Susa
Alexandria
Memphis
EGYPT
Persepolis
Baluchistan Desert
Indus R.
IN
RED SEA
PERSIAN GULF
INDIAN OCEAN

THE CONQUESTS OF ALEXANDER

→ Route of Alexander

☐ Alexander's Empire

he took Susa, the summer capital. Early the next year he entered the great city of Persepolis, from which he took a fortune so large it was supposed to have taken 20,000 mules and 5000 camels to remove it. From there, Alexander moved east to the furthermost parts of the vast Persian Empire. For three years he attacked mountain castle after mountain castle and subdued fierce nomadic tribesmen. In the end, the whole of Asia Minor and the Middle East lay at his feet.

But the desire to conquer and, above all, the thirst for fame led Alexander on. Before his eyes rose the mighty mountains that divided India from the Middle East. Beyond, he was told, lay the Ocean that girdled the world. Into India he marched at the head of his troops, crossing territory so difficult that even today we find his exploit almost unbelievable. Well inside India he fought the most difficult battle of his career, when he faced the Indian King, Porus. The Indian army was several times larger than Alexander's, superbly trained, and included 200 war elephants which terrified Alexander's horses. By using every

tactic in the book, feigning one attack and moving in from an unexpected flank for another, Alexander defeated Porus. But his soldiers had had enough. They had left home eight years before to defeat the Persians. They had marched many thousands of miles and had won a territory of over 2,000,000 square miles, which now includes seventeen modern nations. They had no desire to penetrate further into the vast continent of India, despite their absolute devotion to their leader. Grounding their arms they insisted on returning home. Reluctantly, Alexander agreed. Down the Indus River to the Indian Ocean, along the coast of the Persian Gulf, across burning deserts, always harassed by fierce tribesmen, Alexander led his weary troops. Sending his horse to the rear he marched with his men, refusing water himself when the supplies ran dangerously low. In 323 B.C. the greatest military machine in the ancient world reached Babylon. There Alexander, worn out from his fantastic exertions, died at 33.

With Alexander's death his empire collapsed. The conquests in India returned to their rulers.

94

The face of Alexander the Great engraved on a Greek coin

His generals quickly divided up the Persian Empire. Seleucus founded the Seleucid Empire in Persia; Ptolemy established a dynasty in Egypt; and Antigonus became King of Macedon. The Greek city-states broke up the League of Corinth. Although they became independent once again, they never regained the glory and power that had been theirs before the fatal Peloponnesian Wars. For the next 200 years there was confusion throughout much of what had been Alexander's gigantic empire. Meanwhile in the west a new empire was emerging. Soon it cast its shadow over the ancient world of the Greeks. One hundred and fifty years before the birth of Christ (146 B.C.) Greece became a province of the Empire of Rome.

In the interval which followed the Pelopon-nesian Wars, however, Greek culture had continued to flourish. Greek ideas had followed Alexander's troops and his governors. Greek art and sculpture graced the palaces, temples and luxurious homes of the entire Middle East. Wherever they were situated, the cities of the Middle East were Greek cities, embodying Greek ideals in architecture, law and entertainment. The leading families of Egypt, Syria, Macedonia and other countries, including the new power, Rome, sent their children to Athens to be educated. Athens remained, as it had been, the centre of Greek and Mediterranean civilization. So important was that civilization that the period from Alexander to the Roman conquest is known as the Hellenistic period in world history, from *Hellas,* the word for Greece.

The glory of Greece

Athens and the Athenians

The city of Athens lies on a plain surrounded on three sides by mountains. The plain, which stretches down to the sea, is cut in two by a low ridge which ends abruptly with the flat-topped rock of the Acropolis. It was on the Acropolis (the hill on the left), which commanded the surrounding countryside, that the city first developed. But as Athens grew, the city spread over the plain. By the time of Pericles the Acropolis was used mainly as the site for temples of the gods. Religious processions moved along the Panathenaic Way (as in the model shown here), through the Agora to the temples in the Acropolis.

The city that sprawled at the foot of the Acropolis had a population of 150,000. The city centred on the Agora, or market-place, where the shops and official government buildings were situated. The streets running off the Agora and through the city would disgrace most slums in the modern world. They were narrow, winding alleys, swarming with flies, vermin and refuse. The body of an unwanted infant, usually female, could often be seen at the crossroads, left there by its parents for the dogs or the slave traders.

The homes were much less attractive than those pictured here. Athenian men spent little time at home, preferring life in the Agora or the bath houses, or at evening parties; they were therefore content to spend their sleeping hours in shabby homes with mud walls and few windows. (Burglars simply bored through the mud walls to remove whatever was of value!) Furniture was limited to simple couches (on which the men reclined to eat while the women sat in upright chairs), stools, a few chests, and some clay utensils. There were sleeping quarters, but during the hot season the Greeks often slept on the flat roofs. Food was cooked on an open brazier. The smoke escaped through a hole in the roof, or, in the homes of the wealthy, through pipes made of baked clay. Ordinary homes consisted of a few small cubicles, with drapes for the doorways. The wealthier citizens had floors of stone rather than dirt, a main salon for banquets, a kitchen, dining room, bathrooms, store rooms, work rooms for the slaves, and sleeping quarters upstairs. But even these homes were far from the mansions lived in by other peoples of the ancient world. The Athenian lived outdoors and in company with his fellows.

On the east side of the Agora was the shopping area. Every inch of space was crammed with small stores and workshops. Most of the shops were flimsy buildings, often little more than stalls like the booths at a modern fair. The booths seem to have been grouped according to the material for sale. There was one corner of the market for food, with shops such as that of the fishmonger, seen above slicing a fish for a somewhat worried customer. Other sections of the market would be for wine, pots and furniture, while still others would deal in bulkier goods such as metals and grains.

The Athenians loved to stroll among the shops, talking among themselves or with the merchants, about politics, war and the condition of the crops, as they looked at the merchandise or had their children measured by the shoemaker for a pair of sandals. As one merchant said in court: "My accuser claims that my shop is used as a meeting place by a parcel of ne'er do wells . . . But please note that such charges are no more applicable to me than to any other shopkeeper; nor is there a penny to choose between my customers and theirs. You all like to stroll around and drop in somewhere—at the barber's or the cobbler's or the perfumer's, whichever happens to suit you; and you nearly always pick a shop near the Agora rather than one on the outskirts."

The workshop of the world

The vase painting of Greek boys collecting olives reminds us that although Athens lived largely by trade and commerce, many Athenian citizens lived off the proceeds of their own lands. In fact, 150,000 people (or half the population of the city-state) lived beyond the border of the city in the Attica peninsula. In the early days Attica had consisted mainly of large estates, but by the fifth century B.C. most of the land was cultivated in small farms by independent landlords, usually with the help of a few slaves or labourers. Many historians regard these small landholders as the real backbone of Athens. Sturdy, self-reliant and tough, they probably formed the bulk of the hoplite forces that fought at Marathon. Many wealthy Athenians, like Pericles, owned large estates, but they simply collected the profits made by the farm supervisor using slave-labour.

Nevertheless, by the time of Pericles, Athens could not feed herself. The soil was dry and poor. While little grain could be grown, the mountain slopes yielded rich harvests of olives. Olive oil was highly prized, for it was used as butter, soap and fuel. Figs and grapes were important products, and Greek wine was an important export. Vase paintings often show women making or carrying wine.

Athens then was not self-sufficient agriculturally, and lived more by trade and commerce than by agriculture. The prosperity and importance of Athenian agriculture declined even further after the Persian Wars, for Xerxes destroyed the vineyards and olive groves, which took forty years to reach maturity again. The Athenians then became even more dependent on trade and sea power. Athen's naval supremacy was established at Salamis and she went on to become mistress of the Mediterranean; her ships (such as those shown at right under full sail in a good wind) dominated the ports and trade routes of the known world. In exchange for supplies of foodstuffs Athens sold the products of her mines and workshops. In fact, she became the great workshop of the ancient world. The ships landing at the port of Piraeus carried goods from Athenian colonies, Egypt, Italy and the Near East and even tin from Britain. The docks at Piraeus were to the ancient world what those of London were in the nineteenth century, and what New York is in the twentieth — the meeting place of men and material from all over the world.

The engines of prosperity

The trade and commerce of Athens did not rest on the work of the citizens, but on two other classes in society: resident aliens known as *metics,* and slaves. Only about 40,000 of the 300,000 inhabitants of the state were citizens. There were about 20,000 metics, and the remainder of the population was made up of slaves and women.

The merchant weighing his material (above) was quite possibly a metic, for this group dominated the commercial life of Athens. The metics were important in retailing; they controlled the grain trade and other overseas trading ventures, and they were prominent in building, banking and manufacturing. Many of the most prominent artists, musicians and teachers were also metics. Attracted to Athens by its wealth and its rich culture, the metics were quite prepared to accept the fact that they had no political privileges. This probably did not seem very important to them, for in most other states the people generally lacked any political rights.

Many skilled workers, like this cabinet-maker (below), were slaves. Slaves were equally essential to Athenian prosperity and survival. They provided a large labour force on the farms; they manned the teeming docks at Piraeus and performed the backbreaking work in the mines. A wealthy Athenian might have fifty slaves, and an average citizen from three to a dozen. Slaves did most of the domestic work, cleaning, cooking and waiting on their master.

Slavery was taken for granted in Athens as it was in every ancient society. Slaves had almost no rights. They could be bought and sold. Life in the mines or on the docks could be brutal and short. The slave could be punished severely or tortured, although if he died his master could be brought to trial. On the other hand, many slaves held important positions in society and led decent and prosperous lives. Without slave labour the Athenian economy could not have prospered. Moreover, had not slaves done most of the work, the Athenian citizens would not have developed the world's first democracy or enjoyed the rich cultural and intellectual life that has made the Athens of Pericles one of the wonders of world history.

100

The Athenian woman

A modern woman might argue that the lot of the Athenian woman was worse than that of the slave. The Athenian world was a man's world, and the wife seems to have understood that she was neither to be seen nor heard. Her wedding, which usually took place when she was about fifteen, was a great event in her life even though she had little choice in the selection of a husband. Surrounded by guests, she might leave with her new husband on a chariot. But on her return her task was to raise a family and supervise the domestic chores of the slaves. If the family was too poor to afford slaves, she might at least get outdoors to do the shopping; otherwise she remained inside the house most of the time. She did not attend the frequent parties her husband enjoyed, and even if he entertained at home she was not allowed to enjoy the festivities. Not even the death of her husband could set her free, for he could state in his will whom she must marry after his death. However, while this seems dreary, there is evidence to reveal that the bright and attractive Athenian women often exercised as much power over men as women have done before and since!

101

Growing up in Athens

The painting of the young boy fishing might suggest that the life of the Athenian child was much like that of children today. But nothing could be further from the truth. The Athenians did not have large families. The poor looked on every child as an extra mouth to feed, while the rich were often too selfish to want to spend their money in bringing up and educating the children. There was also fear that the family lands would have to be divided up among so many people that no child would have enough land or wealth to support himself. The poet Hesiod declared, "Try, if you can, to have an only son, to care for the family inheritance: that is the way wealth multiplies in one's halls." The famous philosopher Plato, drawing up plans for his ideal republic, wrote, "The number of children regarded as adequate by law will be one boy and one girl."

The most dangerous period for the Athenian child, at least until he became a man and went off to war, was his first few days. If the family was unwilling to add to its numbers or if the new-born babe looked weak and sickly or deformed, he was placed in an earthenware jar with some bracelets or necklaces (by which he could later be identified if he survived) and left in some isolated spot to die. If he was to be kept, the child was officially accepted into the family on the fifth or seventh day, and on the tenth day was given a name.

For six years the Athenian child lived at home, watched over largely by his mother and a nurse, who was usually a slave. Mother and nurse, and sometimes the father, if he had the time, recited the famous myths and legends, much as parents today read their children fairy tales. Most of the Greek myths contained a moral or were designed to frighten or amuse the youngsters. Babies were given rattles. "As long as the child is occupied with a rattle," wrote the renowned philosopher Aristotle, "nothing else in the house will get broken." Excavations and paintings show that as he grew older the Greek child had tiny chariots as go-carts, toy soldiers, horses on wheels and dolls with moveable limbs. He played with marbles, kites, hoops, balls and swings, and at hide and seek.

At six the boys and girls were separated. The girls stayed at home to learn such domestic arts as weaving, cooking and running the house. Athenians saw no value in educating the women. The boys, however, went off to school until they were eighteen. At first probably only the rich could afford to send their children to schools, but by the fifth century it would appear that there were schools for the poor as well. The historian Herodotus tells us of the roof of one school collapsing and killing 120 boys. But despite the value they placed on education the Greeks did not build schools at public expense. All were private schools. Parents paid fees to the masters, most of whom were badly paid and treated with little respect. (The state did, however, pay the masters for the education of the children of men who had died in battle.) Generally only the rich remained in school until they were eighteen. Children of the poor probably only stayed long enough to learn the three R's. By the end of the fifth century, most male citizens of Athens were able to read and write.

The purpose of Athenian education was not to train boys for a job or a profession, but to make of them men who could play their part as citizens in the city-state. Character-building was of greater importance than professional training. The boys' education consisted of three major parts: the three R's, music and physical training. After the youth had learned to read and write, he was given the great epics of Homer, the *Iliad,* and the *Odyssey.* These great historic poems not only increased his literary ability, but, more important, they provided him with the knowledge a Greek citizen needed. For Homer wrote of war and peace, politics and diplomacy, the value of wisdom and courage, and man's relations with man and the gods. Many a Greek citizen could recite much of the *Iliad* and the *Odyssey* by heart.

The Greeks believed that music was a necessary and basic part of the education of every citizen. Every child had to learn to play the lyre, an instrument with seven strings plucked either with the fingers or a small stick. Less popular was the flute. The children also learned to sing, particularly the ancient ballads. One Greek writer tells us of boys "learning to sing some ancient ballad — in the proper posture, not with the thighs glued together — like 'Pallas, Terrible Stormer of Cities' or 'Fierce Battle-cry from Afar,' keeping to the tune as their fathers knew it. But if anyone started fooling about and putting trills and twiddly bits . . . he would get a sound drubbing for his un-Muse-icality." Music was everywhere in Athens. Men sang on their way to work; poems were recited to music; there was music in the plays. Every Athenian wanted to be able to sing, play or dance.

An education for citizenship

104

Only more unfortunate, perhaps, was the Athenian who was not physically fit. All Greeks placed a high value on physical fitness. This was chiefly because every citizen had to defend his city in time of war. But they also believed that the body as well as the mind had to be fit, strong and alert if a man were to be a good citizen. From the time he was about twelve, the Athenian boy was regularly instructed in athletics. All forms of exercise and sport were included, but the great emphasis was on the five classic sports which made up the *Pentathlon:* wrestling, running, jumping and throwing the discus and the javelin.

For those students who could afford to remain in school, the official end of the Athenian's education came at eighteen. During the following year he received training as a soldier in a city garrison. At the end of the year he was presented with a spear and shield and took a loyalty oath to his city, in which he vowed never to disgrace the sacred arms, never to abandon his comrades in battle and never to let his city down. It was a proud moment in the family's life when the youth then left Athens for a further year at some rougher frontier garrison. Finally, at the end of the year, a *man* returned to Athens to take up his role as a full-fledged citizen.

*In many ways the Agora was the most
important part of Athens, the real centre of
Athenian political life. The Agora lay to the
north of three hills: the citadel or Acropolis;
the Areopagus, site of the city's oldest
law court; and the Pynx where the Assembly
held its meetings. In the Agora were located
the main buildings from which Athenians
carried on the day-to-day running of the
government. In this model of the west side
of the Agora we see the Temple of
Hephaestus (god of fire) at the top of the
photograph. Just below it to the left is the
Council House, or Bouleuterion, where the
Council of 500 met. The round building
known as the Tholos was the administrative
hub of the city. The Tholos housed the
groups of fifty men who governed Athens
for one-tenth of the year. Day and night
there were always some responsible officials
on hand in case of emergency. To the right
of the Tholos was the Metroon complex
which contained the records of state and
housed the shrine of the Mother of the
Gods. To the right of this was the Temple of
Apollo where citizens were registered, and
at the extreme right was the Stoa of Zeus, a
roofed colonnade through which Socrates is
supposed to have walked as he questioned
his students and followers.*

The world's first democracy

About five hundred years before the birth of
Christ the little city-state of Athens had become
the world's first democracy. The word democracy
comes from two Greek words, *demos* (people),
and *kratia* (rule). In modern democracies the
people elect representatives to rule for them. In
Athens the people actually did rule — at least
the 40,000 males who were citizens ruled. To an
Athenian citizen it was unthinkable that someone else should govern for him. Democracy in
Athens meant that all of the citizens could make
their own laws directly. How did this system of
direct democracy work?

Every citizen belonged to the Assembly, which
by the fifth century B.C. had become the most
important political body in Athens. About forty
times a year the members of the Assembly
crowded together at an open air meeting, usually
on a hill called the *Pynx* (a place where people
are packed closely together). As the rulers of
Athens assembled, the meaning of direct democracy became evident. Merchants, country squires
and members of the aristocracy rubbed elbows
with those who qualified as citizens from among
the artisans, fishmongers, sausage-makers and the
unemployed. Brightly-clad Athenian policemen

herded latecomers to the meeting with a rope dipped in red paint. Anyone brushed by the rope could be identified later and fined for his tardiness. Although every citizen could take part in the meetings of the Assembly, usually only those who lived in or near the city attended. Many of these were poor people who looked forward to the payment they received for taking part.

Assembly meetings were usually tense and exciting, for Athenians believed that any member should be free to speak on any matter he wished. But they also felt that other members had a similar freedom to disagree. Often they expressed their disapproval so boisterously, with boos, jeers and catcalls, that it was impossible for a speaker to make himself heard. When the last speaker had had his say, the vote was taken by a show of hands. The decision of the majority became law.

Since mass meetings cannot rule efficiently, a smaller Council of 500 members carried on the day-to-day business of government and decided what business the Assembly would discuss. Council members were not elected but were chosen by lot. Each one had to be over thirty and had to pass a physical and mental fitness test. But 500 is still too large a group to work together effectively. Thus the Council was divided into smaller bodies of fifty men, each of which served for one-tenth of the year. Since no one could become a Councillor more than twice, there was a very good chance that sooner or later most Athenians would serve on the Council. And since a new president of the group was picked each day by lot, every citizen really did have a chance to become President in ancient Athens — if only for a day. Despite the importance of the Council, however, it was the Assembly of all Athenians which had the final authority, for it passed all laws and decided all questions of foreign policy and peace and war.

In addition to the Council and the Assembly there was a board of nine *archons* who carried out judicial and religious duties. Much more important in fifth-century Athens, however, were the ten generals, each one of whom was elected by the Assembly for one year. Since a general could stand for re-election as often as he wished, it was possible for him to become in fact the real head of the state and provide continuous leadership. The brilliant general, Pericles, was able to dominate Athens for thirty years. But Pericles was not a dictator who depended upon military force to stay in power. He had to face the citizens of Athens each year and get himself re-elected. Moreover, the Assembly could ignore his advice or dismiss him from office at any time. The real secret of Pericles' success then was his brilliant oratory and his personal popularity rather than his position as general.

There were also several hundred officials or civil servants who looked after such practical matters as roads, harbours, the planning of festivals and games, and the administration of the empire. They were either picked by lot or elected, but again only for one year. Thus, during their lifetime, most Athenians would fill some official function in their state. Athenians believed that every citizen was capable of playing a part in governing, and that everyone should. Although one historian has described the Athenian system as government by "a rapid succession of amateurs," it was not as amateurish as it may seem to us. Officials who had gained experience by serving in one particular office might be elected or chosen by lot to serve in another. And the Assembly at any time could dismiss a magistrate who was dishonest or who lacked ability.

The basis of Athenian democracy was its legal system which guaranteed the rule of law. Every Athenian was equal before the laws. Every citizen had to obey the law, which was the same for both rich and poor. Everyone had the same opportunity to present his case in court and get a hearing. But many aspects of the Athenian legal system seem very strange. Judicial power was held by 6000 jurymen over thirty years of age who had been selected by lot. At a single trial there might be from 201 to 1001 jurymen. Before these mass juries, both accuser and defendant presented their cases, for there were no lawyers. There was no cross-examination of witnesses. When the case

Each member of the Athenian jury held two ballots—one in each hand—similar to those shown at left and above. The hub of the ballot indicated the verdict. If a juror believed that the accused should be set free, he deposited the ballot with the solid hub in the official voting box, and put the other in a discard bin. If he believed the man guilty, he deposited the ballot with the open hub in the official box.

The arsenal of Athenian democracy

The marble slab shown in this photograph was uncovered during excavations of the Agora in 1952. On the slab is recorded a law passed in 336 B.C. to guard against the seizure of Athens by a dictator. "If anyone rise up against the People with a view to tyranny or join in establishing the tyranny or overthrow the People of the Athenians or the democracy in Athens, whoever kills him who does any of these things shall be blameless." To make certain that everyone became aware of the law the secretary of the Council was instructed to inscribe it on two pieces of stone and to "set one of them by the entrance into the Areopagus . . . and the other in the Assembly." The carved panel above the text shows a personification of the People of Athens receiving a wreath from Democracy.

To prevent corruption, each member of a jury was given a bronze or wooden jurors' ticket like that shown at left. Each ticket contained the name of the juror as well as the jury-section to which he belonged.

Those citizens who volunteered to serve on a jury put their tickets in the slots of a device known as a *Kleroterion* or allotment machine, part of which is shown in the above photograph. Jurors for the day were selected by dropping black and white balls down a tube on the machine. The tickets of those chosen were given to the official in charge, who first identified each man and watched while he selected a bronze ball from a box. The ball indicated the court in which the juror was to serve. The official then put the juror's ticket in a box that would go to that court. This system ensured that the juror would go to the court to which he had been assigned, for he could only recover his ticket and receive his pay in this court.

The Athenian courts were generally able to curb the illegal activities of most ordinary citizens. To provide protection against very powerful men who might be able to seize control of the government, the Athenians invented a device known as *ostracism*, which made it possible to send into exile for ten years any citizen considered dangerous to the state. Every year the Assembly decided whether a vote of ostracism should be held. If so, the citizens gathered on an appointed day in an open part of the Agora. Each man carried a broken piece of a pot or *ostracon* on which he scratched the name of the man who seemed to him most dangerous to the state. If more than 6000 citizens voted, the man whose name was scratched on the greatest number of ostraka was sent into exile. The ostraka shown here not only contain names but also reflect a good deal of feeling as well. The top one reads "Kallixenos the Traitor" while that on the bottom says "Out with Themistocles."

Ostracism was designed to provide a safeguard against tyranny, but it was eventually used by politicians to get rid of powerful rivals. Such misuse led to its abandonment in the late fifth century. Whether or not ostracism served the purpose for which it was intended, the actual ballots proved useful. After the vote was taken they were swept up and used to fill holes in the roads.

was presented, the jury did not retire to consider the arguments but immediately voted. A majority vote decided the case and generally there was no appeal from the verdict.

When the law did not provide a definite punishment for a crime, the jurymen listened while both the accuser and defendant suggested penalties. The jury then voted for one or the other. In 399 B.C., for example, the great philosopher, Socrates, was brought to trial and convicted on the charge of corrupting the youth of Athens and not believing in the city's gods. Since there was no fixed penalty the prosecutor suggested death. Socrates then suggested that his penalty be to receive free meals at public expense for the rest of his life — an honour commonly given those who had made a great contribution to the city. His friends tried to persuade him to change his proposal to a fine. The jury voted for death.

The system of mass juries was one of the weakest features of the Athenian legal system. Often the jurymen were not influenced by the evidence presented as much as they were by appeals to their feelings. Still the juries did give every Athenian a chance to be tried by his fellow citizens, and they certainly involved many Athenians in the administration of justice.

These were the main features of the world's first democracy as it existed during the Age of Pericles. No words better express the pride of Athenians in the government of their city-state than those spoken by Pericles during the life-and-death struggle of Athens with her great rival, Sparta.

> Our constitution is called a democracy because power is in the hands not of a minority but of the whole people. When it is a question of settling private disputes, everyone is equal before the law; when it is a question of putting one person before another in positions of public responsibility, what counts is not membership of a particular class, but the actual ability which the man possesses. . . . Here each individual is interested not only in his own affairs but in the affairs of the state as well. . . . We do not say that a man who takes no interest in politics is a man who minds his own business; we say that he has no business here at all. . . .

The Athenian democracy of which Pericles boasted did not happen accidentally; nor did it arrive overnight. It came about gradually and with many conflicts. At first, Athens, like most of the other city-states, was a monarchy governed by a king assisted by a council of nobles. In the beginning of the Dark Ages the legendary king Theseus of Athens united all Attica under his rule. The Athenians won the loyalty of the conquered people by allowing them to become citizens instead of making them slaves. As the city-state expanded, it became more and more difficult for one person to govern it alone. Gradually the king's powers passed to the leading men of the king's council. Sometimes these aristocrats provided good government that served the interests of all the people in the state, but often small groups of nobles seized control and ruled harshly in their own selfish interests.

By the late seventh century, Athens seemed on the verge of revolt. Many of the common people had little or no property, and small farmers could barely scratch a living from the poor soil. Many had to give up their land. Some fell so deeply into debt that they had to give up their freedom in payment. The common people were not the only Athenians with grievances. The development of commerce and industry led to the growth of a wealthy middle class. This new class resented the fact that they had no political control, and they began to agitate against the aristocratic government. Athenian nobles realized that to preserve their power in the face of growing discontent, they would have to make some reforms.

In 594 B.C. the nobles appointed Solon as archon or chief official. A moderate and courageous man, Solon immediately introduced a number of reforms to end the unrest. To assist the poor, he freed all persons who had been enslaved because they could not pay their debts. To increase the wealth of the state he encouraged trade and industry by inviting foreign craftsmen with new skills to settle in Athens. He also allowed all citizens to attend the Assembly and vote on proposals put before it. To please the middle class he made wealth rather than birth the requirement for

SOLON

holding public office in Athens. By making it possible for many more people to take part in government, Solon set Athens on the road to democracy.

But Solon's reforms left many unsatisfied. The nobles found them too sweeping, the poor too timid. Continued unrest in Athens made it possible for a bold war hero, Peisistratus, to seize power. Peisistratus used his power as tyrant to introduce a series of reforms. He expelled some of the noble families and distributed their lands among the poor peasants. He made loans to farmers to help them improve their vineyards and olive orchards. He encouraged colonization, commerce and manufacturing, and began a programme of building ports, roads and public buildings to give work to the poor and to beautify the city. He also organized athletic, musical and dramatic performances and competitions designed to bind all Athenians more closely together. Everyone benefitted from the improved economic conditions brought about by Peisistratus' policies. As more and more citizens gained wealth, they could take part in government. Thus the reforms of Peisistratus pushed Athens further along the road to democracy.

The men who succeeded Peisistratus lacked his ability and Athens went through another period of unrest. Eventually, in 507 B.C., another uprising of the people brought to power a brilliant reformer named Cleisthenes who gave Athens a new and more democratic system of government. Cleisthenes ended the power of the old aristocracy and provided that all adult males would automatically be members of the Assembly. Cleisthenes also established the Council of 500, which was drawn by lot from all citizens. Although the Council became the chief administrative body, dealing with the day-to-day business of governing Athens, the Assembly of all the citizens remained the supreme authority in the state. It was in this Athenian Assembly that for the first time in history a people governed. When in the Age of Pericles in the fifth century every citizen had an opportunity to hold office in the state, Athens had become the full-fledged democracy described earlier. To a large extent it had been the achievement of three men: Solon, Peisistratus and Cleisthenes.

How shall we judge this first experiment in democracy? The Athenians themselves were well aware that it had weaknesses and were often its harshest critics. As the philosopher Socrates pointed out, it was absurd to select the rulers of a city by lot when no one would similarly select a carpenter or a flute player. Furthermore, this government was in the hands of a minority of 40,000 male citizens out of a population of over 300,000. Women, aliens and slaves had no political rights. And no one could deny that the Athenian Assembly often fell under the spell of speakers who appealed to emotions rather than to reason. But for all its weaknesses the remarkable fact is that the Athenian system worked effectively for 200 years, a longer period than most modern democracies have lasted. Under their democratic constitution Athenians could claim truthfully that they enjoyed freedom of speech, equality before the law and equality of political power.

THE SPARTAN ARMED CAMP

While Athens was creating her democratic system of government, another Greek city-state, Sparta, was following a completely different course. The word spartan today stands for discipline, obedience, prowess in war, and a generally harsh and unpleasant way of life. One of the most famous Spartan legends tells of a young boy who stole a fox and hid it under his cloak. Rather than admit his guilt he allowed the fox to gnaw at his stomach until he suddenly fell dead before the men questioning him. The story may not be true, but every Spartan mother would have been proud to have had such a son. How did a society with such a strange set of values come about?

The Spartans were Dorians (from Doris, in central Greece), a group of invaders who spoke a Greek tongue. They pushed into the Greek peninsula during the early Dark Ages. Eventually they settled in the valley of the Eurotas River in the Peloponnese. The Spartans did not mingle with the people they had conquered or allow them to become their equals as citizens. Instead they made them *helots,* or serfs, and forced them to work on the land. In their new state the Spartans became a privileged upper class, freed from the need to do any work. Only Spartans enjoyed the full rights of citizenship. The helots had no rights at all. A third class of people, the *perioeci* (dwellers round-

The mountains standing guard over the plain of Lacedaemonia suggest the ruggedness of the Spartans themselves and the unchanging nature of their society.

about), were allowed to trade and manage their own affairs but they had no political rights.

As with other Greek city-states, land hunger forced Sparta to try to find new land. But instead of establishing colonies, the Spartans attacked and conquered the neighbouring province of Messenia. Once again the original inhabitants were enslaved and became helots. With the largest territory in Greece, Sparta became prosperous. She developed a flourishing culture and found enjoyment in art, music and dancing. For a time, it seemed that Sparta might become the artistic centre of the Greek world.

But suddenly the peace and prosperity came to an end. In 620 B.C. the Messenians, aided by some of their neighbours, revolted. Only with the greatest efforts were the Spartans able to crush the revolt and survive. The Messenian revolt was a great turning point in Spartan history. It taught the Spartans a lesson they were never to forget. To survive, they decided, they must be strong enough at all times to crush internal rebellion or outside attack. For Sparta's possible enemies outnumbered her by at least ten to one.

The Spartan solution was as simple as it was drastic. Spartan society changed completely. If survival meant being strong, Sparta was prepared to do anything to become strong. At a stroke she banished the "unnecessary and useless" arts which had made Sparta an interesting and exciting place in which to live. Sparta became an armed camp. Every Spartan man, woman and child was expected to make any sacrifice to help create the powerful army which alone could ensure Sparta's survival.

From the cradle to the grave every Spartan devoted his life to the state. If new-born babies showed weaknesses which suggested they would

This small bronze statue of a Spartan warrior (shown here wrapped in his cloak) is one of our few remaining examples of Spartan art. The figure suggests the stern simplicity and discipline of Spartan society as well as the strength which made the Spartan infantryman the greatest soldier of the ancient world.

not become good soldiers or mothers of strong men, they were not reared, but left on the slopes of Mount Taygetus to die. Boys were taken from their homes at the age of twelve and placed in barracks to be trained as soldiers. Here they learned unquestioningly to obey those in authority, to endure physical hardship and to acquire the skills that would enable them to take their place with the greatest soldiers of the ancient world.

No Spartan was allowed to farm or engage in business, for that might take his mind and energies from the all-important task of being a soldier. Foreign trade was discouraged, and foreigners who might bring new ideas were not welcome in Sparta. Since living with his family might distract a man and make him less war-like, it was arranged that all Spartans would spend most of their lives in barracks with their military comrades. In bare mess-halls they ate coarse food and the famous black broth, which, it was boasted, only a Spartan could eat. After sampling some of this brew, a visitor to Sparta was reported to have said, "Now I understand why the Spartans are not afraid to die." During his active military life a Spartan was expected to visit his wife only by stealth. It was claimed that some Spartans had never seen their wives in daylight until their period of military training was completed.

But Spartan women enjoyed a degree of freedom unknown in most of Greece. Their role as the mothers of soldiers made them important in the state and they knew it. In Sparta, unlike Athens, women were encouraged to be seen, and had equal rights with men in everything but voting. Other Greeks were critical of Spartan women, who were, they said, "bold, masculine, over-bearing to their husbands . . . and speaking openly on even the most important subjects." But the Spartans knew what they were doing. No modern mother is likely to have said to her son as he left for battle the words attributed to one Spartan mother: "Come back with your shield or on it."

Sparta's system of government was simple and fitted the needs of a nation in arms. The Spartans did not experiment with new systems of government. Since Sparta discouraged trade and industry, there developed no middle class that might oppose the nobles. Thus Sparta remained basically an aristocracy. Although Sparta had two hereditary kings, the real power was in the hands of an aristocratic council. The Council was elected from nobles over sixty years of age. It framed laws which it placed before the assembly of free citizens. The Assembly could do no more than shout their approval or disapproval of the measures submitted. By the sixth century, however, officials known as *ephors* (overseers) gave the citizens greater control over government. Every year the Assembly elected five ephors who presided over it, sat as judges with kings and council, and had the final word in deciding what the custom or law of the state was. The ephors, in most respects ran the state. The Council and the Assembly generally supported their policies.

The Spartan way of life has often been condemned. It has even been seen as the forerunner of later dictatorships. Certainly it is true that personal liberty, family life and the arts were sacrificed. The main Spartan concern was to produce soldiers who could protect the state from revolution or invasion. But it is also true that throughout the rest of Greece Sparta was generally admired. Why was this? For one thing, other Greeks did not think that the Spartans lived under a tyranny but rather under a regime that they had chosen and accepted themselves. Although few Athenians could have put up with the Spartan system, they admired such Spartan ideals as respect for authority, simplicity, moderation, willingness to serve the state, and the denial of personal pleasure. Above all, the Greeks admired the heroic way in which the Spartans actually lived up to their ideals. And when we consider what Sparta stood for, we can realize how much of the Spartan view of life has become an accepted part of our own civilization. It has often been said that Sparta left the world no creative art. The Spartans themselves did not think so. They would have agreed with a modern historian who wrote: "Sparta created not things in words or stone but men."

The war that saved the Western world

The mountains look on Marathon—
And Marathon looks on the sea,
And musing there an hour alone,
I dreamt that Greece might still be free;
For standing on the Persians' grave,
I could not deem myself a slave.

So wrote the English poet Lord Byron about 150 years ago after standing near this site, which was one of the most famous battlefields in history. He was brooding over the plight of Greece, which at the time was dominated by a ruthless foreign power. He then recalled the famous Battle of Marathon in which a handful of Greeks had repelled a foreign invader and preserved the freedom of the entire Greek world. Ever since that Greek victory, the very word Marathon has inspired men in the constant fight for freedom against oppression.

Marathon today

114

In the Battle of Marathon the forces of Darius, the mighty king of the vast Persian Empire, were pitted against the little city-state of Athens. Darius invaded Greece partly because he wanted to expand his empire and also because he wanted to punish Athens for having sent forces to help his rebellious subjects in the Greek Ionian colonies of Asia Minor. The great Persian king, seen in this carved relief holding audience in his court, had every reason to feel confident. His invading armada of 600 ships carried a huge army of experienced soldiers. As the fleet entered the Bay of Marathon and the soldiers alighted, there were few men in Greece who would have dared predict that the little Athenian army had any chance of victory. The presence of Sparta's hoplites would certainly have made some difference. But the Spartans had remained at home, refusing, for religious reasons, to start a campaign before the full moon. For Athens the outlook could scarcely have been blacker.

The miracle of Marathon was due largely to one man, the general Miltiades. Leading his army from the city, he stationed it on a slope overlooking the plain of Marathon. For several days, according to the Greek historian Herodotus, who wrote of the Persian Wars, the Greeks observed the Persians encamped on the seashore below. When it appeared that the Persians intended to re-embark in their ships and sail for undefended Athens, Miltiades took the initiative. As his hoplite infantrymen (such as those shown on this Greek vase) charged down the hillside, the Persians stared at them in amazement. The Athenians seemed "bereft of their senses, and bent upon their own destruction." But the daring assault was successful beyond any expectation. After a hard day's fighting more than 6000 Persians lay dead

on the beach. The remainder had been driven into the sea or back to their boats. The victory had cost fewer than 200 Athenian lives. To the Greeks, it seemed clear that their gods and heroes had been fighting at their side. After the battle many an Athenian soldier claimed that he had seen the ghost of Theseus leading the Athenian charge. In spite of the Greeks' amazing victory Miltiades knew there was no time for relaxation, for part of the Persian fleet had sailed in the direction of Athens. He raced his exhausted troops back to the city. When the Persian fleet reached Athens and found the hoplites drawn up in battle array on the shore, the ships turned and headed for home. By doing the impossible, a handful of Athenians had saved the entire Greek world from disaster.

THRACE

MACEDONIA

MT. OLYMPUS

MT. ATHOS

SEA OF MARMARA

HELLESPONT (DARDANELLES)

PERSIAN EMPIRE

Thermopylae

AEGEAN SEA

Delphi

Thebes

Plataea

Marathon

Salamis

Athens

Sardis

SAMOS

ASIA MINOR

DELOS

Mycale

Sparta

RHODES

MEDITERRANEAN SEA

- - - → } Xerxes' routes 480 B.C.
———→

———→ Darius' route 490 B.C.

X   Battle sites

GREEK AGAINST PERSIAN

For the moment Athens had been saved, but Persian power had not been destroyed. The time would come when the mighty Persians would try again. One man who had fought the Persians at Marathon and who realized the danger better than most was Themistocles, who soon became the leading statesman of Athens. The son of a merchant, he knew that Athens lived by trade, and that she must control the sea lanes to survive. He also agreed with the Athenian who wrote that "as most of us gain our livelihood from

the sea, all the time we are engaged upon our ordinary day-to-day business we are learning the art of naval warfare." With great difficulty Themistocles convinced his country-men that Athens should pour all her resources into the construction of a vast navy, and let other Greek states be responsible for facing the Persians on land. Fortunately, the discovery of a rich vein of silver in southern Attica provided the money necessary to build a fleet of two hundred warships, called *triremes* because they had three banks of oars.

The construction of the Athenian navy came none too soon, for in 480 B.C., ten years after Marathon, the Persians returned to the attack. The new Persian leader was Xerxes (shown, at right in the relief below, while he was still crown prince), who hoped to avenge the defeat of his father, Darius. For years Xerxes had gathered his forces, until a host of 200,000 men from forty-six races, and a fleet of 800 ships had been assembled. So determined was he to conquer Greece that when a storm destroyed the bridge the Persians had built across the Hellespont, the mile of water which separated Europe from Asia Minor, he became enraged. According to the story told by Herodotus, he "gave orders that the Hellespont should receive three hundred lashes . . . and that the overseers of the work should lose their heads."

A stronger bridge was soon built, however, and the army passed over into Europe. Herodotus goes on to recount that "the crossing continued during seven days and seven nights, without rest or pause." Well might a man who lived near the Hellespont ask, "Why, O Jove, dost thou, in the likeness of a Persian man, and with the name of Xerxes instead of thine own, lead the whole race of mankind to the destruction of Greece? It would have been as easy for thee to destroy it without their aid!"

through a secret pass, Leonidas realized that his position was hopeless. Rather than have his entire force destroyed, the Spartan King ordered the main body of his force to retreat and prepared to defend the pass with 300 men.

Savagely whipped into battle by their commanders, the Persians repeatedly threw themselves against the Spartan spears and shields. Although thousands of Persians suffered the fate of the warrior shown below, the issue was never in doubt. When Leonidas was killed, his followers withdrew to the narrowest part of the pass. Here, wrote Herodotus, "they defended themselves to the last, such as still had swords using them, and others resisting with their hands and teeth; till the barbarians . . . overwhelmed them and buried the remnant which was left beneath showers of missile weapons." A later epitaph at Thermopylae commemorated Spartan heroism:

> Go, stranger, and to Lacedaemon tell
> That here, obeying her behests, we fell.

The Persian horde moved easily through northern Greece. Finally they arrived at Thermopylae, a pass through the mountains which guarded southern Greece. Defending the pass were King Leonidas of Sparta (above) and 7000 soldiers. Time after time the Greeks threw back the Persians, inflicting such losses, wrote Herodotus, that Xerxes, "who was watching the battle, thrice leaped from the throne upon which he sat, in terror for his army." But when a Greek traitor led a picked band of Persian soldiers to the rear of the Greek position

The Persian victory opened the way for the conquest of Attica and Athens. Themistocles persuaded the Athenians to fight their next battle with the Persians on the sea, and hastily recruited all able-bodied Athenians to man the 200 triremes that had been built. The triremes were approximately 150 feet long and each one could carry 170 rowers and thirty soldiers. Many of the rowers were slaves who had been promised their freedom if they fought with distinction. The ships were built with a reinforced bow which was to serve as a battering ram. Greek tactics included a manoeuvre in which the trireme would row at full speed toward an enemy vessel, only to change course at the last moment. Just as their ship brushed alongside the enemy, the Greek rowers were to raise their oars and let the prow of their ship snap off the oars of the Persians. While the crippled ship wallowed helplessly, the Athenians were to turn about and ram it amidships. If this tactic failed, the Athenian plan was to board and capture the enemy vessel.

The whole system relied heavily on the greater manoeuvrability of the Athenian triremes. Themistocles realized that they would have a greater advantage in shallow and narrow waters than on the open sea. Thus he hoped to entice the much larger Persian fleet into the narrow channel between the island of Salamis and the mainland. When one of his slaves pretended to be a traitor and told the Persians that Themistocles would order his fleet to retreat without fighting, the trap had been set. The Greeks back-watered as the enemy fleet approached, and the eager Persians pressed forward. Once the Persians had been lured into the narrow channel at Salamis, the Greeks reversed direction and rowed quickly toward them. The Persians were packed too tightly to manoeuvre, and the faster and lighter triremes with their bronze-tipped prows took a heavy toll. By the end of the day-long battle much of the Persian fleet had been battered or boarded, and the rest of Xerxes' vessels were in full flight. Leaving a large army in northern Greece to continue the war in the spring, the Persian Emperor left for home.

The Greek warship shown here has only two banks of oars out, but the scale of the ship and the battering rams at and below the water-line can be clearly seen.

While the Persians waited for spring, the Greeks were busy gathering a force from all over the peninsula. When the Persians moved south, they faced a united Greek force at Plataea. For a time the issue was in doubt, for both sides fought with skill and bravery. The hoplites, armed with swords and spears, were constantly harassed by the fine Persian cavalry. At one point, however, the Persians wrongly concluded that the Greeks were retreating. The commander led his infantry against the solid wall of the hoplites. The Persian infantry was cut to ribbons and the commander was killed.

After the battle what remained of the Persian army fled to Asia Minor, never again to attack the Greeks. Today, reliefs on the ruins of the great Persian capital at Persepolis boast of the great triumphs of Darius and Xerxes. But there are no reliefs to commemorate the campaign against the Greeks.

The victory of Greece had incalculable effects on the future history of Western civilization. Greece saved itself and the European world from the domination of an Asiatic power. Understandably, their amazing victory in the face of overwhelming odds inspired a great feeling of pride and confidence in the Greeks. Yet tragedy lay ahead, for the Greek states that had united to withstand the Persians were soon locked in a brutal struggle among themselves. But despite the events that followed, nothing could dim the glory of Marathon, Thermopylae and Salamis, names that have continued to inspire men like Lord Byron who have believed in freedom.

119

The Greek way

Victory over the Persians not only saved the Greek world, it also inspired a great cultural development. The fifth century B.C. is the golden age of Greece and one of the great periods of Western civilization. As one historian has written, "Greece left some of the most magnificent works of art and literary monuments ever bequeathed by one civilization to another." In parliaments and on street corners we still discuss ideas that were first discussed by the Greeks. Modern buildings still show the influence of Greek architecture. Adults and children still enjoy the literature that excited ancient Greeks. Audiences applaud performances of plays first produced in the open-air Greek theatres. As the heirs of Western civilization we are all partly Greek.

In many ways religion was the base on which the Greeks built their culture. It inspired their buildings, art and literature. But while religion inspired the Greeks, it did not control their thoughts or actions. The Greeks were mainly concerned about man, and even gave their gods human form. There were no pyramids built as royal tombs. Priests were public officials, servants of the state and its people, not their masters. There was no fixed creed or set of religious teachings which all Greeks had to believe. As a result, the Greeks were far freer to explore new ideas and express their thoughts than any other people in the ancient world.

RELIGION

Like early peoples everywhere, the first people who lived in Greece believed in a host of gods, great and small, friendly and hostile, who were usually associated with the elements of nature. When the people we know as Greeks first moved into the Aegean world of these earlier settlers, they brought with them a whole new family of sky gods. The mightiest was Zeus (left), king of gods and men, who ruled heaven and earth from Mount Olympus. Like his brothers and sisters, Zeus was supposed to have been eaten by his father. But his mother had fed her husband a stone instead. Zeus later forced his father to cough up his brothers and sisters, who joined Zeus in a successful battle for control of the universe. Zeus and his brothers then drew lots for their share of the universe. Poseidon received the sea, and Hades the underworld. Zeus himself was Lord of the Sky, the Rain-god, and the Cloud-gatherer who wielded the awesome thunderbolt. Thunder and lightning were signs of his anger. So real was Zeus to the Greeks that they did not say "It rains," but "Zeus rains" or "Zeus thunders."

With Zeus on Mount Olympus lived the family of gods, twelve of whom are seen in this Roman relief. From left to right they are Hestia, sister of Zeus and goddess of the hearth; Hephaestus, son of Hera and possibly of Zeus, who was thrown out of Olympus because Hera was ashamed of his lameness and who became the god of fire and handicrafts; Aphrodite, daughter of Zeus, and goddess of love and beauty; Ares, son of Zeus, and god of war, who was detested by Zeus and Hera but was popular with Hades since he helped to increase the population of the underworld; Demeter, sister of Zeus, and goddess of the crops, who once turned the world into a frozen mass when Hades carried off her daughter, Persephone, into the underworld; Hermes, son of Zeus, messenger between the gods and mortals, and protector of thieves and mischief makers, who on the day he was born stole Apollo's flocks; Hera, wife of Zeus, and protector of marriage and married women, who spent most of the time jealously watching Zeus fall in love with one woman after another; Poseidon, brother of Zeus, and god of the sea and of earthquakes, who had a splendid golden palace under the sea but who usually lived on Olympus; Athena, the goddess of wisdom, who sprang fully grown from the brow of Zeus and who was regarded in Athens as the protectress of culture, art and the rule of law; Zeus, whose bird was the eagle and whose tree was the mighty oak; Artemis, daughter of Zeus, goddess of the moon and guardian of cities, and an expert with the bow and arrow; and Apollo, son of Zeus, god of the sun, god of truth, patron of music, medicine and prophecy. Apollo has been called "the most Greek of all the Gods," for he came the closest to representing the Greek ideal of man and god. It was Apollo who established the famous oracle at Delphi.

Their Olympian religion does not seem to have had much effect on the way the Greeks behaved. Since the gods were more interested in ceremony than in good conduct, Greeks like the warrior seen below paid particular attention to the correct performance of such religious ceremonies as offering a sacrifice before leaving for battle. But while the Greeks believed that the gods were powerful, they did not fear them very much. It was difficult to fear gods who were very much like ordinary people and who often showed such human vices as dishonesty, quarrelsomeness and jealousy. And the Greeks did not believe that there was a heaven or paradise to reward those who lived righteously. Whether they had led good or evil lives, Greeks could look forward only to a shadowy kind of existence among the ghosts of Hades' underworld. To the Greeks, the gods were very much like people except that they were larger, stronger, more intelligent and immortal. The gods often interfered in their daily lives, particularly to punish the sin of pride (hubris), but they could generally be kept happy through sacrifices and ceremonies in their honour. Over the centuries, Greek religious ideas changed and developed. In time, many Greeks moved away from the rather shallow beliefs and practices of the Olympian religion and developed ideas that were extremely advanced.

The patron goddess of Athens was Athena whom the citizens honoured with festivals, gifts and sacrifices. Her main festival was the Panathena, a very happy as well as sacred occasion which was held every four years. In return for such honours as they paid Athena, the Athenians expected the goddess to protect their city and to make sure they were victorious in war. Every city had its own Olympian god, and worship was usually a public rather than a personal matter. In a Greek city-state, therefore, it was often difficult to distinguish between government and religion.

On the slopes of Mount Parnassus at Delphi in central Greece stand these ruins of the famous shrine of the popular god Apollo. God of the sun, it was he who created day by drawing his sun-chariot across the sky. Apollo was a very likable young person, "the god of perpetual youth." Poets and sculptors pictured him as handsome, athletic and intelligent. Because of his purity he was god of healing and he also had the gift of prophecy.

At Delphi, Apollo established the oracle, an order of prophets through which he gave advice to people who came from all parts of Greece. In this painting, a priestess seated on a three-legged stool speaks for Apollo in answer to the questions of a visitor. Although the words of the oracle were sometimes confusing and the advice unsound, the shrine at Delphi was respected by all Greeks. Enemies were even prepared to forget their differences for a time while they visited Delphi.

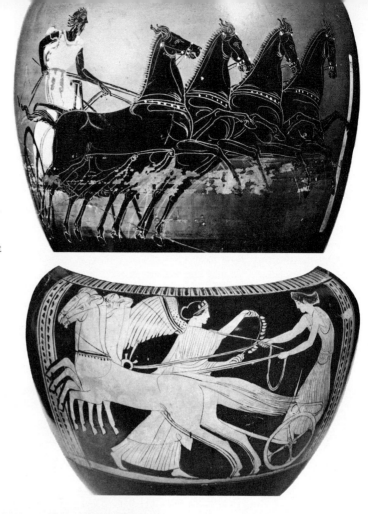

Among the most famous religious festivals in Greece were the Olympic games, first held, according to legend, in 776 B.C. at Olympia in the western Peloponnesus. Held every four years in honour of Zeus, the games opened with a thrilling four-horse chariot race accompanied by so many spills and mishaps that few contestants managed to finish.

The Olympic games were the most famous of a number of *Pan-hellenic* ceremonies which attracted Greeks from all over the disunited peninsula. Here they could all worship the gods together. Even wars were stopped long enough to permit participants to travel safely to and from the games. In addition to athletic contests, they also included musical and literary competitions. Whatever the form of contest, the laurel wreath of victory was among the most highly prized awards a Greek could hope to receive.

As an increasing number of Greeks became dissatisfied with the religion of the Olympian gods, they turned to "mystery religions." These religions were popular because they gave individuals a feeling of personal contact with some power greater than themselves. The mystery religions grew out of spring festivals which celebrated the return of life each spring, and they centred around the worship of gods who had died and had risen from the dead. Dionysius was one of the most popular of the gods who symbolized eternal life. His worship eventually attracted followers from all parts of Greece. Sometimes his followers, intoxicated with wine, reached a state of emotional frenzy in which they danced and leaped about to the sound of wild music, and sometimes even tore apart and ate the flesh of animals. All of the mystery religions offered to cleanse their followers from sin through some elaborate ceremony. Those who had been purified could gain everlasting life by leading pure, moral lives.

ART AND ARCHITECTURE

Greek art, like Greek literature, was closely connected with religion. The most enduring example of Greek artistic genius is its architecture. Since the most important buildings were designed to honour the gods who protected the city, many of the finest examples of Greek architecture were located on the Acropolis of Athens. Here every citizen could enjoy them and share a common feeling of pride in their creation.

The crowning glory of the whole Acropolis was the Parthenon, seen in this photograph from the Propylaea, a magnificent gate and stairway leading to the Acropolis. Made from marble quarried near Athens, the Propylaea glistened with many colours as it reflected the rays of the sun in the clear Athenian sky. The Parthenon was built in honour of the goddess Athena and was one of the largest of Greek temples. Even in a ruined state the great marble structure gives an impression of great beauty, dignity and simplicity. Athenian architects and builders worked hard to achieve this impression of perfection. The inner chamber of the temple is surrounded by simple fluted columns which support the roof. Each column is made up of a number of drums or cylinders so skilfully put together that one can scarcely see the joints. The designers of the temple carefully worked out the exact number and size of columns needed to leave an impression of perfect unity, harmony and balance. To make sure that the Parthenon would look perfect from any angle, they made the columns lean inward slightly, bulge in the centre and taper towards the top. They also made sure that the middle of the horizontal lines around the temple were higher than the ends so that the structure would not seem to sag.

On the north side of the Acropolis stands another famous temple known as the Erechtheum, after a legendary hero-king, Erechtheus. The temple was built to house a number of relics connected with Athens' early history. It contained the tomb of Cecrops, first king of Athens; the first olive tree, special gift of Athena; the shrine of Erechtheus; and the golden armour captured from the Persians at the Battle of Plataea. The temple also provided a home for Athena. To include all of these sacred objects in their proper places, it was necessary for the Erechtheum to take an unusual shape. Instead of columns which usually encircle the main hall of a Greek temple, there were porches on three sides. Above we see the most beautiful and unusual of the porches, the famous Porch of the Maidens. Instead of the usual type of columns, six beautifully sculptured maidens support the roof.

On the very cliff's edge of the Acropolis stood this little temple to Victorious Athena. One of the most charming examples of Greek creative art, the slender temple was built when Athens was at the height of her power, and was dedicated to Athena in her role as goddess of victory. The little temple with its graceful and well-proportioned columns added a welcome touch of brightness to the solemn Acropolis. The small chamber behind the columns housed a statue of Athena. Well-preserved relief figures on the front of the temple show gods grouped around Athena; reliefs on the sides celebrate Athenian victories over the Persians.

In many ways the relief figures
used to decorate the temples were
the best examples of Greek creative
art. Certainly sculpture was the art
form which the Greeks most enjoyed.
Often their figures honoured the
gods, recalled great victories or
recorded festivals and ceremonies.
Whatever the purpose, however, the
form of the statue was usually man.
The greatest Greek sculptors
concentrated on creating the perfect
human form. Not content to portray
man exactly as he was, they set out to
create the perfect human body, the
ideal figure without a single flaw. A
favourite subject was the Greek
athlete. This statue of a discus
thrower from Athens captures
superbly the combination of beauty,
skill and strength which Greek
athletes tried to attain. Looking at
the statue we feel somehow that
this is the athlete as he should be.

For ten long years the Greeks lay siege to Troy. Although the plains outside the city rang with the clang of armour and the dying cries of many a brave warrior on his way to Hades, neither side could win a decisive victory. The Greeks could not break through the walls of Troy; nor could the Trojans drive the Greeks away. Throughout the war the gods also took part, now giving the advantage to one side, now to the other. Zeus, Apollo and Aphrodite supported the Trojans while Hera, Poseidon and Athena fought for the Greeks. One of the most dramatic events of the war was the duel between Paris' brother Hector, son of Priam and noblest of the Trojan warriors, and the mighty Greek hero, Achilles, who could only be killed by a wound in the heel. The climax of their conflict is illustrated in the painting below. When Hector first saw the dreadful Achilles running towards him over the plain, he lost heart and took to his heels. Three times Achilles chased Hector around the walls of the city before the Trojan determined to face his enemy and let the gods decide the outcome. Although Hector fought bravely, he could not withstand the furious strength of Achilles who, helped by the gods, at length drove his spear through the Trojan's neck. Despite Hector's dying plea that his body be returned to his father and mother for burial, the vengeful Achilles dragged the dead hero's body behind his chariot across the plains to the Greek ships.

The earliest known Greek literature is found in two great epic poems, the *Iliad* and the *Odyssey*, believed to have been written by a poet and minstrel named Homer in the eighth century B.C. Although we know little about Homer himself, his famous poems, written about events which occurred during the dark ages of the twelfth century B.C., are among the most wonderful adventure stories ever told. The *Iliad* tells mainly of the dramatic events of a few weeks in the ten-year siege of Troy by the Greeks.

The Trojan War broke out when the handsome Paris, son of King Priam of Troy, persuaded the beautiful Helen (seen in the painting above with her husband, Menelaus, King of Sparta) to leave her home and go with him to Troy. The action of Paris was particularly shocking to the Greeks because he had been a guest in the home of Menelaus and had therefore broken the sacred bond between guest and host which bound them to help, not harm, each other. When Menelaus found Helen gone, he appealed to the other Greek rulers to help him get her back and to punish Paris and the Trojans. The Greek rulers responded eagerly, for many of them had wooed Helen before she married Menelaus and they had promised to help him if anyone ever tried to take her away. Within a short time a thousand-ship armada carried a great army to the Trojan shores. Although the Greek ranks included such famous heroes as Achilles, Ajax and the wily Odysseus, their task was not to be an easy one, for the Trojans had great warriors of their own and Troy was strongly fortified.

Eventually Achilles, moved to pity by the pleas of the old King, Priam, surrendered Hector's body to his father. But with the death of their hero, Hector, and with the later death of Paris, who himself had slain Achilles, the Trojans had lost much of their zest for battle. No longer did they come out and fight the Greeks upon the plains but remained like prisoners behind their city walls. It seemed that the war would last forever, for the Greeks could not break their way through.

At last, with the help of the goddess Athena, the crafty Odysseus devised a plan. The Greeks built a huge wooden horse which they left on the beach, thus leading the Trojans to think it was either an offering to the gods to ensure their safe return to Greece or a token of peace left for them. Then, after secretly hiding the best of their warriors in the belly of the horse, they pretended to sail for their homeland. Despite warnings that the horse was some kind of Greek trick, the Trojans dragged it into the city. That night the war-weary Trojans feasted and celebrated, never dreaming that the destruction of their city was close at hand. When finally the city lay in exhausted sleep, the Greeks stealthily crept from their pine horse and opened the gates of Troy to their comrades, who had returned to the beaches under cover of night. Within a short time the famous ancient city lay in flaming ruins, with many of her citizens the victims of Greek swords. So ended the most famous war in all Western history, made unforgettable through the lines of Homer's *Iliad*.

Homer's second great poem, the *Odyssey*, is the story of the homeward voyage from Troy of Odysseus, King of Ithaca, who had played an important part in the Greek victory. Because he had angered Poseidon, god of the sea, by blinding his son, Polyphemus, Odysseus was not allowed to return home immediately. For ten eventful years he wandered from place to place, overcoming impossible obstacles, enduring terrible suffering and surviving incredible mishaps. Retold in many different forms—radio and television, plays and movies—the *Odyssey* continues to thrill audiences of all ages. Wherever there are libraries and books, there probably will be people who can explain how Odysseus and his men escaped from the giant one-eyed Cyclopes, or how they managed the hazardous passage between the great whirlpool, Charybdis, and the many-headed monster Scylla. The vase painting at left illustrates one of the most famous incidents in the nightmarish homeward voyage. Tied to the mast of his ship, Odysseus is able to hear the irresistibly sweet songs of the Sirens or sea-nymphs without being drawn to them. To make sure that he could listen to their singing without being drawn to his doom, Odysseus had his men's ears stopped up with wax and he himself was secured to the mast. Despite his frantic shouts and signals to be set free, his sailors rowed on until Odysseus had recovered from the spell cast by the Sirens.

After ten years of wandering, Odysseus did manage to return to Ithaca and rejoin his faithful wife, Penelope, and their son, Telemachus, both of whom are shown in this painting. During Odysseus' absence a horde of worthless suitors had descended upon the King's palace, each one trying to persuade Penelope to marry him. But Penelope steadfastly refused, insisting that she had to complete the weaving of a shroud for Odysseus' father, the aged Laertes, who must die soon. The suitors agreed to wait until the work was finished. But each night Penelope unravelled what she had woven during the day. Eventually, however, the suitors discovered her trick and demanded that she make up her mind. Penelope devised an archery contest and agreed to marry the man who would win it using the bow of Odysseus. On the appointed day, all of the suitors tried without success to string the bow. Even the strongest among them found it too stiff. Then Odysseus, who had appeared at the feast disguised as a beggar, took the bow, strung it with ease and began to shoot down the suitors one by one. When his arrows were gone, he finished the rest with spear and sword. The story of the *Odyssey* ends with the hero happily reunited with his wife and son.

130

For about two centuries Greek poets tended to imitate Homer. Then about 600 B.C. they began to produce a new kind of poetry, called *lyric* because it was often sung to the accompaniment of a lyre. In this Greek vase painting, Apollo, the master musician among the Olympians, plays on his golden lyre while his twin sister, Artemis, looks on. Unlike the epics, lyric poetry was concerned with the feelings and problems of ordinary people rather than with the heroic achievements of gods and warriors. One of the greatest of Greek lyric poets was Pindar (c. 518-438 B.C.) who often composed poems or odes in honour of victorious athletes in the festivals.

During the fifth century B.C. the Greeks produced the first plays in Western history. Greek plays probably grew out of religious ceremonies in various districts, held in honour of such gods as Dionysius, the wine god.
In the early ceremonies, a chorus of actors tried to illustrate some event in the life of the god through songs and dances. Characters and plots were added about 500 B.C. Although the plays were based on well-known stories, the dramatists often wrote lines for the actors which expressed their own ideas and feelings about man and the world.

Greek plays were performed in theatres which were very much different from ours. They were usually staged out-of-doors in some natural or artificial amphitheatre. By modern standards the theatres were enormous. Tier upon tier of seats rose upwards in much the same way as a modern football "bowl." In this great horseshoe-shaped theatre at Epidaurus in the Peloponnesus there were fifty-five rows of seats in two sections, where 14,000 people could watch a performance.

131

Greek actors faced many problems in playing before such large audiences in great open-air theatres. They could not speak in natural voices, for they would never have been heard even in the clear Athenian air. Instead they spoke very loudly in majestic tones through large masks which were equipped with brass megaphones. The masks also enabled a member of the audience far from the stage to identify a character quickly, for each one was moulded to represent the feeling or character the actor was trying to portray. Some suggested youth, age, fear, hate, pride, anger or laughter. As a further aid to recognition the actors also used padding and wore high wedged boots. Greek audiences did not expect the realism of a modern stage in which scenery, set and costumes are often very close to the "real thing." They were quite happy to let their imaginations run free and had no difficulty filling in the details.

In the fifth century B.C. three writers of tragic plays towered above the rest. They were Aeschylus (525-456 B.C.), Sophocles (496-406 B.C.) and Euripides (480-406 B.C.). All three took their plots from myths and legends which were well known to their audiences, but each one used the familiar story to achieve a different effect. Aeschylus was mainly concerned with justice and law. He stressed the terrible things that happened when man disobeyed the will of the gods. Sophocles emphasized man in his plays and often showed how too much of even a good quality can lead to a man's suffering and downfall. Euripides used his plays to raise all kinds of questions. He expresses the doubts of a critical age which no longer accepted the gods of early Greece. He portrays the gods as sometimes mean and nasty tyrants rather than as protectors of the people. Euripides' main concern was for ordinary people and he tried to show man as he really was. Sophocles is supposed to have said: "I depict men as they ought to be, but Euripides portrays them as they are." Although Euripides' doubts about Greek religion and values made him unpopular in his own lifetime, he has since become the most popular of the Greek dramatists. His plays, like *Iphigenia in Aulis,* still delight modern Greek audiences like the one shown in this photograph.

After they had seen one or more tragedies, Greek audiences usually expected lighter entertainment. This was provided by comedies, which by the fifth century B.C. often combined entertainment and education on current events. The best writer of comedy was Aristophanes (450-385 B.C.), who delighted his audiences by poking fun at the politicians, democratic institutions and many of the customs of his fellow Athenians. Toward the end of the century a new form of comedy arose; this form is illustrated in the work of the playwright Menander, whose plays provided a witty commentary on everyday life. This photograph of an ancient marble relief shows Menander with the masks used in the *Dyskolos* or *The Curmudgeon,* his only comedy which has survived intact. Not until 1957 was a complete copy of the play discovered on an old piece of papyrus. The plot of the comedy is the familiar one of a young man who pursues a maiden against her father's wishes. Menander is holding the mask used by the young man, while those of the girl and her father rest on the table in front of him.

For many years poetry was the most important form of Greek literature. Prose writing did not come into its own until the fifth century B.C. with the writing of two outstanding historians, Herodotus and Thucydides. Herodotus (485-425 B.C.), who has been called the "Father of History" wrote brilliantly of the war between the Greeks and Persians. He roamed the world gathering an immense amount of material, fact and fiction, about the peoples involved in the struggle. His curiosity was boundless and his writing reflects his great interest and delight in the customs, lands and lives of different peoples. Although Herodotus tried to write accurate history, he could not resist telling a good story whether it was true or not.

Thus, his *Histories* are crammed with fascinating folklore and anecdotes about prophets, statesmen and kings. For example, he reported that King Croesus of Lydia was condemned to be burned on a funeral pyre after he had been defeated by the Persians. But the god Apollo intervened and sent rain which put out the fire and saved the king. The Greek vase shown here gives another version of the same incident and shows Croesus voluntarily sacrificing himself.

The other great Greek historian, Thucydides (c. 460-c. 400 B.C.) who wrote about the Peloponnesian Wars was much more critical in his approach and tried never to let his personal feelings get in the way of his judgement and accuracy.

133

pupil, looked on, Socrates actually left no writings. We learn of his ideas mainly from Plato's *Dialogues*, which record talks between Socrates and his pupils. Socrates believed that there was such a thing as Truth and that man could find it if he tried. To help his pupils find the truth, Socrates asked them endless questions designed first of all to reveal their errors or lack of knowledge. Then, through further questions he tried to lead them on to discover the truth for themselves about such matters as love, hate, justice and the gods. Socrates believed that man should act according to the teaching of his own conscience. He should not obey without question laws made by the state. Socrates upheld this belief at the cost of his life.

Accused of corrupting Athenian youth, he might have saved himself by saying that he had been wrong. Instead he made this speech:

> Athenians, I am not going to argue for my own sake . . . but for yours. . . . For if you kill me, you will not easily find a successor to me, who, if I may use such a ludicrous figure of speech, am a sort of gadfly, given to the state by God: and the state is a great and noble steed who is tardy in his motions owing to his very size, and requires to be stirred into life. I am that gadfly which God has attached to the state, and all day long and in all places am always fastening upon you, arousing and persuading and reproaching you. You will not easily find another like me, and therefore I would advise you to spare me.

But the Court found Socrates guilty and sentenced him to die by drinking hemlock. As was the Athenian custom, he was allowed to suggest his own sentence. When he proposed that Athens give him free meals for life, Socrates had pronounced his own death sentence. Calmly draining his cup of poison, he talked quietly with his friends until he died.

PHILOSOPHY AND THOUGHT

While Greek artists and writers were producing works that have inspired men, Greek philosophers were developing ideas that have shaped the thinking of Western civilization. Among many great thinkers in the Greek world three tower above the rest: Socrates (469-399 B.C.), Plato (429-347 B.C.) and Aristotle (384-322 B.C.).

Son of a stonemason, the short, snub-nosed Socrates had served as a tough and courageous soldier in the Peloponnesian Wars. Although this picture from a medieval book shows Socrates writing while Plato, his

The death of Socrates so angered Plato that he left Athens for ten years. When he returned, he founded a famous school called the *Academy*. (Here he is seen teaching, a stick in his hand.) Like Socrates, Plato also sought Truth, which he believed was unchanging. The world of truth to Plato was a spiritual world, a world of Ideas. To him, ideas were the only real things, the only things that never changed. Physical things like trees or buildings or rivers were changing all the time. No one tree was as it had been the day before; nor was it like any other tree. All material objects that we see in this world, like horses, tables and chairs are really only reflections of the Idea of a horse, table or chair, he thought. Through thought and reason, Plato believed, everyone could obtain some understanding of the perfect world of Ideas and so come nearer to the truth.

Like most Greeks, Plato was also interested in politics. In his famous book, *The Republic,* Plato claimed that the best state would be one in which everyone did the job he was best able to do. There would be a warrior class to do the fighting and a peasant or lower class to do the routine work. The ruler would have to be a philosopher-king, for only a very wise person would be able to recognize what his subjects could do best and organize their work for the benefit of all. The ruler would regulate every aspect of life. He would, for example, supervise the training of the classes and control the economic system so that everyone received only what he was worth. He would also carefully arrange marriages in the best interests of the state. There would be no families. Plato's perfect society was to be a dictatorship of wise men designed to avoid the weaknesses he saw in Athenian society. Although few in the West admire Plato's ideal state, his *Republic* is still widely read as the first blueprint for a planned society and government.

Perhaps the greatest philosopher of Greece and, many believe, the greatest of all time, was Plato's pupil, Aristotle. After serving as the tutor of Alexander the Great, Aristotle returned to Athens where he set up his own school known as the *Lyceum*. He was interested in almost every field of human knowledge. His works included studies on art, biology, logic, mathematics, physics, astronomy, politics and many other subjects. In his scientific work, Aristotle based his conclusions upon observation and experiment. First he tried to collect all the information he could about the natural world. Then he tried to arrange his evidence so that he could explain how the whole natural world operated. For example, in order to determine which political systems were best, Aristotle studied the histories of 152 different states. From the evidence provided by these studies he came to a number of conclusions which he wrote about in his famous book *Politics*. He concluded that man was a "political animal" who could not fulfil his true nature unless he were a member of a state. The main purpose of the state was to promote virtue.

Aristotle's most famous doctrine was the idea of the "Golden Mean." "Virtue," he said, "is the mean between two vices, that which depends upon excess and that which depends upon defect." Thus, in his use of money, a virtuous man is neither wasteful nor miserly. Courage is the mean between rashness and cowardice. So influential were Aristotle's ideas that they continued to dominate the minds of Western philosophers for nearly 2000 years.

Their boundless curiosity about man and the universe also led the Greeks to great achievements in the field of mathematics. One of the greatest mathematicians was Pythagoras (c. 582-507 B.C.) , whose name is associated in the minds of millions of students with the famous theorem, "the square on the hypotenuse of a right-angled triangle is equal to the sum of the squares on the other two sides." Pythagoras, seen in this relief sculpture, also discovered that musical sounds were a matter of mathematical proportions. The shorter a string, the higher would be the note. Such discoveries increased Greek interest in all kinds of mathematics, for if music could be explained in terms of mathematics, what could not be? Even before Pythagoras there had been thinkers who sought through mathematics to unlock the mysteries of the world. One such person was Thales (c. 624-547 B.C.) from Miletus, who believed that the mystery of life could be explained in terms of some "world stuff" from which all else was formed. He decided that water was the basic "world stuff"; everything was made of water and everything returned to water. Other Greeks suggested fire, air and a combination of these elements. In the early fourth century B.C. a scholar, Democritus, developed an atomic theory to explain the nature of the physical world. Everything in the universe, he said, is made up of tiny particles or atoms floating about in space. Accidentally these atoms combine to form beings and objects, and eventually decompose to become floating particles again. Although the Greeks put great emphasis on a knowledge of mathematics — a sign above Plato's door read, "Let no man enter who knows no geometry" — they also increased their knowledge of astronomy, physics, geography and botany. The Greeks placed such reliance on observation that they are often credited with the discovery of the scientific method.

Among the scientists who relied upon observation were physicians like the one who cured the varicose veins of this grateful patient (shown here presenting a model of his cured leg to Asclepius, god of healing). The most famous Greek doctor was Hippocrates (c. 460-377 B.C.), who insisted that cures should be sought in science, not in gods. The only way to learn about disease, he maintained, was to observe sick people carefully and compare their symptoms with other recorded cases. From such observations doctors should try to determine the cause and nature of the disease and prescribe treatment. Hippocrates stressed that disease was due to natural causes and not to evil spirits and the like, as many doctors had claimed. Such men were quacks, he charged, and were practising a craft, not a science. Under the influence of Hippocrates the practice of medicine in Greece was growing into a science.

Modern man can only marvel at the miracle of Greece and Greek culture. The words of C.M. Bowra, a gifted Oxford scholar, come as close as those of anyone to summing up the greatness of man in ancient Greece. What he wrote of literature is true of Greece as a whole, and especially of the golden age of Athens. ". . . in its unfailing sense of the real values of life . . . , Greek literature has passed into the spiritual life of the world. . . . The spirit that breathes through these works is that of a people who believed in the dignity of man and displayed its belief in every word it wrote. . . . How did they do it? We do not know. They were the Greeks."

ROME: A STATE IN ARMS

From City-state to Empire
The Roman achievement
The City of God

From City-state to Empire

Despite the brilliance of their civilization, the Greeks had failed to bring unity and peace to the Mediterranean world. Alexander the Great had come close. His conquests and marches had spread Greek culture throughout the ancient world. But when his Empire began to crumble not long after his death, Alexander's dream of world unity collapsed with it. It remained for a new western power, Rome, to try to succeed where the Greeks and Alexander had failed.

The Romans were the greatest conquerors and empire builders of the ancient world. By nature they were not a fierce and warlike people. They do not seem at first to have had great ambitions to rule over anyone else. Yet, two centuries after the birth of Christ, the Roman Empire reached from the Atlantic Ocean in the west to the Fertile Crescent in the east, and from Africa in the south to Britain in the north.

In these lands lived almost 90,000,000 people. In some ways they were among the most fortunate people of all time, for they enjoyed more peace and order than did most earlier peoples. They also had great material comforts, for the Romans were the great engineers and builders of the ancient world. Many of their magnificent buildings, roads and aqueducts still stand as monuments to their creative genius.

In the fifth century A.D. the Roman Empire collapsed, as every great empire in history eventually has done. But the influence of the Roman Empire has never disappeared. It lives today in many of the laws, institutions, languages and ideas of Western civilization. To appreciate fully our debt to Rome we must study Rome's history, for only then can we understand how and why a little city-state in Italy became the ruler of the Mediterranean world.

The Roman Forum: Capital of an Empire

THE CONQUEST OF ITALY

After Rome had become a great world power, Roman writers tried to provide exciting accounts of the origins of their people. One of Rome's greatest poets explained that Rome had been founded by a Trojan hero, Aeneas. With a small band of brave followers he had fled from ruined Troy, and after many adventures reached the plain of Latium in Italy. Another early legend states that Rome was founded in 753 B.C. by two brothers, Romulus and Remus, twin sons of the god Mars. As infants they had been thrown into the Tiber River. Miraculously they had survived and had been raised by a she-wolf. In time they became strong leaders and established the city of Rome.

These stories are much more interesting than the facts. In truth, Rome was no different at first from dozens of other little cities in the peninsula

Suggesting the greatness of Imperial Rome is Trajan's column, one of the most famous landmarks in the city. The stone pillar rises to a height of a hundred feet. It recalls the achievements of the emperor, Trajan (A.D. 98-117), under whom the Roman Empire reached its greatest extent. Seen here is a portion of the three- to four-foot wide continuous band of carved relief figures which spirals upward. The band of relief provides a story carved in stone of Trajan's campaigns in Dacia. As the central figure in the stirring account of Roman military success, Trajan appears often among the 2500 figures on the column. At the foot of the column where the story begins, he can be seen leading a column of Roman soldiers from the wall of a fortified city across the Danube River. Father Danube watches from a nearby cave. As the story rapidly unfolds, Trajan can be seen in many different activities — planning a campaign, taking part in a religious ceremony, directing the building of fortifications and questioning a spy. The great stone column gives a more lively, interesting and detailed account of a Roman military campaign than can be found in any single printed document.

of Italy. Barbaric tribesmen had been living on the site of Rome some 2000 years before the birth of Christ. Although we do not know the exact date, Rome seems to have been founded no later than 1000 B.C. by the Latins, people from the north who had been pushing into Italy for about a thousand years. Rome was an ideal centre of settlement. The Tiber River was both a shield which discouraged invaders and a highway for trade. Seven surrounding hills provided additional defence.

One of the great turning points in Rome's history occurred about 650 B.C. when the Etruscans, a people to the north of Rome, conquered the settlement on the Tiber. We know little about the mysterious Etruscans because we have not been able to find a key to their language. We do know that they were a highly civilized, fun-loving people and that they had a great effect on Roman history. Under Etruscan rule, Rome became a prosperous city-state under a strong king. The Etruscans taught the Romans improved methods of farming, building, manufacturing and trading. As a result, the Romans increased in wealth, and their city became increasingly important. But although they had benefitted from the Etruscans, the Romans revolted against them. According to tradition, in 509 B.C. the Romans drove the last Etruscan king from the throne.

In the two and a half centuries after the defeat of the Etruscans the little city of Rome gradually came to control the whole peninsula of Italy. The Romans had not planned to expand in this way. They simply wanted to survive, to protect their boundaries from ambitious and warlike neighbours. To do this it was often necessary to wage war. After the Etruscans' domination ended in the region of the Tiber, many of their former subject peoples fought with each other for as much of the best land as they could get. Barbarous mountain tribesmen from eastern Italy were another danger. Previously held in check by the Etruscans, they now launched continuous raids from their mountain strongholds upon the better lands of west-central Italy. From the north came waves of invaders from Gaul. On one occasion in

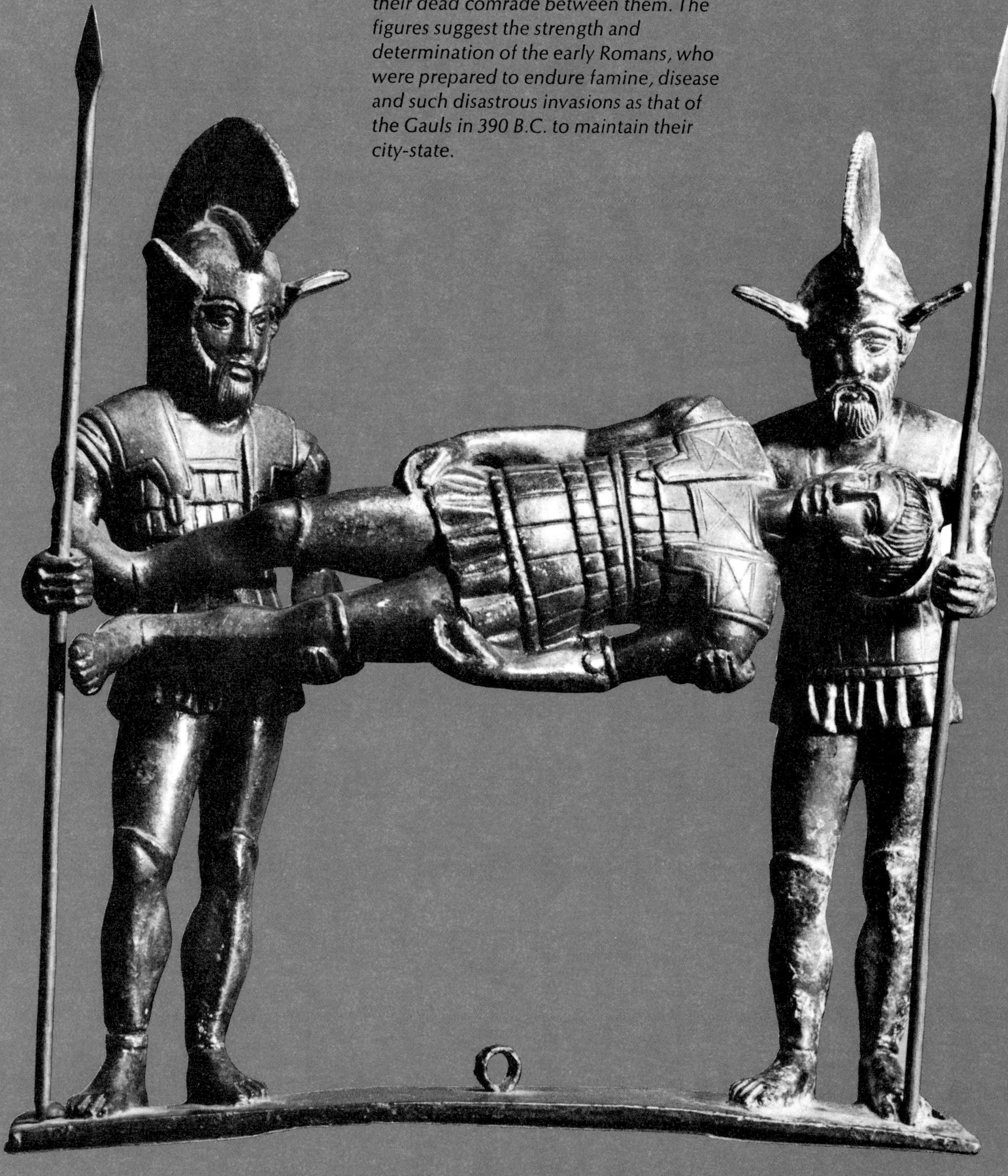

These figures form the handle of the lid of a fourth-century B.C. bronze container found in Latium. Roman soldiers, who fought almost continuously throughout the fifth and fourth centuries B.C. to preserve Rome, were dressed and equipped very much like those shown here supporting their dead comrade between them. The figures suggest the strength and determination of the early Romans, who were prepared to endure famine, disease and such disastrous invasions as that of the Gauls in 390 B.C. to maintain their city-state.

390 B.C. an invading party of wild Gauls defeated the Roman army and destroyed Rome. But the determined Romans refused to give up. They constantly tried to keep their closest neighbours under control, either by making them allies or subjects. As a result, Rome's borders began to expand and she constantly found herself with new neighbours on her frontiers. Feeling that if she did not conquer them, they might conquer her, Rome was led on to further expansion.

The desire for security was not the only reason for expansion. As Rome's population grew, there was an increasing need for more land. And once Romans had tasted victory, many were moved by greed, personal ambition or the love of fighting. No one reason explains completely why Rome fought for more territory. The important thing is that by 265 B.C. Rome had established her supremacy over Italy.

It was no accident that Rome succeeded in dominating the Italian peninsula. There are many reasons to explain why the Romans succeeded where other city-states would have failed. For one thing, the Romans prized, and were forced to develop, those qualities of character that would tend to make them successful. From their earliest years Romans learned to value hard work, loyalty, courage and a serious approach to life. The family was the most important unit in society. The Roman father ruled over it as a dictator, controlling every action of its members. He could sell his sons into slavery or even put them to death if they misbehaved. Not surprisingly, under this kind of discipline, the Romans became accustomed to obey, and learned to respect authority without questioning it.

The qualities that the Romans admired and tried to develop were the very qualities desirable in first-rate soldiers. Without her excellent army Rome could never have conquered Italy. The basic unit of the Roman army was the *legion* of 3600 men. The legion was often divided into more manageable units or *maniples* (handfuls) of 60 to 120 men. Equipped with iron-tipped javelins, short swords, helmets, shields and lances, the Roman legion in time became the toughest

The practical Romans were much more interested in winning battles than in cutting dashing figures on a parade square. The typical legionary seen here is equipped to perform efficiently on the battlefield. The Romans were never too proud to learn from their enemies or neighbours. The helmet shape came originally from Greece, and the mail tunic from Gaul; the short sword was modelled on those used by the Celts in Spain.

and most effective fighting force of ancient times. No other army could boast of higher morale. This spirit was kept at a high level by a combination of harsh punishment and generous rewards. If a legion backed down or mutinied, it might suffer the horrible punishment of decimation (the execution of every tenth man). But for the first soldier who mounted the wall during the assault on a city there was a crown of gold.

But brave and dedicated soldiers do not alone account for Rome's successful expansion. Roman politicians also tried to make certain that their enemies would never unite against Rome. Their basic policy was to "divide and rule." Sometimes they made an alliance with one possible enemy against another. On other occasions they prevented enemies from uniting against Rome by occupying land between them.

Even more impressive than the actual conquest of other peoples in battle was Rome's ability to maintain control over them afterwards. One of the main reasons for Rome's success in this was her generous policy towards subject peoples. She did not rule over the other Italian cities as a conqueror or demand payment from them. Instead she offered them friendship and formed treaties of alliance. Sometimes she offered them some of the benefits of Roman citizenship. In return, the conquered tribe or city was expected to give Rome military assistance. Although Rome controlled their relations with other countries, she allowed the defeated peoples almost complete control over their own local affairs. Through this sensible and restrained policy Rome changed enemies into friends and allies, and eventually united all Italy under her rule.

THE ROMAN REPUBLIC

Perhaps the most important single reason explaining Rome's successful conquest of Italy was the system of government she developed during the two and a half centuries of expansion. Without an efficient system of government Rome could not have survived the constant years of warfare. And if the government had not been just, it could not have inspired the constant devotion of

These relief figures from the column of Augustus show a group of Senators on their way to a session. Bound together by ties of family, wealth and privilege, they enjoyed such great power that they were said to rule Rome "as though it were a conquered city obedient to their whims." Since they worked in great secrecy, we know little about the way they made many of their great decisions. We do know that they used their almost unlimited power without much thought for the welfare of the mass of the people, and that they often showed little respect for the laws of the Republic. We also know that within the Senate there was a sort of inner group of about twenty men, who, for the most part, controlled the actions of the larger body.

the citizens. The Romans did not keep the same system of government throughout the entire period. As they came to rule more and more territory, they had to create a more complicated form of government than had been necessary for running a small city-state. Throughout these years, too, there was an almost continuous struggle between the two classes of Roman citizens for control of the government. On the one hand were the *patricians*, wealthy, land-owning aristocrats who enjoyed special rights and privileges; on the other were the *plebeians*, the ordinary citizens of Rome — city workers, craftsmen and farmers.

When the Etruscans had been driven from Rome, political power fell into the hands of the small number of patricians, since they had led the revolt. The patricians set up a *republic*, a form of government in which, in theory at least, the people and not a king governed. In fact, however, the patricians themselves controlled the government. The chief officials in the Roman Republic were two *consuls* who replaced the Etruscan kings and had supreme power over the state and army. Possibly to prevent any one man from becoming too powerful, either consul could veto or reject the acts of the other. To assist the consuls there were a number of other officials or magistrates. These men handled such matters as finance, the courts, roads and buildings, and

the organizing of the city's police force.

More influential than the magistrates was the Senate, composed at first of about 300 members. Senators were chosen mainly from the patrician class and held office for life. Originally the Senate was supposed merely to give wise advice on the running of the state. But since it was composed largely of former consuls and magistrates, the Senate in fact had great authority and really did run the state. The early Republic also had two assemblies in which all Roman citizens were represented. But these assemblies had few real powers and were controlled for the most part by the patricians. In the early Republic, most of Rome's citizens were members of the plebeian class, and as such had no power in government and no chance to gain it.

In addition to this lack of political power, the plebeians had many other grievances. Illness,

crop failure or other disasters often forced them to borrow and fall deeply into debt. As in Greece, failure to repay these debts could result in enslavement for the plebeian and his family. Among their other complaints was the law which forbade marriages between plebeians and patricians.

The early centuries of the Roman Republic were thus marked by the struggle of the plebs for a greater voice in government and for social equality. They had one great advantage. These were the years when Rome was fighting for her life, and the plebeian farmer and soldier were necessary to provide food and to defend the city. When Rome began to expand throughout the Italian peninsula, the ordinary Roman citizen became even more important. The plebeians soon realized that they were the key to Rome's survival and pressed the patricians to grant them reforms. Since the patricians also realized how important the plebeians were, they gradually and wisely agreed to share some of their power with the great mass of the citizens.

The first and perhaps the most important plebeian gain occurred about 470 B.C. when the plebeians forced the patricians to agree to the election of special officials known as *tribunes*. Originally the tribunes' function was to protect plebeians from injustice by the patrician government. Later, they were given the power to block the acts or measures of magistrates or senators. Another important plebeian gain was a written code of law known as the Twelve Tables. The important thing about the code was that it was written. The laws themselves did little to increase the liberties of the plebeians, but they did let the people know what legal rights they had. Before the law had been set down in this way, patrician judges had often interpreted it as they wished, probably to the advantage of patricians rather than plebeians. Eventually, the plebeians also gained an assembly of their own. In time, this assembly became the most important law-making body, for its decisions had to be obeyed by plebeians and patricians alike. By the end of the third century B.C. the plebeians had also won the right to hold the higher offices in the state, and in 362 B.C. the first plebeian consul was elected.

Yet, even after these reforms had been made, the Roman Republic was not in practice ruled by the mass of its citizens. Since there was no payment for taking part in government, the great mass of Romans could not afford to hold political office. Thus only the wealthy plebeians benefitted from the reforms. They soon joined with the old aristocrats to form a new ruling class in control of the high offices and the Senate. Although the citizens in the assemblies had won considerable power, they seldom used it. As before, the aristocratic Senate dominated the government of Rome. But if the government was not democratic, it worked. For the most part, the mass of Roman citizens were content with, even proud of, their government. For under aristocratic leadership the little city-state on the Tiber came to dominate all Italy.

ROME VERSUS CARTHAGE

In becoming ruler of Italy, Rome had also become a major military power in the Mediterranean. Whether she liked it or not, she could neither ignore, nor be ignored by, the other Mediterranean powers, Egypt, Syria, Macedonia and Carthage. For many years after 265 B.C. Rome's main aim was to uphold her position among these powers. In the end, she fought and conquered them all and welded them into the greatest empire of ancient time.

Rome's first enemy outside Italy was the African city-state of Carthage. Originally a Phoenician colony, Carthage had become the greatest naval and commercial power in the western Mediterranean. When the two first faced each other in war, she was three times the size of Rome and boasted the most powerful battle fleet in the world. Carthage also controlled the islands of Sardinia and Corsica and the western part of Sicily. The two powers clashed when Carthage threatened the Greek cities of Syracuse and Messana on the eastern coast. This attempt to bring all of the island of Sicily into her empire alarmed the Romans. They determined to check this expanding power on their very doorstep. The First Punic War (from the Latin word meaning Phoenician) broke out in 264 B.C. and dragged on for twenty-three years.

The Romans liked to say "Rome loses battles, but never a war." Against Carthage they proved it. The main fighting took place in Sicily and on the seas. At first the greatest sea power in the world naturally had the advantage. But within an amazingly short time, the resourceful Roman farmers had built a navy of one hundred five-decked ships of war, using a captured Carthaginian battleship as a model. Eventually they became reasonably good sailors and developed effective naval tactics which enabled them to board enemy vessels and engage in hand-to-hand combat. In this kind of fighting, the Roman legionary had no match.

Finally, in 241 B.C. the Romans defeated the Carthaginians and forced them to seek peace. The peace treaty gave Rome her first territory outside of Italy; the island of Sicily became her first overseas province. Rome had taken her first step along the road to an overseas empire.

The treaty was merely a truce. It was inevitable that Rome and Carthage would fight again, for Carthage, though beaten, had not been destroyed. A young Carthaginian nobleman, Hannibal, resolved that Carthage, not Rome, would be master of the western Mediterranean. As a young boy he had sworn an oath of undying hatred to Rome. When he became leader of the Carthaginians, Hannibal established strong forces in Spain in preparation for the overland invasion of Italy. The Second Punic War broke out in 218 B.C.

The Roman navy originated during the first war against Carthage. It soon developed into a powerful fighting force, really a sea-going part of the Roman legion fighting on water rather than land. Since the Romans had the best infantry soldiers in the world, they tried to make warfare at sea as much like a land battle as possible, in order that their soldiers could be used to the best advantage. Roman war galleys were rowed by slaves so that infantrymen like those shown here could reach the battle fresh, board the enemy ship and destroy its often exhausted crew of rowers.

when Hannibal attacked a city in Spain that was allied to Rome.

Rome angrily declared war and prepared to cross the Mediterranean and invade North Africa. But Hannibal wrecked these plans by striking first. Moving with unbelievable speed he marched across Spain, crossed the Rhone River and struggled through the rugged Alps. Before the Romans could catch their breath, he was in northern Italy. Strengthened by recruits picked up along the way and using elephants as his tank corps, Hannibal marched victoriously towards Rome. At Lake Trasimeno he outmanoeuvered, trapped and slaughtered a Roman army. Shocked by the disaster, the Romans appointed a new commander, Fabius. Refusing to engage in open battle with Hannibal's main army, Fabius was content merely to threaten the Carthaginians. This sound strategy of delay annoyed both Hannibal and, surprisingly, the Romans. Impatient to destroy the daring invader, they demanded immediate action. The cautious Fabius was dismissed. The new commander, Varro, enthusiastically led the Roman army to its greatest defeat. At the Battle of Cannae, Hannibal again showed his military genius, trapping and destroying almost an entire Roman army. Only 10,000 of an original 50,000 Roman soldiers escaped death or capture.

Despite this disaster the Romans did not lose heart. Although Syracuse in Sicily, and Macedonia now joined the Carthaginians, most of Rome's allies in Italy remained loyal. The dogged Romans sent armies against Syracuse and Macedonia and into Spain and Africa. Hannibal soon found himself cut off from supplies and reinforcements. Even so, he campaigned brilliantly. But Rome refused to go down, and eventually took the offensive against Carthage herself. Although Hannibal returned to lead the defence, the Romans under an able young general, Scipio, completely defeated the Carthaginian forces at the Battle of Zama in 202 B.C. They had no choice but to make peace.

For Carthage the defeat was disastrous. She had to surrender Spain and her Mediterranean islands, destroy her fleet and pay a huge tribute to Rome. In addition, she had to promise never to go to war against any state in the future without Rome's permission. Rome had become ruler of the western Mediterranean, a world power with a growing empire.

THE PROBLEMS OF EMPIRE

No sooner had Rome defeated Carthage than

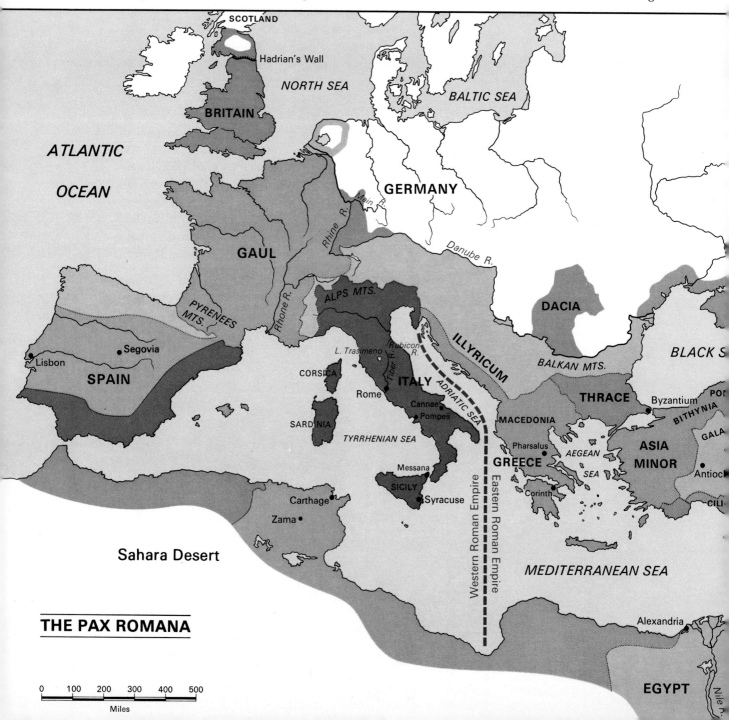

THE PAX ROMANA

0   100   200   300   400   500

Miles

she became involved with the two great powers of the eastern Mediterranean, Macedonia and Syria. Exhausted as she was, Rome had no desire to continue fighting; nor did she particularly wish to gain a great empire. But she was determined to defend the powerful position she had won in the western Mediterranean. Convinced that it was threatened by Macedonia and Syria, Rome went to war with these powers. At the end of the conflict Macedonia was defeated. She became a province of the Empire in 148 B.C. The Greek states were added to the Empire shortly after. Fifteen years later, Asia Minor also came under Roman control. Thus, by 133 B.C. the little city-state on the Tiber had expanded to include Asia Minor, Macedonia and Greece in the east, and Sicily, Sardinia, Corsica, southern Gaul, parts of Spain and the north coast of Africa in the west. The Mediterranean Sea had become a Roman lake.

During this period of expansion and wars, Rome changed. At first she had fought only to defend herself. Now she tried to find excuses to attack others. The old ideals tended to be forgotten in the desire for wealth, fame and empire. A third war with Carthage showed a new Roman ruthlessness and brutality. After the Second Punic War, Carthage was no threat to Rome. But the old hatred and fear remained. When Carthage showed signs of renewed strength, many Romans became alarmed. One Roman aristocrat helped

EXPANSION OF ROME:—

to 201 B.C.

to 44 B.C.

to A.D. 14

to A.D. 117

Rome's amazing success in expanding her empire is not difficult to explain. The same skills that led to the creation of the world's finest roads, bridges and aqueducts also helped the Romans to become resourceful and efficient soldiers. Primitive peoples had little chance of withstanding attacks by well trained legionaries. Besides having personal fighting skills, the soldiers were equipped with a great variety of war machines which could hurl a deadly rain of stones and spears among enemy ranks. In this relief Roman soldiers prepare to use a series of mechanical slings to assist their offence.

to keep this fear alive by ending every speech he made, whatever the subject, with the words, "Carthage must be destroyed." Rome eventually found an excuse to declare war in 149 B.C. After a three-year siege she completely destroyed the city and sold its surviving citizens into slavery. In a final act of vengeance, the Romans sowed the ground with salt so that nothing could grow there again.

Rome's wars and conquests created many problems. It was one thing to gain an empire; it was another matter to rule it effectively. It soon became clear that Rome was not doing a very good job of governing hers. She had organized most of her new lands into provinces ruled by governors appointed by the Senate. Although some governed well, there were others who were greedy and cruel. The government at Rome took little interest in the actions of its officials in the provinces so long as the tribute money poured into Rome and the territories remained under control. Such misgovernment, however, eventually led to rebellions which proved very serious because Rome at that time did not have a permanent army to defend her empire.

Another problem was the appearance in Rome of a new class known as the *equites* or knights. These were wealthy businessmen and bankers who had made a great deal of money as the result of Rome's conquests. They made great profits from lending money, collecting taxes in the provinces, supplying the army and working on government contracts. Thus the knights had great economic power in Rome. But they lacked political influence. Increasingly they resented the fact that a small number of aristocrats in the Senate were the real rulers of Rome. The agitation of the knights for political power kept Rome in a continual state of unrest.

There were other causes of unrest arising out of the wars of expansion. Although these wars had brought wealth to Rome, the wealth was not distributed among all the people. The rich tended to become richer and the poor poorer. Particularly hard hit were Rome's small independent farmers. Great quantities of tribute grain poured into Italy, where it was sold at much lower prices than Italian grain. Small farmers could not compete; nor did they have the money necessary to change from grain growing to vine and olive culture, or sheep or cattle grazing. To add to their difficulties, much of the land was being bought up by a small number of rich men, often former generals and governors who had made great profits from Rome's conquests. A plentiful supply of slaves captured in foreign wars gave these new landowners all the cheap labour they needed. Faced with this competition, the small Roman farmer often had to give up his own land. Sometimes he worked as a farmer on a large estate. More often he drifted to the city where he joined a growing mass of jobless, desperate and often violent men. The sturdy farmers, once the backbone of Rome, had become a mob depending upon the government for food and entertainment ("bread and circuses"). The Roman Republic was sick.

By the end of the second century B.C. it was clear that drastic reforms would be needed to cure Rome's ills. The Senate, now little more than a rich man's club, was concerned only with protecting its power and wealth. Faced with these problems, two young brothers of a noble and respected Roman family, Tiberius and Gaius Gracchus, offered a reform programme. Tiberius was elected tribune in 133 B.C. He was convinced that Rome's main problem was the decline of her small farmers. To improve their lot, he proposed to distribute some of the farming lands belonging to the state among the poor and landless people of Rome. However, the great landowners in the Senate (many of whom were controlling or profiting from the state lands) opposed such a distribution. They started a riot in which Tiberius and many of his followers were killed. A few years later his younger brother, Gaius Gracchus, proposed even more sweeping land reforms. His programme included the building of roads and the founding of settlements and colonies, including

The man who did most to change Rome's citizen army into a professional standing army was a general named Marius who defended Rome brilliantly against northern barbarian invaders during the last century of the Republic. He was elected to the consulate seven times. The soldiers of the new army sometimes referred to themselves as "Marius' mules." When they were not fighting, they were at work on an endless variety of jobs which included the building of roads and bridges and fortifications such as the timber ones being prepared by the legionaries in this relief. The Romans probably invented the military practice of "digging in," for they never went into battle or retired for the night without preparing some kind of fortified position.

one near Carthage, to provide new opportunities for Rome's jobless and poor. He also created a court to try dishonest governors of the provinces. Once again the Senate opposed the reforms and to prevent capture and public execution, Gaius took his own life.

The failure of the Gracchi brothers marked the end of peaceful and orderly attempts to solve Rome's problems. As rival groups fought for power, Rome went through a century of corruption, murder and civil war. At the same time she became involved in wars on many fronts outside Italy — in Asia, Spain, Gaul, Macedonia and Thrace. Naturally the army became increasingly important both in the defence of Rome and in the struggle for power within Rome. During this period the army changed from a militia of citizens who fought for the length of the campaign to a force of professional soldiers who remained in the army for many years. As a result, the soldiers began to feel a greater loyalty to their general than to Rome. Thus, political power in Rome often passed to the general who could control the legions, as the career of Sulla showed. Sulla was an aristocrat supported by the Senate. He had been elected consul in 88 B.C. After putting down a rebellion in Asia, Sulla returned in triumph to Rome only to find his political opponents in control of the government. Backed by his legions, Sulla seized power, made himself dictator, ruthlessly slaughtered thousands of his opponents and seized their property.

Disorders following Sulla's death paved the way for three men to gain complete control of Rome. The first was Pompey, a brilliant soldier who had won great fame by clearing the Mediterranean Sea of the pirates who had become a menace to Roman trade. He had also defeated Rome's enemies in the eastern Mediterranean and enlarged Rome's empire by creating the new provinces of Bithynia and Pontus, Cilicia and Syria. Pompey also added immense booty to Rome's treasury. As a result of his conquests, Roman power in the east extended from the Black Sea to the borders of Egypt. The second man was Crassus, a friendly but ambitious mil-

When Julius Caesar (100 B.C. - 44 B.C.) threw in his lot with the other two members of the First Triumvirate, he had already shown some of the qualities that would make him one of the most famous of all Romans. He had travelled widely throughout the Mediterranean world and had managed to stay alive despite the attempts of his enemies to be rid of him. He had also demonstrated great political skill in a number of important positions, and had managed to build up a great fortune which he had used to win great popularity. His later conquest of Gaul with its huge resources was one of the greatest achievements of the century and revealed Caesar as a military genius. His brilliant account of the Gallic War is both clear and vigorous. During his campaigns in Gaul Caesar had also launched two invasions of Britain, in 55 and 54 B.C. But although he claimed to have conquered Britain, his campaigns had not been decisive, and it was left to his successors to make Britain part of the Empire.

lionaire. He had helped to defeat Spartacus, who for six years had terrorized Italy with an army of 90,000 run-away slaves. Finally there was Julius Caesar, a young and ambitious politician and soldier.

In 60 B.C. the three formed a secret alliance (which has since become known as the First Triumvirate, or, Rule of Three Men). Their purpose was to join their forces to further their own personal ambitions. At first all went well. Pompey was rewarded for his eastern conquests. Crassus received a military command in the east. Caesar became a consul and secured command of the armies in Gaul. The conquest of Gaul would not only put an end to the annoying raids from the north, but also give Caesar a chance to gain fame and an army. Within eight years the brilliant Caesar had conquered the entire country, and Rome's empire now included all the territories west of the Rhine. Moreover, Caesar now commanded a great army of thirteen legions composed of troops fanatically loyal to their general.

Not everyone rejoiced in Caesar's triumphs. Crassus had been killed in battle and was no longer a rival. But Pompey watched Caesar's

Although Caesar's accounts of his exploits in Gaul are generally accurate, he often left out details that would not have been flattering to him. Scenes like this one from the Antonine column in Rome must have been common, for the legionaries expected to be left free to plunder after a victory over the barbarians. Many a barbarian father was slain before the eyes of wife and child before they were sold as slaves.

After Caesar had driven Pompey's supporters from Italy, he followed them to the Greek peninsula where he defeated them at Pharsalus. Pompey then fled to Egypt where he was killed at the order of the reigning Ptolemy. When Caesar arrived shortly afterwards, he immediately became involved with the beautiful Cleopatra, sister of the young ruler. In the power struggle between the two, Caesar sided with Cleopatra and installed her upon the throne. Caesar then went on to defeat the armies still ranged against him in North Africa and Spain. When he returned to Rome, he was in a stronger position than any Roman had ever been before.

One of the most important achievements of Augustus was the creation of a new professional army made up of twenty-eight legions of citizens. Each legion contained 6000 heavy infantry made up of sixty centuries of one hundred men, each commanded by an officer known as a centurion. The legion was the basic unit of the Roman army. Augustus also organized an equal number of smaller units composed of non-citizens who received citizenship at the end of their service. These units provided the army with such special troops as archers, cavalry and slingers. Many troops became highly skilled in the important task of building bridges (such as the log bridge shown here) to provide for the rapid crossing of streams and rivers.

In the east, Augustus began the slow process of bringing Galatia, Pontus and Judaea into the Empire. He ruled over Egypt directly as the successor of the Pharaoh. In the west his armies completed the conquest of the lands bordering the Danube. At the end of his reign three great rivers marked the boundaries of the Roman Empire: the Rhine, the Danube and the Euphrates.

growing power with increasing alarm. Hoping to gain control of Rome, he won the support of the Senate in opposition to Caesar. The conflict between the two former allies reached a peak in 49 B.C. The Senate ordered Caesar to disband his army after completing the conquest of Gaul. Caesar defiantly refused. Instead he made his own bid to control Rome. Crossing the Rubicon River from Gaul, he pushed almost unopposed through Italy. During the next few years, he crushed all opposition to him within the Roman world and greatly enlarged its extent. By 45 B.C. he had become the sole ruler of the Roman world.

During the short time he spent in Rome, Caesar accomplished a great deal. He founded new colonies where Rome's poor might find better opportunities. He planned great public works to make new jobs. He reformed the civil service and the system of local government. He introduced the Julian calendar, the forerunner of our own. But despite these and other reforms, Caesar made enemies among men who felt he was becoming too powerful. As he went to a meeting of the Senate on March 15, 44 B.C., a band of conspirators stabbed him to death.

The murder of Caesar solved nothing, for his assassins had no definite plans for the future. In the confusion that followed his death a second triumvirate arose consisting of Mark Antony, Caesar's friend; Octavian, Caesar's eighteen-year-old great nephew and heir; and Lepidus, an influential Roman politician. After destroying their enemies, the three divided the Roman world among them. As before, there developed a new struggle for power. Finally in 31 B.C., Octavian defeated his enemies and at the age of thirty-two became the sole master of the Roman world.

The triumph of Octavian, who took the new name Augustus in 27 B.C., ended a century of bloodshed and kept the Roman Empire from breaking up. It also marked the beginning of a great new period in Roman history. Augustus established a new system of government but made sure that it appeared much the same as the old. He knew very well that the old Republican government could not manage the affairs of a great empire. Under his new system of imperial government, Augustus was the all powerful ruler of the whole Empire.

For forty-one years Augustus ran the affairs of Rome and the Empire efficiently. He developed a large civil service composed of able men, particularly from the lower classes. These men dealt with the day-to-day matters of government, and became increasingly important and influential. Augustus also carefully supervised his government officials in the provinces, where for years there had been complaints of corruption and injustice. He improved the finances of the Empire by introducing new taxes. He also reformed the system of tax collection. He launched a great building programme within Rome which not only provided work for many people but also beautified the city. He boasted, not without accuracy, "I found a Rome of brick and left it of marble." To ensure order and security in the city Augustus established for the first time a fire department and a police force.

Augustus was interested in more than material matters. To strengthen religion, he encouraged the worship of the old gods and spent great sums building new temples to them. To raise moral standards he had strict laws passed regulating personal conduct, punishing bachelors, discouraging luxury and encouraging large families. His vision was of a new Rome with the virtues of the old. If he was not successful in his aim, his efficient rule gave Rome peace, prosperity and cultural development. It was Augustus who more than anyone else laid the foundations for the greatness of Imperial Rome.

The eighty-four emperors who ruled after Augustus were a mixed lot. Some were able and efficient rulers who worked for the welfare of their subjects. Others had little ability. A few were downright villains. Perhaps the worst of these was Nero, who became Emperor at the age of sixteen. He is best remembered for his murders, including that of his mother, his persecution of the Christians and his madness. He is also accused of starting a great fire in Rome and then playing his fiddle while it burned. It is not certain that

Early in the second century A.D. the Roman Empire reached its greatest extent. By the year 100 a series of emperors had pushed the Roman occupation of Germany as far as the Main River and had gained control of Britain as far north as Scotland. Some of the most dramatic developments took place in the reign of Trajan. Between 100 and 106 he conquered and colonized Dacia, a region beyond the Danube, using tactics like those employed by the legionaries (above) who have linked their shields over their heads to provide protection against missiles thrown by defending Dacian soldiers. Somewhat later Trajan conquered Armenia and Parthia, thus pushing the imperial boundaries to the Persian Gulf and the Caspian Sea.

he actually did this. But it seems likely that he was both evil enough and had sufficient musical talent! Nero loved nothing better than to sing and play the lyre in public. It would be impossible and tedious to list the names and achievements of each emperor. None of them made serious changes in the system of government established by Augustus. Like him they personally controlled the most important matters of state, the finances, the army and the growing civil service. But while the Roman citizens had little control over government, the system generally was efficient. For many years the people of Rome's great empire enjoyed the blessing of peace and considerable prosperity.

THE FALL OF ROME

By the end of the second century A.D., however, there were signs that all was not well with Rome. There were serious economic problems. Trade throughout the Empire had declined as small industries in towns and cities began to produce most of the goods their citizens needed. Since fewer people could make money from exchanging goods, there was a general decline in prosperity. A shortage of gold and silver from which to make coins speeded up the decline of trade. Agriculture was also in a weakened condition. Poor farming methods had exhausted the soil and therefore reduced the amount of food available. The food shortage came at the same time as the demand for food increased, for more people had moved from the country to enjoy the free bread and entertainment of the city. To make matters worse, as times became more difficult for most people, their taxes steadily increased.

Rome also faced serious political problems. The growth of the imperial system of government had left ordinary Roman citizens with no say in their government. As a result, they tended to lose their sense of pride and patriotism. The great mass of people in the cities had no concern for the future of the Empire. Even among wealthy aristocrats there seemed to be more interest in having a good time than in good government. At

The Emperor Hadrian, who succeeded Trajan, adopted a defensive rather than an offensive policy. One of his first acts was to give up Trajan's conquests east of the Euphrates. He felt that the cost of governing them would be too great a burden on the Empire's resources. His policy was to protect and improve existing provinces. In line with this policy he ordered the building of a great fortified wall across Britain from the mouth of the Tyne to the Solway Firth, to provide the Roman province with protection against wild tribes to the north. Known as Hadrian's Wall, the structure extended for seventy-three miles across the country and linked fourteen forts. At one-mile intervals this northern frontier of the Empire was manned by garrisons of one hundred men.

the very time when outstanding political leaders were most needed, Rome produced some of her very worst. One reason for this was the fact that there was no definite system for selecting emperors. Under the circumstances it was natural for the strongest power in the Empire to make the choice. That meant the army. For half a century, a number of emperors acted as little more than puppets worked by the troops who had put them in power. Army control led to lawlessness and the breakdown of the central government.

This political failure could not have happened at a worse time. On all sides barbarian invaders began to strike across the boundaries of Rome's empire into Gaul, Spain and the Balkans. One indication of Rome's decline is the fact that some barbarian troops were even invited into the Empire to help defend it against other barbarians.

Towards the end of the third, and in the early years of the fourth centuries, two emperors, Diocletian and Constantine, tried with some success to solve Rome's problems and halt its decline. Their method was to control and regulate every aspect of life within the Empire. They fixed the amount of wages a person might earn and set prices at which goods had to be sold. They made tenant farmers stay on the land in order to increase food production and stop the flow of people to the cities. Others had to do whatever work the government directed, whether they wished to or not. Conditions improved, but the Empire became a police-state with an army of spies to report any signs of unrest and rebellion.

The reign of Constantine is remembered for two main developments. It was he who finally

From the end of the second century much of Rome's energy was spent trying to hold back invading barbarians on every frontier. This contemporary relief depicting the horrible fate of German prisoners suggests the brutality of Roman officers as well as the seriousness of the barbarian threat.

allowed Christianity to exist as a lawful religion and gave it an equal standing with other religions within the Empire. Constantine himself became a Christian in A.D. 337. By the end of the fourth century, Christianity had become the official religion of the Empire and the government even began to persecute pagans or unbelievers. From an insignificant cult that had appeared in Rome during the time of Augustus, Christianity had become the state religion.

Constantine also transferred his capital from Rome to Byzantium which he renamed Constantinople. This act was a recognition that the eastern territories were now much more important to the Roman Empire in every way than were those in the west. Towards the end of the fourth century the Empire was divided into two distinct parts, the Eastern Roman Empire called the Byzantine Empire with its capital at Constantinople, and the Western Roman Empire with its capital at Rome. The Eastern Empire lasted until the eleventh century, but the Western Empire soon fell. When historians speak of the "fall of Rome," they are referring to the fall of the Western, the least important, part of the Empire. Constantinople remained a strong centre of civilization long after Rome had fallen to invading barbarians.

The achievements of Diocletian and Constantine delayed, but they could not prevent, the collapse of the Western Empire. After they died, the old economic, political and military problems reappeared. In a way the new religion, Christianity, hastened the decline, for it taught men that the welfare of their souls was more important than saving the Empire. Historians still argue about the causes of Rome's collapse. While they cannot agree about which was most important, they admit that no one factor can explain the collapse. There were many causes and they were related. For example, the failure to control the army undoubtedly caused political breakdown. At the same time the army became more powerful because of weak political leadership.

At any rate, for a variety of reasons, the Western Empire by the beginning of the fifth century was in utter confusion. Faced by attacking barbarians in Gaul, Spain and Africa, it lay helpless. Finally in A.D. 410 Rome itself was sacked by barbarian Visigoths. When a German became Emperor in A.D. 476, it was clear that the Western Roman Empire was at an end. This did not mean the destruction of the civilization Rome had developed. It continued to flourish in the East, and the barbarians themselves adopted much of the civilization of the people they had defeated.

The Roman achievement

A great historian once wrote that if he had to choose a time in history when the human race was happiest he would pick the period between A.D. 96 and 180. Not everyone would agree with this choice. But there is no doubt that for a great many of the 70 to 90 million people in the forty-three provinces of Rome's empire, life during the first two centuries was good. It was a time of general peace and stability known as the *Pax Romana*. In some respects it was the closest men have ever come to achieving the ideal of one united world. As one poet expressed it, "Rome had made a city where once there was a world." It was not a great exaggeration, for Rome's empire at its height included most of what was known of the Western world. And despite its great size, the Empire had many of the qualities of a closely-knit city. From the Atlantic shores of Spain in the west to the Caspian Sea in the east, and from Hadrian's Wall in Britain to Egypt in the south, people lived under one system of government, used the same kind of money and were protected by a common Roman law. Linking the far-flung parts of the Empire physically were 50,000 miles of the finest roads built until very recent times.

THE GOVERNMENT OF AN EMPIRE

It was during the reign of Augustus that the main features of imperial government for Rome and the Empire were gradually set up. For the 200 years that followed, the system remained, with only a few changes. Augustus knew when he seized power in Rome that the system of government under the Republic was unsatisfactory. While the Republican system had worked well for a small city-state, it was incapable of ruling so vast a territory as Rome had become. Signs of weakness were everywhere. For a hundred years Romans had fought each other in bloody civil wars. The army was unreliable. Senators were often lazy and dishonest. In many parts of the Empire subject peo-

Augustus, meaning the "revered one," was the name conferred on Gaius Octavius in 27 B.C. when he became the real ruler of Rome. Octavius, the grand-nephew of Julius Caesar, was born in Rome in 63 B.C. and was adopted by Caesar in 44 B.C. Augustus was handsome and dignified, and despite his great power had a very modest manner. His favourite motto apparently was "Make haste slowly." Although he lived until A.D. 14, he never enjoyed good health.

159

ples increasingly resented the bad government of Roman officials. Clearly, Rome needed a strong ruler who could restore honest and efficient government at home and bring order and justice to the provinces of Rome's growing empire. Augustus understood Rome's problems and believed that he could cure them. Yet he also knew that the Romans would not submit happily to the government of a dictator based on military power alone. Aware of their respect for the old habits and traditions, Augustus tried to establish his position on the basis of law. He hoped to obtain all of the power he needed, while at the same time keeping the forms or machinery of the old system of government.

His first move came in 27 B.C. After having put an end to the fighting within Rome, he dramatically gave up all of his powers to the people and the Senate. He was, he claimed, restoring the Republic. But the Senate, fearing renewed violence, quickly gave Augustus many official positions and titles which carried with them great powers. For example, they gave him control of the consuls and assemblies, the army, the state religion and many of the provinces in the Empire. The Senate also declared that Augustus was *princeps* or the first citizen of Rome. It was no empty title, for it carried with it such prestige that the princeps or emperor was the real power in the state. No other individual or group had nearly as much authority.

The system of imperial government worked out by Augustus continued almost unchanged for the next two centuries, during which the Roman Empire was at its peak. The emperors who followed Augustus exercised almost complete control over Rome. Yet on the surface it seemed that he had restored the ancient Republic. In theory, all power still came from the people and the Senate. Officials were still elected to the old offices of state. Senators met as they always had, although increasingly they played little active part in government. The assemblies came together on occasion. But while the names and forms remained the same, the old institutions of the Republic lacked any real authority. Their main job was to act as

rubber stamps, granting each emperor his great powers at the beginning of his reign and legalizing his decrees.

Great powers alone did not ensure good government. The emperor needed loyal and able servants to help him in the actual running of the state. Here again Augustus had taken the lead by creating a well organized and efficient civil service. Like any modern civil service, that of imperial Rome was organized into departments which were responsible for such matters as finance and justice. At the head of each department was a senior official of ability and experience. Usually he was a member of the equites or knights, though he might be a senator. Under him were a host of lesser officials with clearly stated duties to perform. Most of these men were capable plebeians or even educated slaves. The entire civil service was controlled from a central office in Rome, which was responsible to the emperor. At its best, throughout the second century, the civil service was efficient and honest and served the Empire well.

Just as important as the civil service was the army, upon which the safety of the Empire depended. For the first two centuries after the establishment of the Empire the Roman legions were an unbreakable shield against invasion. In the minds of most men it was unthinkable that the Roman army could ever be defeated. In many ways the army, like the civil service, was the creation of Augustus. He had built a permanent professional army. It was made up of men who enlisted for long periods of sixteen to twenty years. For such men, the army was no part-time job. It was a permanent profession which paid them well and provided them with good pensions at the end of their service. Discipline was strict, but by and large, the officers were able and just. And there was great satisfaction in serving with men who had good reason to be proud of their fighting ability. The main core of the army was made up of Roman citizens, but an increasing number of auxiliary troops were recruited from among Rome's subjects in the provinces outside Italy.

While Roman soldiers protected the provinces and maintained order, governors appointed by the emperor ruled over them. Augustus had also taken the first steps to improve the system of government in the provinces. To reduce dishonesty and disorder, he chose governors carefully on the basis of ability and character and paid them good salaries. Then he kept a watchful eye on their conduct. He appointed a special body of tax collectors who were directly responsible to the emperor and had to give a detailed account of their work. As a result of such policies, the government of the provinces during the first two centuries was generally efficient, orderly and honest..

One reason for the success of Rome's policy towards the provinces was the freedom given local communities to run their own affairs. Emperors encouraged the development of city-states throughout the Empire. In each city-state, local officials looked after such day-to-day matters as policing, courts, public buildings and the collection of local taxes. But while the emperors encouraged such activities, they did not hesitate to interfere when they found local policies in conflict with the interests of Rome. These occasions showed clearly that the final authority throughout the Roman Empire rested with the emperor at Rome.

Although the emperors during the first two centuries had almost unlimited powers, they were not usually tyrants. Most of them had a strong sense of duty and believed that their power should be used for the good of their subjects. A deep respect for the law also kept emperors from misusing their powers.

Among the greatest glories of Rome was its law. It is impossible to talk about Roman government without also considering Roman law. From the earliest times the Romans believed that a state could not exist without laws. At first the Roman law was simply unwritten custom. For more than a thousand years it was changed and modified. Eventually it developed into a complicated code of laws which has influenced the legal systems of

161

almost every country in the Western world. Our very word "justice" comes from the Roman word for law, *ius*. Many people believe that Rome's most enduring contribution to Western civilization was her law.

About 450 B.C., after demands from the plebeians, the early customs of Rome were first brought together and written down in the Twelve Tables. The Tables were drawn up to meet the needs of Roman citizens living in a small agricultural community. They were concerned with what we call civil matters — property rights, wills, the conduct of citizens and the rights of individuals. At that time, however, even murder was considered a civil matter, and it was up to the relatives of the murdered person to take legal action against the murderer. It was not until the period of the late Empire that there developed a definite code of laws to deal with criminal matters. These laws were based on the notion that a crime such as murder was an offence against the state and that it was the duty of the state to bring the accused to justice.

Although Roman law continued to be based on the Twelve Tables, it changed and grew as Rome itself changed and expanded. Sometimes changes occurred as the result of acts of the assemblies or Senate, or through decisions of emperors. An even more important source of "new" law were the rulings of judges. Eventually these judgements created a large body of "case law" based on precedent, the decisions of judges in previous similar cases.

In addition to this case law, there gradually developed a body of law to govern the subject peoples of Rome's empire. This was known as *ius gentium* or the law of the nations, in contrast to the *ius civile* or the civil law which applied only to Roman citizens. However, by the third century, when Rome had given citizenship to most people in the Empire, there were repeated attempts to create a single law that would be the same for all parts of the Empire. The most famous of the legal codes which attempted to organize the whole body of Roman law was completed by the Eastern Emperor Justinian in the sixth century. This

Intelligent and industrious, Justinian (A.D. 527-565) was the greatest of the Byzantine emperors. In addition to his legal reforms, he tried with some success to reconquer the lost or western half of the Roman Empire. He added North Africa, Italy south of the Alps, the Mediterranean islands and part of Spain to the Eastern Empire. But his campaigns left the state so exhausted financially and militarily that it was not able to resist later invaders from east and west. Justinian also tried to strengthen and unify the Christian Church. (Christianity by now was the official religion of the Empire.) He believed that unity in religion was necessary to the well-being of the state. But he was unable to end the religious disputes which constantly threatened to weaken the Byzantine Empire. One of his greatest achievements was the building of Santa Sophia, one of the world's most beautiful churches, and long regarded as one of the wonders of the world.

unified system of Roman law was known as the *Corpus Iuris Civilis* or Body of the Civil Law. Many scholars believe that Rome's chief contribution to Western civilization has been the principles and ideas contained in such legal codes as Justinian's. Certainly, there is scarcely a nation in the Western world that has not been influenced in some way by the Roman law. Oddly enough, Justinian's code was completed some fifty years after the western part of the Roman Empire had collapsed before the barbarians.

The Romans were the first to admit that their law was not perfect. Then, as now, some judges were incompetent and some punishments brutal and absurd. The Romans recognized the need for continuing efforts to improve the law so that it could best serve the needs of all men. They recognized also that changing conditions often required changes in the law, but they felt that there were certain principles that must always be upheld. It was these principles, rather than any particular laws, that have made the Roman law important to us. Among the most important of these was the belief that justice must be impartial, that it must be the same for everyone, rich as well as poor. Other Roman principles that still form a part of most law codes in the Western world are the right of an accused person to defend himself before he can be convicted; the need for the prosecution to prove guilt rather than for the accused to prove his innocence; freedom of conscience, or the right of a person to think what he wishes.

Among the many blessings of the people who lived within the boundaries of Rome's empire then, the greatest was probably the enjoyment of a common Roman law. The law protected the rights of everyone, not only against individuals but against the state itself. It gave orphans and slaves some protection against inhuman treatment. The law was the basis of the humane system of government which united millions of people of different races and kept them at peace.

LIFE IN THE EMPIRE

Sound government encouraged prosperity within the Empire. Most of its inhabitants made their living by farming, which provided the economic foundation of the Empire. There was a steady demand for the products of the soil. People of the growing cities needed food, as did the soldiers of every province. Agricultural production was also stimulated by the technical skill of the Romans. In almost every part of the Empire they increased the amount of land under cultivation. In Egypt they increased the size of the harvests by improving the ancient methods of agriculture. In many other parts of Africa they raised crops on land which today is parched and unproductive.

The most prosperous agricultural units were

The large estates, each one with its magnificent villa, were not confined to Italy itself. They existed in Gaul (France) and Britain, and in the territories conquered by the Romans in Africa and the Near East. This Roman mosaic shows a villa in Tunisia in North Africa.

The oldest and most famous of all Roman roads was the Appian Way. Begun in 312 B.C., the Appian Way headed in a straight line south towards Capua, defying hills and marshes. Roads like this linked the hub of the Empire with its outposts on the Rhine, the Danube and far-away Britain. Mileposts along the road indicated the distance to Rome or to the nearest provincial capital.

That rivers were no obstacle to Roman engineers is clearly seen in this modern picture of a magnificent Roman bridge spanning a river in Spain.

the large estates owned by rich landowners. Such men concentrated on the large-scale production of grain, grapes, olives and cattle. This made it more difficult for small landowners to survive. Thus, more of these small farmers were forced to give up their land and work as tenants on the big estates. The estates often became industrial units as well, manufacturing and selling such products as pottery and utensils to the surrounding countryside and to nearby cities.

Much of the Empire's prosperity was due to a tremendous increase in trade and industry. Many factors stimulated the rise of trade. Good government and peace meant that merchants could travel safely throughout the Empire. A single money system which Augustus had established for the whole Empire made the exchange of goods easy. There were practically no customs barriers or taxes between districts, so that trade could move freely from one province to another. Differences in language presented few problems, for Latin

164

was generally understood in the west, as was Greek in the east. Futhermore, excellent roads and sea lanes provided a first-rate system of communications.

Roman roads were of immense importance in trade. Originally built to make the movement of troops fast and easy, the roads soon carried a flourishing commerce. Early in the second century about 50,000 miles of roads stretched from the Tigris River in the east to Spain in the west. In Britain alone, on the very outskirts of the Empire, there were 6500 miles of highway, the best roads Britain was to know until the eighteenth century. The roads were engineering and technological marvels, rightly regarded as Rome's greatest single physical accomplishment. A typical Roman road was forty feet wide and from three to five feet thick. It was constructed with layers of stone, the cracks between them filled with a mortar over a gravel surface. Perhaps Rome's greatest contribution to technology was the invention and use of concrete. Roman roads were crowned or rounded on top to allow water to run off; drainage ditches ensured that the foundations would not crumble. In their attempts to make the roads as straight as possible, Roman engineers bridged valleys and swamps and cut through mountains. Many of their roads do not vary from a straight line more than half a mile over a twenty-mile stretch. Built to last, many Roman roads, particularly in southern Europe, are still in use today.

Along with the roads, the sea lanes also helped to increase trade and commerce. The Roman navy policed the seaways so effectively that goods moved safely by sea from all parts of the Empire. So thoroughly did the navy control the Mediterranean that during the first two centuries of the Empire, it did not have to fight a single major battle. Piracy almost ceased to exist. There is no doubt that much of the Empire's prosperity was due to the navy's control of the Mediterranean Sea.

A Roman relief (above) shows ships at sea. Below, the owner of a grain ship watches the loading of his vessel before it sets out for Rome or some other great city in the Empire.

In addition to these factors, trade naturally expanded as the Empire grew during the first century after its establishment. Within a short time traders carried a wide variety of goods over the Empire's roads and seaways. The newly won territories in North Africa and Europe provided new sources of raw materials, as well as some manufactured articles and an abundance of slaves. At the same time they bought some luxury articles from Rome. From Britain came supplies of tin and leather. Gaul sent pottery, rough textiles and wine. More important than any of the other western territories was Spain whose mines produced immensely valuable gold, silver, copper, lead and iron. The Spanish provinces were also important sources of timber, grain, olives and rope.

In the east, Egypt became a very important part of the Empire's trading system and economic life. Each year from the Nile granary came some 20,000,000 bushels of grain to feed the growing population of Italian cities.

The great port of Alexandria at the mouth of the Nile became a bustling centre of commerce, second only to Rome itself. Through its harbour passed goods — grain, wine and tools — on their way to Arabia, East Africa and the Far East. Westbound through Alexandria came such luxury products as ivory and tortoise shell from Africa, perfumes, spices and pearls from India, and even silk from China. It took silk about a year to reach the Roman world by Persia and India, and it required a pound of gold to purchase a pound of

silk. Although there is evidence of considerable contact between Roman merchants and Indians and Chinese, there is no indication that Roman civilization had much effect upon, or was itself influenced by, the civilizations of the Far East.

The growth of trade and industry was reflected by the growth of cities. The older cities of the eastern part of the Empire had been centres of civilization for a long time. During the *Pax Romana* many of them rivalled Rome in importance. In addition to Alexandria, such cities as Antioch, the capital of Syria, Corinth and Constantinople became even larger and more prosperous urban centres than they had been. In the more backward provinces of the Western Empire new kinds of cities developed under Roman direction. Some-times former military camps became centres of trade, industry and civilized life. In Britain, the Latin word for camp, *castra,* survives in names like Manchester and Lancaster. In many ways the new cities of the west were "little Romes" built according to a standard Roman plan. The market place, known as the forum, stood at the centre of each town. Beyond it were temples, guild-halls, and a senate house — centres of religious, commercial and political life. Each town could usually boast an assortment of theatres, gymnasia, baths and libraries. The orderly design of the main streets would have delighted a modern town planner. A good water supply and system of sanitation were taken for granted. Indeed, Rome's famous sewer, the *Cloaca Maxima,* is still in use.

The city:
Rome and Pompeii

Although great cities dotted the Roman Empire, the greatest by far was Rome itself. The centre of government, trade and religion was the Roman *Forum,* the ruins of which can be seen here. In the early days of the city the Forum was largely a commercial centre, but around its edges arose the oldest temples in the city. Next came such buildings as the Senate House. Eventually the Forum became the political centre of Rome.

In the left foreground can be seen part of the Arch dedicated to the Emperor Tiberius. Through the Arch ran the *Via Sacra,* along which great processions made their way through the Forum. The building (to the left of the Via Sacra) with the marble columns and broad stairs is the temple of Antoninus and Faustina, built in honour of the Emperor Antoninus Pius and his wife. In the right foreground stand columns from the temple of Saturn, which housed the state treasury.

In his comedy, *Curculo,* the Roman writer Plautus provided a fascinating picture of life in the Forum. The description has been retold by De Ruggiero, an expert on the Forum: "There is the famous scene in which the poet takes the spectator through the best known parts of the Forum and its immediate neighbourhood, pointing out the characteristics of each, as represented in the people who frequented it. There in the *Comitium* where the judges sit and the orators make their speeches from the platform, you can see the perjurers, the liars, the braggarts . . .; beside the shops, old and new, in front of the basilica are the strumpets, the bankers, the usurers, the brokers; in the lowest part of the Forum, the serious-minded and the gentlemen who conduct themselves quietly. . . ; higher up are the gossips and scandal-mongers . . . everywhere the rabble of idle vagabonds, the men about town — the type that are either deep in gaming or spreading false rumours . . . and with them those credulous and simple-minded people who crowd the Forum and Comitium in time of crisis, when fantastic portents are being reported, to hear exactly where a rain of blood or milk has fallen, or what remains of the immense swarm of bees that was seen overhead, and to prognosticate good news or bad if there is a rainbow or three suns appear above the temple of Saturn. . . ."

The Forum also witnessed many of the most dramatic events in the history of ancient Rome: the assassination of Caesar, Mark Antony's speech in honour of Caesar, Cicero's famous speeches, and the great parades of victorious generals who marched up the Via Sacra at the head of their troops.

Since by the time of Caesar the old Roman Forum was too small, the new "forum of Caesar" was begun. Augustus prided himself on the new public buildings he had constructed and the old ones he had restored. Later emperors added a host of magnificent buildings. By the fourth century, Imperial Rome, from the air, would have looked much like the model here. Dominating the new heart of the city was the gigantic *Colosseum,* built by Emperor Vespasian and his son Titus between A.D. 70 and 80 on a site formerly used by Nero for a lake in his villa. While the Colosseum could seat almost 50,000 people it was dwarfed by the *Circus Maximus* which had 300,000 seats. The scene of chariot races, gladiator fights and mock battles between thousands of soldiers, the Circus was almost as dangerous for spectators as for performers. It was destroyed by fire several times, and the banks of seats collapsed at least twice, killing 1112 people on the first occasion and 13,000 on another. Up from the Colosseum is the Roman Forum with the *Basilica Julia* shown at the far end. Beyond that lies the sacred Capitoline Hill with the temple of Jupiter. On the edge of the Forum was the Palatine Hill, where Rome was supposed to have been founded by Romulus. Augustus moved his residence there in 44 B.C. Thereafter almost all the emperors lived there, so that the Hill became one immense royal palace. Other striking buildings which graced the new forum were the Temple of Claudius, the theatre of Marcellus, and Trajan's Forum.

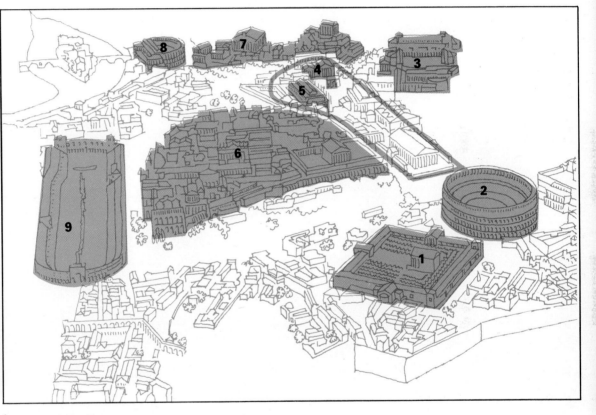

1. Temple of Claudius
2. Colosseum
3. Trajan's Forum
4. Curia (Senate House)
5. Basilica Julia
6. Palatine Hill
7. Capitoline Hill
8. Theatre of Marcellus
9. Circus Maximus

The tragedy of Pompeii

A tragedy almost 2000 years ago made it possible for us to walk down the streets and into the homes and shops of an ancient Roman city. In A.D. 79 Mount Vesuvius, in southern Italy, erupted and buried the town of Pompeii and many of its 20,000 inhabitants under twenty feet of lava and ash. A century ago the work of rediscovery began. As the ash and lava were removed, streets and homes, shops and public baths, and even the skeletons of people who were buried alive or suffocated were found just as they had been on that fateful afternoon in August.

Pompeii was not a large city; it has been compared to a reasonably prosperous suburb of a large modern city. Like all Roman cities it had a forum, seen here with Vesuvius rising menacingly in the background. Along the paved streets were a wide variety of shops in which lived the merchants and artisans. Behind some of them were bakeries like the one seen (p. 171) with its ovens and millstones. The wealthier inhabitants, however, had separate homes. A typical house was enclosed within high windowless walls and the inhabitants enjoyed complete privacy. The house centred on an open courtyard, usually decorated with a fountain and statues. Inside, the walls were decorated with vivid paintings. (The painting of Alexander at Issus came from a home in Pompeii.) Even behind the water trough can be seen the outline of what once was a colourful wall painting.

To supply water to the cities of the Empire the Romans constructed aqueducts, some of which were built on two or three tiers of arches. Rome, for example, received its water supply from eleven aqueducts which ran from ten to fifty miles and carried about 25,000,000 gallons of water a day. The famous aqueduct at Segovia, Spain, still provides part of the city's water supply. More famous is the Pont du Gard, seen here, a combined aqueduct and bridge over the Gard River in southern France. Built in the first century B.C., the Pont du Gard is about 900 feet long and towers 160 feet above the ground. The lowest tier is still used as a bridge.

EVERYDAY LIFE IN ROME

Roman society was made of up definite classes, but the barriers between them were not rigid. It was possible for someone at the bottom of the social ladder to move to the top. For example, the brilliant Roman general, Marius, was the son of a small plebeian farmer. Early Roman society had been dominated by wealthy landowners. During the period of the early Empire, however, the aristocracy expanded. The top level of society now included not only rich landowners, but also leaders in business and commerce and important government officials. Into the ranks of this new nobility came non-native Romans — Spaniards, Africans, Greeks, Gauls and even Britons.

Below this upper class was a group which included smaller landowners, and artisans of all kinds, usually organized into guilds. Thus, there were, for example, metal workers' guilds and physicians' guilds. In some respects the guilds resembled trade unions, charging dues, bargaining for higher wages and sometimes even striking. Also included in this group were shop owners and minor officials. Lowest in the social scale were the unemployed members of the city mobs, the agricultural workers, and, at the very bottom, the astonishingly large number of slaves.

Depending upon one's social class, life in the Empire could be very pleasant or extremely difficult. For the wealthy it was a good life. In addition to a large and luxurious town house with running water and central heating, a rich Roman would often have a great sprawling estate or a villa in the country. A villa often had a sunny promenade for strolling, an aviary filled with rare birds, a fish pond, a wrestling ground and a garden filled with ivy-covered Greek statues, often hastily created by sculptors of little skill.

Food merchants grew prosperous simply by meeting the needs of their wealthy clients. Always there was a demand for newer delicacies Among the favorite dishes was whole roast boar, carried from the kitchen by four or five slaves, or roast peacock served on a silver tray decorated with the peacock's tail feathers. A not unusual meal might include whole fish cooked in a sea of shrimp, meats with spiced vegetables, meats with sauces, oysters with sauces, pigeons and broiled blackbirds, Spanish wildfowl stuffed with Indian rice, peaches from Persia and Greek wine drunk from golden goblets. A dinner party was a great event customarily lasting several hours and often accompanied by professional entertainment. At length the guests arose, often pale from overeating, depending upon their slaves to help them stagger safely home.

Only a small number within the Empire enjoyed the pleasures which wealth could buy. The poor and unemployed lived in crowded conditions with few material comforts. Most of Rome's population lived in slum-like conditions on the streets or in fire-trap tenements. These box-like structures were often six storeys high and frequently collapsed or burned to the ground. A walk at night through the mud-filled alleys of the poor districts of Rome was no exercise for a sensible person. Poverty, hunger and suffering had made such areas rabbit warrens of every imaginable kind of crime. Without work, the mob depended upon the state for food. Every month they lined up for the wooden tickets which would entitle them to free grain from the state. The state also provided them with amusement, no doubt hoping to keep them from rebelling against their hopeless conditions. Roman writers constantly expressed their contempt for these unfortunate creatures whose only interest in life was "bread and circuses."

During the Empire there were more than a hundred holidays a year in Rome. On these days emperors, public officials or rich men staged their famous public shows or circuses. In Rome the greatest stadia were the Colosseum which could hold 50,000 people and the Circus Maximus where a quarter of a million spectators could cheer the violent spectacles. The main event at the Circus was the chariot race, in which teams of horses pulled their light vehicles around a tight track at breakneck speed. Although accidents were common, the chariot races were good clean fun compared with many other events. At least the participants in these races were not matched against unequal opponents.

Romans at work

A Roman relief shows a small Roman town, with the homes resembling modern two- and three-storey apartment buildings separated by narrow streets.

A Roman butcher is seen here at work on the head of a pig. The rest of the animal hangs on hooks behind him.

MARCIO SEMP

A shopkeeper displays his ware of cutlery, including small sickles and knives, to a customer.

A draper and his assistant hold up a bolt of cloth for inspection by two wealthy customers and their slaves. Clothing was not bought ready-made in Rome.

The millstones in the bakery at Pompeii were probably turned by slaves or workmen. The stones in the large flour-mill pictured here are being turned by a horse, as a workman collects the flour.

Two workmen pull a small boat loaded with wine along an internal waterway in Italy or the Empire, as a third steers.

The furious excitement of the chariot race was captured in this contemporary relief. The four-horse chariots raced around the Circus Maximus as frenzied onlookers cheered them on. The charioteers were the great sports heroes of the day. One of the greatest, a man named Dilcles, entered 4257 races, finishing first 1462 times and winning the equivalent of more than a million dollars.

Before the contests began, the gladiators marched in front of the emperor's seat and shouted "Hail Emperor, we who are about to die, salute you." Gladiators who were reluctant to fight were spurred into action by trainers armed with whips and red-hot pokers, much as a quiet bull is spurred on in a modern bull fight. Victorious gladiators sometimes became popular heroes; after a long string of victories such a hero might be awarded a wooden sword, the symbol of his freedom. Few were so fortunate. Gladiators wounded in combat could ask for mercy by dropping their shields and raising their arms. As a rule the spectators decided, basing their decision upon how well he had fought. The emperor made the final gesture that determined his fate. Thumbs down meant death. In one year the Emperor Claudius set 19,000 criminals at each other's throats, and in four months Trajan displayed 10,000 gladiators to celebrate his military victories. The gladiator fights and the inhuman struggles between men and wild animals were held in the giant Colosseum. As the modern ruins show (page 178), the area below the floor of the Colosseum was a network of cells and cages where people and animals were kept until it was their turn to appear before the bloodthirsty crowd.

Among the most brutal events were the gladiator fights. The gladiators were usually specially trained slaves or criminals who often fought to the death in the arena before the shrieking crowds. Gladiators normally fought in the afternoons, after business hours, so that everyone could attend the show. Animal events were held in the mornings. Sometimes these were harmless and amusing. Trained monkeys drove chariots, and elephants performed such tricks as kneeling and writing with their trunks. Then there were contests which pitted animals against animals—bears against buffalo, for example, or elephants fighting with rhinoceros. Often, men fought against wild and starving animals, either in single combat or in contests involving groups of men and packs of animals. So many beasts were slaughtered — as many as 5000 in a single day — that armies of hunters were kept busy hunting new supplies. Capturing wild animals alive was no easy task, but the Romans became so skilful at it that some species were almost wiped out.

A popular activity was to send men and women, particularly early Christians, into the arenas to be torn apart by the beasts. The evil emperor Nero began such large-scale persecution following a great fire in the year A.D. 64. He decided to blame the fire on the Christians, the innocent though troublesome followers of the strange religion which had begun in Palestine and which was spreading throughout the Empire. On Nero's orders, great numbers of Christians were thrown to the lions to entertain the howling Roman masses. Others were crucified or dipped into pitch and set afire to illuminate the night chariot races. Other emperors followed Nero's savage example. But despite the persecution the number of Christians continued to grow.

Brutality was not confined to the arenas. Many a condemned criminal found himself on the stage of a theatre playing the part of an actor who had been condemned to death in a play. Instead of watching the tame spectacle of an actor pretending to be killed, the audience was treated to the real thing as the criminal was often tortured and killed before their eyes. Such ghastly entertain-

In their architecture the Romans loved size
for its own sake. Most of their work is
impressive because of the size and scale.
Few better illustrations of Roman
architecture can be given than the picture
of the arch of Constantine (above) or this
modern photograph of the Colosseum seen
through the Arch of Titus (right). (The relief
on the inside of the arch shows the source
of some of the pictures seen earlier in the
section on Rome.) About half of the
Colosseum still stands. The outside wall is
about 160 feet high. The interior is so
skilfully constructed that a spectator had
a clear view of all the action regardless
of where he sat.

ment at the state's expense probably helped to keep the masses under control. But the price was high, for all who watched could not help but become brutalized.

One class of poor within the Empire was probably even worse off than the poor or unemployed masses of the cities. These were the farm workers who toiled for a bare living on the lands of the large farmers. Many of the labourers had once been small landowners who had been forced to give up their lands through debt or other causes. They became tenant farmers working their landlords' farms for a tiny fraction of the crops they produced. During the general prosperity of the first two centuries of the Empire, their condition grew steadily worse, although their work did much to support the rest of Roman society.

At the very bottom of Roman society were the slaves. Slavery had existed since the days of the early Republic but with Rome's expansion and the large number of prisoners of war which resulted from it, the number of slaves increased greatly. At first the treatment of slaves was unbelievably bad. They were not regarded as people at all. The harsh Roman aristocrat, Cato, in a book on agriculture listed three kinds of farm tools: voiceless ones (wagons and plows), inarticulate ones (oxen and mules) and speaking ones (slaves). Over the years the lot of most slaves improved somewhat, but there were many whose lives held little but misery. Worst off were those who dug in the mines or worked on construction projects or the great landed estates. Harshly treated and half-starved, they often welcomed death as the only relief from their suffering.

Most slaves lived in the cities, and while their condition was not particularly happy, there is evidence to suggest that their lives were not just an endless round of hardship. Many were household servants. Even a lower middle class household could usually boast a few slaves, while a wealthy man might own 1000. Emperors had as many as 20,000. Slaves performed an endless variety of tasks. They were cooks and bakers, porters and waiters, barbers and valets, street cleaners and aqueduct repairmen, entertainers and clerks.

Many slaves were skilled men who became an important part of a wealthy household as craftsmen. Some rich men hired out their craftsmen-slaves or even established them in business, the slave receiving a share of the money he earned. In this way a slave could save his money and buy his freedom. He then became what was known as a freedman, and could even acquire slaves of his own. Talented freedmen often held important positions in the administration of the Empire.

Among the most important functions performed by slaves was that of education. Most of the teachers were well-educated Greeks who taught the children of the wealthy in their homes or in schools. (For the poor there were no schools.) At elementary schools children of well-to-do Romans learned the three R's — reading, writing and arithmetic — and graduated at the age of twelve or thirteen. At this point the girl's formal education ceased and she remained at home where she often received individual instruction from a slave. Boys advanced to a secondary school

A Roman relief shows a goatherd, who was probably one of Cato's "speaking" farm implements. If not a slave, he may have been one of the farmers who no longer owned his own land but worked on a rich man's villa.

M·CORNELIO·M·F·PAESTATIO·P·   ·FECI·R·

There were certain similarities between growing up in ancient Rome and growing up today. The father finds he has little to do with the baby while he is very young. Soon, however, the child becomes old enough to enjoy playing with his father's beard. There are a few years of freedom for playing games and pretending to be a famous charioteer in the Circus Maximus. When the youth faces his first duties, however, he finds that his father is a patient but stern taskmaster when it comes to reciting his lessons.

where they studied such subjects as grammar, history, geography and astronomy. At sixteen they graduated, were accepted as men and citizens, and either took their place in society or went on to more advanced studies. The final stage in the education of a rich man's son was to travel to the great centres of Greek civilization, particularly Athens.

Life in the early centuries of the Roman Empire presented many contrasts. It seems likely that more people within its boundaries enjoyed a higher standard of living and were better governed than ever before. At the same time, there were inequalities. Some lived in selfish luxury, while others starved. Some lived in idleness, while others toiled endlessly to support them. In other words, as with every society, the Roman Empire had its strengths and weaknesses. Yet whatever one's final verdict, it cannot be denied that under

Roman imperial rule the whole Mediterranean region became more unified and more civilized.

ROMAN CULTURE

At the same time as the Romans were establishing their system of government for the Empire, they were also making their greatest cultural advances. Much of Roman culture was Greek in origin. Most Romans greatly admired the Greeks whom they had conquered. From them the Romans borrowed or imitated a great deal, particularly in the fields of art, literature, science and philosophy. In doing so, they helped to preserve and spread the Greek cultural heritage. In other areas, the practical Romans were much more creative, and as we have seen, they excelled in engineering, law and administration.

The best Roman literature was produced between the first century B.C. and the second century A.D. Most writers followed Greek examples, both in the way they wrote and in the subjects they chose. However, the best Roman literature has a distinctive quality, and rivals that of the Greek masters. The fact that it was written in Latin is also important. Knowledge of Greek soon died out in the Western Empire, so that Latin was the language through which the Western world learned about ancient cultures.

It is generally agreed that Rome's greatest writer was the poet Virgil. Virgil grew up during the period of the civil wars in Rome, which ended with the triumph of Augustus. Eventually Augustus noticed his work and made it possible for him to spend all of his time writing. Virgil's greatest poem is the *Aeneid,* which is very much like the great epic poems of Homer. In the *Aeneid* Virgil tells of the adventures of the Trojan hero, Aeneas. After the Greek siege of Troy, Aeneas sets out, at the order of the gods, to found a new city that would one day rule the world. In other words, Rome's rise to world power was according to a divine plan. In carrying out the orders of the gods, Aeneas has many difficulties, but like the ideal Roman which he represents, his bravery, courage and patriotism enable him to overcome all obstacles. Virgil hoped to support the policies of Augustus by praising the virtues which had made Rome great, the old virtues of bravery, industry, simplicity and self-control which Augustus was trying to restore.

The greatest prose writer was a middle-class Roman lawyer named Cicero. An active politician, Cicero wrote a great many forceful speeches

In this Tunisian mosaic the famous Roman poet Virgil is seen holding the Aeneid. *Standing on either side of him are figures representing the muses or spirits of tragedy and epic. The epic is a narrative form of poetry celebrating heroic deeds, and to this class the* Aeneid *belonged.*

which remain as models of the way to use words to persuade. Among his most famous speeches were four which he delivered as consul in 63 B.C. against a schemer named Catiline, who tried to overthrow the government. As well as his speeches, Cicero wrote many essays on a wide variety of topics, and almost 800 letters. These letters not only reveal an intensely interesting person but also tell a great deal about contemporary Roman society and politics. Few prose writers in history have ever written with such genius on such a wide range of subjects. Cicero was also a man of courage and conviction. After the murder of Caesar, he supported the forces of Republicanism and vigorously opposed Mark Antony's bid for power despite the risks of attacking so powerful a figure:

> You grieve, senators, that three armies of the Roman people have been slaughtered. Antony slaughtered them. You mourn the noblest of your citizens. Antony robbed us of them too. The authority of this, our order, has been overthrown. Antony overthrew it. In a word, all we have seen afterwards (and what evil have we not seen), if we reason rightly, we shall credit to Antony alone.

It is not difficult to understand why Cicero was among those killed when Antony and his partners in the Second Triumvirate came to power.

In the visual arts, as in literature, the Romans borrowed heavily from the Greeks. In fact they not only borrowed Greek ideas, they actually stole a great many Greek works of art. Victorious returning armies brought back thousands of statues, columns and paintings. For many years the Roman sculptors were content to copy famous Greek productions. Some of the best Greek sculpture, in fact, exists today only in Roman copies. In time, the Romans developed a sculpture of their own, which at its best realistically portrayed personalities or events. The bas-relief work carved on a number of triumphal arches and columns (such as those seen earlier) shows historical scenes with great clarity.

Although Roman architecture was also based on Greek models, the Romans added features

One of the Romans' most celebrated thefts was the capture of the contents of the temple in Jerusalem. In A.D. 70 the Romans **ruthlessly suppressed a Jewish revolt,** destroyed the temple and carried off its treasures. The details were recorded in stone in the Roman Forum on the Arch of Titus, the conqueror of Jerusalem. In this relief, Roman soldiers follow Titus, and among them are manacled Jewish prisoners. On their shoulders they carry the Table of the Bread of the Presence, on top of which is the cup of Yahweh and underneath, two silver trumpets. A second group of soldiers are carrying the seven-branched candlestick: "And thou shalt make a candlestick of pure gold. . . . And thou shalt make the seven lamps thereof." (Exodus)

of their own. They used the arch and the dome which had been developed in the Near East, and changed them to form the basis of their great structures. These techniques made it possible for the Romans to build more varied structures than had been possible for the Greeks, who had relied on columns. The use of the arch and the discovery of concrete also enabled the Romans to engineer their great miracles, the aqueducts and bridges.

Although the Romans contributed a great deal in such practical arts as building, they made no real progress in science or scientific thought. Here again the practical Romans were imitators rather than creators. They did not usually seek new knowledge for its own sake, but they were excellent at collecting and organizing useful information. To Romans, the interesting and important thing was to use or apply the principles which had already been discovered. For the most part they were not interested in learning to use the scientific method employed by the Greeks. Certainly though, the technical skills developed and passed on by Roman engineers, builders and artisans were no little contribution to the development of Western civilization.

In no area was Roman borrowing more obvious than in religion. The early Romans, like most primitive peoples, worshipped spirits connected with nature and the family. From the Greeks they learned to think of these spirts or gods in human form. The Romans, in fact, merely took for their own many of the important Greek gods and by giving them Latin names made them Roman. Thus Zeus became Jupiter and Athena, Minerva.

The worship of their gods did not arouse strong religious feelings among the Roman people. For the most part they were content to leave religion to the priests. There was little emphasis on formal worship. A man in need of a favour would make a vow to some god. But he would carry out his promise only if the god first granted his request. The obvious weaknesses of this religion caused it to decline. As men became better educated, they looked with contempt upon the old gods. During the early Empire an increasing number of Romans turned to new religions from the east. Most of these appealed to the emotions and offered their believers a personal saviour and a life after death. The fact that the imperial government did not pass laws making these religions illegal encouraged their spread. One religion from the east, Christianity, was not tolerated. It was not that its teaching clashed with Roman religious ideas, but that Roman authorities believed that the Christians were a threat to peace and order. Despite persecution, however, Christianity, and indeed many of the other eastern religions, survived and spread. The effects proved to be serious, for all the religions emphasized the importance of preparing for life after death rather than dealing with the existing problems of the Roman Empire. These problems were so serious, however, that they demanded the fullest attention if Rome was to survive.

The City of God

A Roman citizen, writing to his nephew who was with the army in Syria, observed, "Our slaves are getting much excited about this so-called Messiah, and a few of them, who openly talked of the new kingdom (whatever that means) have been crucified. I would like to know the truth about all these rumours. . . . " In his letter the nephew replied, "A few days ago a pedlar came . . . to the camp. I bought some of his olives and I asked him whether he had ever heard of the famous Messiah who was killed when he was young. He said that he remembered it very clearly, because his father had taken him to Golgotha (a hill just outside the city) to see the execution, and to show him what became of the enemies of the laws of the people of Judaea."

The Roman soldier was, of course, writing about Jesus of Nazareth, who was born in the town of Bethlehem in Palestine. All that we know about the life of Jesus is found in the first four books of the New Testament, the gospels of Matthew, Mark, Luke and John. Their stories of Christ's life differ in some detail, but in general the story of Jesus is the same in all four gospels.

(The following picture essay uses texts from the Bible, ancient and medieval drawings, and the results of the work of modern scholars to trace the history of early Christianity.)

"And Joseph also went up from Galilee, out of the city of Nazareth, into Judaea, unto the city of David, which is called Bethlehem. . . . And she, Mary, brought forth her first-born son, and wrapped him in swaddling clothes, and laid him in a manger, because there was no room for them in the inn. And there were in the same country shepherds abiding in the field, keeping watch over their flock by night. And, lo, the angel of the Lord came upon them, and the glory of the Lord shone round about them: and they were sore afraid. And the angel said unto them, Fear not: for, behold, I bring you good tidings of great joy, which shall be to all people. For unto you is born this day in the city of David a saviour which is Christ the Lord." Like the medieval artist who illustrated a prayer book with this painting of the angel and the shepherds, almost everyone in the Western world knows the story told by St. Luke of the birth of Jesus.

184

According to St. Matthew, after the birth of Jesus, Joseph and Mary fled into Egypt following a warning from an angel that Herod the Great, King of Judaea, had heard of the young child and wished to destroy him. Later, the family returned from Egypt and settled in Nazareth. There the young boy grew up, learning his father's skills as a carpenter or mason. He was brought up in a pious Jewish home and learned to read and write in the synagogue. He was an able student, and enjoyed discussing religious matters with his elders. St. Luke wrote that when he was twelve Jesus strayed from his parents during a visit to Jerusalem. He was later found in the temple engaged in an earnest discussion or argument with the learned men of the temple. "And when they saw him, they were amazed: and his mother said unto him, Son, why hast thou thus dealt with us? Behold, thy father and I have sought thee sorrowing. And he said unto them, How is it that ye sought me? Wist ye not that I must be about my Father's business? And they understood not the saying which he spake unto them."

Jesus was about thirty years old when John the Baptist, a prophet, began preaching in Palestine. John called on the people to repent and turn from their sinful ways, predicting that the Kingdom of Heaven was at hand and that a Messiah or leader would soon come to lead his people. "Then cometh Jesus from Galilee to Jordan unto John, to be baptized of him. But John forbade him, saying, I have need to be baptized of thee, and comest thou to me?" But Jesus insisted and was baptized by John in the Jordan River, supposedly where this photograph was taken. "And, lo, the heavens were opened unto him, and he saw the Spirit of God descending like a dove, and lighting upon him: and lo a voice from heaven, saying, This is my beloved Son, in whom I am well pleased." Such is the story told by St. Matthew.

This drawing of bread and a fish, found in a cave under the city of Rome, refers to the famous story in the Gospels which tells of Jesus turning a loaf of bread and some fishes into enough food for a huge crowd of his followers. After his baptism he had gone into the wilderness by himself, where he fasted, prayed and meditated for forty days and nights. Then he travelled about Palestine, preaching in synagogues, on hillsides and in village squares. Christ's teachings attracted many followers. He taught of a kind and loving God and of an after-life in Heaven that could be attained by all just, moral and believing people. He called on people to love their neighbours and their enemies, as well as God. He illustrated his teachings with simple but clear parables such as those of the Prodigal Son and the Good Samaritan. The Bible also recounts how his fame spread as he worked miracles in healing the sick, the blind and the lame. The core of the teaching of Jesus is found in the Sermon on the Mount, where he expressed such ideas as "Blessed are the merciful, for they shall obtain mercy. Blessed are the pure in heart, for they shall see God. Blessed are the peacemakers, for they shall be called the children of God."

As the fame of Jesus spread, he gained many followers who hailed him as King of the Jews and as the Son of God. He also gained many enemies, among them Roman officials who feared rebellion and, more important, many Jewish religious officials who disputed his message. Finally, in A.D. 30, according to most historians, Jesus visited Jerusalem to challenge his opponents. He secured the approval of many people when he expelled the money changers and cattle dealers from the temple. However, he angered the priests by engaging in an open debate with them on complex religious questions. On the evening after he and his twelve disciples had eaten the famous Last Supper, they withdrew to the slopes of the Mount of Olives. But one of the disciples, Judas Iscariot, betrayed to the authorities their resting place outside the city. Here, Judas thought, they were far away from the crowds that might support Jesus if an attempt was made to arrest him. During the night Jesus was seized in the Garden of Gethsemane, at the foot of the Mount, where gnarled and ancient olive trees still stand today.

187

Tragedy at Calvary

This casket of wood and ivory, made in A.D. 360, dramatically tells the rest of the story. Jesus can be seen standing in the garden, after Judas had identified him by kissing him. Then, according to St. Luke, "Jesus said unto the chief priests, and captains of the temple, and the elders, which were come to him, Be ye come out, as against a thief, with swords and staves? When I was daily with you in the temple, ye stretched forth no hands against me: but this is your hour, and the power of darkness. Then they took him, and led him, and brought him into the high priest's house." To the right in the top column, Peter is shown denying that he knew Christ: "And Peter remembered the word of the Lord, how he had said unto him, Before the cock crow, thou shalt deny me thrice." In the bottom column Jesus is brought before the high priests and then before Pontius Pilate, the Roman Governor, who is shown washing his hands. The Roman heard the charges, but saw little cause for the execution of Jesus. Finally, however, he yielded to the demands of Jesus' enemies and agreed to the sentence of death.

Jesus was sentenced to be crucified, along with two criminals. Under Roman law a man sentenced to be crucified was first beaten with thongs or weighted chains. This fourteenth-century illustration from an English prayer book shows Jesus being scourged or beaten. He was then placed on the cross at Calvary. On the cross Pontius Pilate had his men place a sign to ridicule Jesus, on which was written: "Jesus of Nazareth, the King of the Jews." The first letters of the Latin version spelled out *I.N.R.I.*, initials that were to become the symbol of Christ's supreme position among Christians. The Book of St. Luke tells the story of the crucifixion: "And when they were come to the place, which is called Calvary, there they crucified him, and the male-factors, one on the right hand, and the other on the left. Then said Jesus, Father, forgive them; for they know not what they do. . . . And it was about the sixth hour, and there was a darkness over all the earth until the ninth hour. And the sun was darkened, and the veil of the temple was rent in the midst. And when Jesus had cried with a loud voice, he said, Father, into thy hands I commend my spirit: and having said thus, he gave up the ghost."

Although the bodies of executed criminals were usually thrown into pits, Pilate released the body of Christ to a man named Joseph of Arimathea. St. Luke wrote: "And he took it down, and wrapped it in linen, and laid it in a sepulchre that was hewn in stone, wherein never man before was laid."

An illustration in a twelfth-century prayer book retells the central story of the Christian religion. When, after resting on the Sabbath, Jesus' friends returned to his tomb, they found the stone guarding the entrance rolled away and the sepulchre empty. They were convinced that Jesus had risen from the dead and ascended to heaven. His disciples taught that he was the Son of God who had died to save mankind, and then risen from the dead. Just as Christ had risen, so could the faithful members of his Church.

The enthusiasm of the early Christians was increased by the belief that Jesus would soon return to establish the Kingdom of God on earth. One of the most devoted of the early disciples was Peter, one of the twelve apostles, who, like the men shown here, was a fisherman on the Sea of Galilee. Peter travelled about the eastern Mediterranean preaching. Apparently he was so successful in healing the sick that a magician offered him money for the secret of his miraculous powers. Peter finally made his way to Rome itself where he played a leading role in establishing a Christian community in the heart of the Roman Empire.

Perhaps the man who did most to promote the growth of Christianity was Saul of Tarsus, later known as Paul. A Jewish tent-maker, St. Paul was at first opposed to the Christians. In fact, the short, broad-shouldered man was well-known for hunting down Christian believers in Jerusalem and the nearby villages.

One day while he was going from Jerusalem to Damascus to begin new attacks on Christians, he saw a vision and heard Christ ask, "Why persecutest thou me?" As is portrayed in this picture from an early medieval Bible, Paul fell down blinded on the road to Damascus and had to be led by the hand into the city. There he was healed by Ananias, who had received Christ's command to cure Paul. With his sight recovered, Paul became a Christian, convinced that he had been chosen to spread the gospel to all peoples. Between A.D. 47 and 59 he travelled over 8000 miles throughout the Mediterranean world from Spain to Palestine.

Not only did Paul convert men of all races and classes to Christianity, he also established countless new churches. His letters to Christians throughout the Roman Empire, such as those to the Ephesians and the Corinthians, make up an important part of the New Testament. The letters were full of religious enthusiasm and practical advice. They did much to strengthen and guide the new Christian communities through their most difficult early years. In transforming Christianity into a world religion and in carrying Christianity out of Palestine to people throughout the Roman world, Paul is rightly considered one of the greatest missionaries of all time.

When Peter and Paul first arrived in Rome, there was little opposition to Christianity. The average Roman citizen, while accepting the gods of his fathers, was not greatly concerned about the ideas and doctrines of religion. Slowly, however, the attitude of the Romans changed. The Christians condemned worldly success, wealth and war. They insisted that their God was the only god, and that the gods of the Romans were false. They refused to pay homage to the emperor (since that meant accepting him as a god), take oaths in the law courts or join the army. So long as the Empire was growing in size and wealth, the Romans were merely amused by the Christian prophecy that it would fall because of the sinfulness of the Roman way of life. But as conditions worsened in Rome, opposition to this kind of criticism increased. Active persecution of the Christians began under Nero, when the evil emperor was searching for a scapegoat for the great fire, which he may have set himself. Both Peter and Paul were executed during or shortly after this wave of persecution. By A.D. 100 it was unlawful to be a Christian, and anyone confessing the Christian faith could be tortured and put to death. Christians moved underground in a very real sense. The chapel seen here, for example, was built underground on the Appian Way about a mile and a half from the gates of the city.

Yet Roman policy was still not as harsh as it was to become. As the Emperor Trajan wrote: "The Christians are not to be sought out; but if brought before you, and the crime is proved, they must be punished." But when the Empire began its rapid decline in the third century, there was much harsher and more determined persecution. Thousands of Christians died in mass executions or were thrown into the arena to be destroyed by wild animals before the bloodthirsty mob.

THE CITY OF GOD

It is sometimes said that "the blood of martyrs is the seed of the Church." In the Roman Empire this seemed to be true. More and more people turned to Christianity, perhaps impressed by the courage and faith of the Christians. This illustration from an eleventh-century manuscript tells the famous story of Constantine's conversion to Christianity during a bitter military campaign in 312. One version is that the worried general had a dream in which he was told to mark a Christian emblem on the shields of his troops, while another states that he saw a cross in the sky with the words "By this you shall conquer." At any event, Constantine was triumphant at the battle of Mulvian Bridge. His victory sealed his belief in the power of the Christian God to bring success. The Emperor Constantine granted Christians the right to worship, and made Christianity equal to other religions. A few years later he made Sunday a legal holiday and day of prayer.

The final triumph came in 380 when the Emperor Theodosius declared Christianity to be the official religion of the Empire. The wooden carving below vividly illustrates the victory of Christianity. The building is meant to represent the Empire. Beneath the cross stand the emperor and an angel, and below them stand respectful senators and ordinary Romans.

The Christian Church needed more than the blood of martyrs to survive; it also needed practical organization. The apostles, like Peter and John who had lived with Christ, had naturally been the first leaders of the Christian community; their successors were men who were deliberately chosen and set apart to continue their work. These new leaders were called bishops, meaning overseers. Each one had control over all churches within his district or diocese. Under the bishops were priests who preached, advised the people and administered the sacraments, such as those connected with baptism, marriage, confession and death.

While there were many important dioceses in the early days of the Church, the one at Rome soon became the most important. St. Peter and St. Paul had founded the diocese of Rome, and Christians placed great emphasis on the words of St. Matthew which reported Christ as saying: "thou art Peter, and upon this rock I will build my church . . . And I will give unto thee the keys of the kingdom of heaven. . . ." This twelfth-century picture shows Christ handing the keys to Peter. St. Peter became the first bishop of Rome. Later bishops of the city claimed that, like Peter, they received their authority directly from Christ. As the Roman Empire in the west weakened and then collapsed, the diocese of Rome provided the only stable and effective government of the Church. By the seventh century, with western Europe overrun by barbarians, the western bishops were organized under the bishop of Rome (the Pope), who had emerged as the supreme head of the western Church. In the east, the Church, centred at Constantinople under the strict control of the emperor, developed its own practices and beliefs.

193

refused to celebrate Mass while the Emperor Theodosius, who had just slaughtered 7000 innocent people, was in the church. The Emperor was forced to repent. In bringing about his repentence St. Ambrose had established the principle that in matters of faith and moral conduct political rulers must obey the Church authorities. St. Jerome was a great scholar whose translation of the Old and New Testament, known as the Vulgate, is still used today in the Roman Catholic Church.

The greatest of the Church Fathers was St. Augustine, shown here as he was imagined by a sixteenth-century artist. As a young man St. Augustine had led an enjoyable but sinful life. But under the influence of his mother and St. Ambrose he became a Christian at the age of thirty-two, and soon turned his great mind to writing. While his book *Confessions* is one of the greatest accounts of a personal religious experience, his most outstanding work is *The City of God*. The book was written partly to challenge the charges that Christianity had led to Rome's decline. He argued that non-Christian empires had fallen in the past. Moreover, he said, all history was the unfolding of God's plan and could best be explained as a continuing battle between the City of God, the saved, and the City of Earth, those who rejected God. Ultimately, the City of God would triumph. St. Augustine was the most important Churchman since St. Paul.

The bishops were responsible for determining correct religious doctrines. It was they who developed the short summary of the Christian faith known as the Apostles' Creed. The work of certain bishops was so outstanding that they have become known as the Church Fathers. The three most famous in the early church were St. Ambrose, St. Jerome and St. Augustine, all of whom lived in the fourth century. St. Ambrose

---

In five hundred years, a short time in the early history of the Western world, Christianity had undergone an amazing growth and triumph. As the Roman Empire collapsed, the Christian Church alone remained firm to its principles. By A.D. 500 the Roman Empire in the west was in ruins. But the Church had escaped the wreckage and had expanded in size and strength. It was to be one of the rocks upon which a new civilization in the west would be built.

The two worlds of medieval man — the mounted knight and the monastery of Mont Saint-Michel, a fortress to God on an island rock off the coast of Normandy.

THE BIRTH OF A NEW CIVILIZATION: MEDIEVAL EUROPE

The Dark Ages: A.D. 400-1000
The medieval monarchies:
    the emergence of England and France
The medieval Church
Moslem and Crusader
Village and town
Towards a new world:
    1300-1450

Introduction

Today when we speak of the Western world we think of western Europe and the countries in the Americas and elsewhere that were once colonies of the western European nations. In ancient times no one spoke of a region called Europe. The Greek and Roman empires were thought of as Mediterranean empires. While their capitals were in Europe, their most important territories were in the Near East and northern Africa. The Roman Empire included what is now Britain, France, western Germany and Spain. But Britain, France and Germany were among the least important parts of the giant Empire.

In the 500 years between the fall of Rome and A.D. 1000, the emergence of the first truly Western or European civilization came about. Western Europe was in part an offspring of the civilizations of the ancient world. For example, it became a Christian society, owed much to Rome, and later absorbed Greek ideals of freedom and beauty. But it was also a new civilization. It was not based on the Mediterranean, but the lands and rivers of northwestern Europe. Its people were of different origins from those of the ancient world and they developed in different ways. By A.D. 1000, the foundation of that society had been laid amidst the ashes of the Roman Empire. In the three or four hundred years that followed, the new European civilization slowly became increasingly self-confident, rich and powerful. By 1450, a thousand years after the fall of Rome, western Europe was about to discover, conquer, settle and provide an example for much of the earth.

The thousand years following the fall of Rome, the period in which western Europe took its shape, are usually called the Middle Ages, from which comes the word *medieval*. Accustomed to the rapid and almost miraculous developments of our own age, many people look upon medieval Europe as a backward civilization hardly worth studying. Nothing could be further from the truth. In creating a new civilization from the wreckage of the Roman Empire, medieval man created the modern world. He developed methods of agriculture which lasted until our own day. Through his use of such sources of power as wind, water and the horse, he was able to replace manpower more effectively than had any earlier society. He was the first to build an advanced civilization without the use of slave labour. He developed his own languages and created his own universities. He kept Christianity alive. He created works of art and architecture as magnificent and inspiring as those of the ancients. And, above all, he developed laws and forms of government that were to provide the basis of modern Western democracy and human freedom and liberty.

The Dark Ages: A.D. 400-1000

For centuries Rome had possessed the strength to defend the frontiers of its empire. Roman legions and fortified posts circled the giant Empire from Hadrian's Wall in Britain, along the banks of the Rhine and the Danube rivers to the Black Sea, and through the deserts and oases of the Middle East and northern Africa. Outside the Empire, envious of the good land and riches protected by the swords and shields of the legionaries, were peoples much less civilized. The most important were the Germanic peoples—Saxons, Franks, Vandals and Goths. These tribes lined the frontiers of the Empire from the mouth of the Rhine River in the north to the lower reaches of the Danube in the south.

THE FALL OF ROME

With increasing difficulty Roman generals had kept these restless, nomadic and warlike Germanic peoples—usually called barbarians—outside the frontier. The Romans' success was due partly to the fact that the barbarians had made no united effort to crack the Roman defences. But late in the fourth century, the barbarians themselves were attacked by a more savage people, the Huns, who had swept out of Central Asia. In A.D. 375 the Ostrogoths (East Goths) were savagely overwhelmed. The terrified Visigoths (West Goths) fled before the Huns and successfully begged for permission to settle across the Danube within the Roman Empire. But a few years later, angered by the treatment given them by the Romans, they rose in revolt. At Adrianople in 378 they destroyed a great Roman army. The defences of the Empire had crumbled.

In the years that followed, barbarian hordes moved across the frontier from north to south. From Adrianople the Visigoths moved westward, ravaging Greece and destroying Rome itself. Finally they moved into Gaul and Spain. Here the Romans stopped their plundering by granting them land for a permanent settlement. Another Germanic group, the Vandals, also roamed across Europe. Eventually they founded a new settlement in Spain, and later another in Africa, where they established a capital at Carthage. There they built a fleet and raided the shores of Italy. In 455 they even sacked Rome.

As Roman troops withdrew from Britain early in the fifth century to defend the heart of the Empire, Jutes, Angles and Saxons from northern Europe sailed across the North Sea to conquer Britain. The Franks crossed the Rhine and became masters of what is now northwest Germany, Holland, Belgium and France. The Huns themselves crossed the defenceless borders of the Empire, conquering large sections of eastern Europe and subjecting the Germanic peoples to their rule. Under their fierce leader, Attila, they swept into central Europe, leaving a trail of destruction in their wake. Finally in 451 they were defeated by the Roman army near Troyes in France. Persuaded by the Pope not to attack Rome, the Huns returned eastward and disappeared from the pages of history.

Finally in A.D. 476, new barbarian invaders deposed the Emperor in Rome and placed a German, Odoacer, in his place.

The Roman Empire in the west was no more, but the Empire in the east survived the barbarian

Pope Gregory the Great (590-604) described the distress in Italy as the Lombards followed Goths and Vandals in overrunning the countryside. In 593 he wrote, "Everywhere we observe strife; everywhere we hear groans. Cities are destroyed, fortresses are turned over, fields are depopulated, the land has returned to solitude. There is no farmer in the fields, nor hardly any inhabitants in the cities. The survivors, poor dregs of humanity, are daily crushed down without cessation. . . . Some are carried off to captivity, some are left limbless, some are killed. . . . See what has befallen Rome, once mistress of the world."

One of the greatest Churchmen in history, Gregory the Great himself did much to strengthen the Church and keep civilization alive amidst the barbarism that surrounded him. Pope Gregory is usually shown with a dove, representing the Holy Ghost, whispering in his ear.

attacks. Although the territories had suffered to some extent, troops of the Eastern Empire had usually withstood the barbarians successfully. The strong fortress city of Constantinople could not be taken. From Constantinople, the great Emperor Justinian hoped to reconquer the lost territories in the west. Ten years of hard fighting subdued the Vandals in North Africa. Another decade of destructive warfare, which left Rome itself in a shambles, won some control over Italy. But Gaul, Spain and Britain remained firmly in the hands of the barbarians. Moreover, soon after Justinian's death another German tribe, the Lombards, conquered much of Italy. Before long, North Africa and Spain were to fall before the attacks of a new group of invaders, the Moslems.

Early in the seventh century the wandering tribes of Arabia were united or conquered by the prophet Mohammed, who founded the religion of Islam. The Moslems, or followers of Islam,

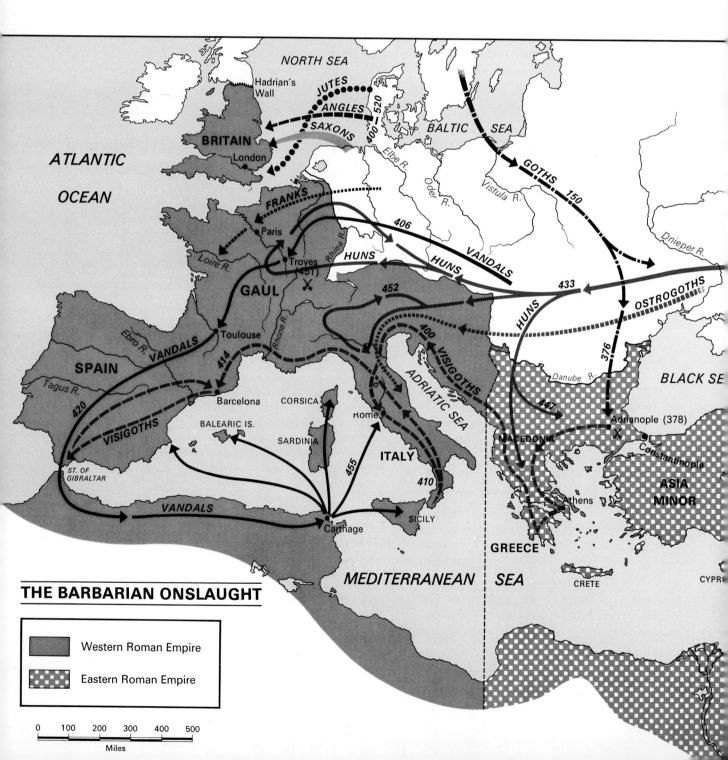

THE BARBARIAN ONSLAUGHT

Western Roman Empire

Eastern Roman Empire

0 100 200 300 400 500
Miles

exploded out of the Arabian deserts and oasis. Within a hundred years they had conquered most of the Middle East, moved beyond the borders of India and China, and swept westward across North Africa. Moving north, they conquered Spain and advanced into France. There in 732, just a century after Mohammed had founded Islam, an advance Moslem raiding party was stopped by Charles Martel, leader of the Franks. Western Europe had been saved, but it was even more isolated than before. The Mediterranean, highway of the ancient world, was now under Moslem control.

THE INVADERS

We know very little about the century of invasions, or the few hundred years following them. As a result they have been labelled the Dark Ages, dark for civilization because the mighty structure of the Roman Empire crumbled, and dark for the historian because he knows so little. For the most part, the barbarians were illiterate heathens when they burst through the borders of the Empire. In the northwest, in what is now Germany, England and northern France, the invaders drove everything before them and settled on the land themselves. In southern France, Spain and Italy they defeated the inhabitants, but there were not enough of them to settle on all the land. As a result, the old residents remained and generally outnumbered the newcomers. For this reason the present inhabitants of northern and southern Europe are quite different.

The invaders were mainly agricultural people. As they moved into the Empire they destroyed the old commercial life. Towns disappeared and stone buildings crumbled. Roads were left unrepaired; later, their stones were often used for buildings. At first, however, the barbarians erected wooden stockades. While the newcomers often took over the villages they found, many of them were destroyed or were overrun by forests, or became swampland once again. The amount of cultivated land declined drastically. As trade and commerce disappeared, the small village or manor became the basis of economic life. But the village farmers no longer produced a surplus of goods to sell. The villages were simply local communities trying desperately to produce enough food and other necessities for their inhabitants.

The system of government of the Germanic barbarians was just as primitive as their economy. They were organized in tribes under a chieftain, who was often elected by members of the tribe. Major decisions were made by the chief or the king and a council of all men old enough to bear

199

arms. The council members showed their approval of a proposal by clashing their weapons on their shields. Here were the elements of an early democratic system which was to be important in the future of Western civilization. Certainly the members of the Germanic tribes appear to have had a greater voice in their own government than the citizens of the Roman Empire.

Unlike many earlier peoples the Germans had no written laws. Law was simply the custom of the tribe, handed down from generation to generation. These customs or laws were binding on all men, including the king. Some of their methods of determining guilt strike us as being very superstitious and primitive. A man accused of a crime, for example, might have to prove his innocence through trial by battle or by undergoing the ordeal. If he lost the battle he was judged guilty. In the ordeal by water, he was bound hand and foot and thrown into a body of water. If he floated, he was considered guilty, for the Germans believed that the gods had rejected him as an evil spirit. (If he sank he was judged innocent, although by then it might be too late!) In the ordeal by fire the accused would be asked to carry a hot rock or a piece of iron a number of paces. The wound was then bound up. If it had healed after a few days, the man was proclaimed innocent; if it had not, he was guilty. However, the barbarians had a more civilized and more customary means of determining guilt or innocence. This was the practice in which the accused could prove his innocence by finding a number of his neighbours to swear on oath that he was of good character and not a criminal. (The number needed depended on the seriousness of the crime.) From this use of neighbours, rather than judges who listened to the facts and made a decision, grew the jury system a few centuries later.

Once settled on the conquered land, the barbarians united to form small kingdoms under the strongest leader, or a man they might elect as king. In England, for example, the Anglo-Saxon invaders gradually formed seven kingdoms, which together were known as the *Heptarchy*. These kingdoms seemed to enjoy fighting each other for land and wealth as much as they had enjoyed battling the Romans and Celts. On the continent, the most important early political development was the attempt of a Frankish king, Clovis (468-511), to unite all the Franks in one kingdom. A cruel and violent warrior, Clovis conquered most of Gaul and western Germany. But after his death, his kingdom fell apart. For almost 200 years his successors fought for power. During these centuries the story of the Frankish kingdom is one of scandal and intrigue, murder and assassination.

THE CAROLINGIAN EMPIRE

By about 700 the strongest and most able men in the kingdom of the Franks were members of the Carolingian family, named after Carolus (Charles) or Charlemagne, its most famous member. An early and very able Carolingian was Charles Martel, who had stopped the Moslem advance on Europe. He and his son Pepin restored some order to the kingdom, and in 751 Pepin took the title of King of the Franks. But the greatest Carolingian, and one of the greatest figures in history, was Pepin's youngest son, Charles the Great or Charlemagne, who ruled from 771 to 814.

Charlemagne was determined not only to unite the Franks, but to re-establish the old Roman Empire. A brilliant warrior-statesman, he and his generals conducted fifty-five military campaigns. On his death, the Carolingian Empire covered much of western Europe. Spain remained firmly Moslem; Britain was not attacked by the Franks, and Sicily and part of Italy remained attached to the Byzantine Empire. In the east he conquered lands that had never been taken by the Romans. He had also served as protector and ally of the Pope. On Christmas Day, A.D. 800 in Rome, he was crowned Emperor by a grateful Pope. The assembled people cried, "Charles the most pious Augustus, crowned by God, great and pacific Emperor, long life and victory." Although the ceremony had not re-established the Roman Empire, there was once again an Emperor. But the important fact is that the man crowned Emperor was Germanic. His capital was not at Rome or on the

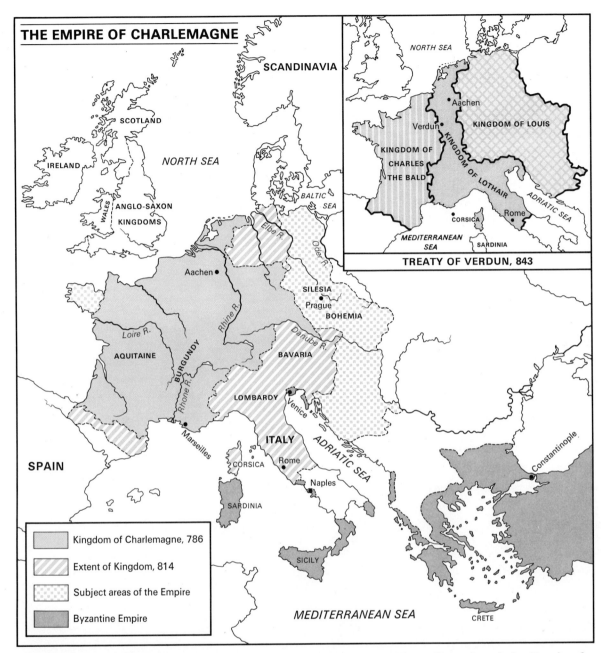

THE EMPIRE OF CHARLEMAGNE

SCANDINAVIA

SCOTLAND

IRELAND

NORTH SEA

WALES

ANGLO-SAXON

KINGDOMS

BALTIC SEA

Elbe R.

Oder R.

Aachen

SILESIA

Prague

BOHEMIA

Loire R.

Rhine R.

Danube R.

AQUITAINE

BURGUNDY

BAVARIA

Rhone R.

LOMBARDY

Venice

Marseilles

ADRIATIC SEA

Constantinople

SPAIN

CORSICA

Rome

ITALY

Naples

SARDINIA

SICILY

CRETE

MEDITERRANEAN SEA

TREATY OF VERDUN, 843

NORTH SEA

Aachen

Verdun

KINGDOM OF LOUIS

KINGDOM OF CHARLES THE BALD

KINGDOM OF LOTHAIR

ADRIATIC SEA

CORSICA

Rome

MEDITERRANEAN SEA

SARDINIA

Legend:
- Kingdom of Charlemagne, 786
- Extent of Kingdom, 814
- Subject areas of the Empire
- Byzantine Empire

Mediterranean, but at Aachen near the mouth of the Rhine.

Charlemagne's empire appeared to be more united than it was in fact. However solid they may have appeared, the foundations were shaky. Charlemagne had neither the money, the troops, the transportation system nor the administration to govern the Empire effectively for long. Particularly serious was the fact that most people within the Empire generally gave their loyalty to local leaders. Therefore, the unity of the Empire depended upon the Emperor's ability to win these local loyalties to himself. When Charlemagne died in 814 his empire began to crumble. His three grandsons fought over their inheritance. The result was further destruction and dislocation in an already battered Europe. Finally, in 843 in the Treaty of Verdun, the three brothers divided the Empire: Charles took the west, Louis the east, and Lothair a strip in the middle. From this division there came in time the modern states of France and Germany. Lothair's kingdom was fought over until the twentieth century.

The division of the Empire came at a time when western Europe was once again being attacked from all sides. The Moslems returned to the attack, making swift raids into Italy and southern France. From fortresses which they built near Rome and Marseilles they moved inland in sudden raids on merchants or manors. In the east, a new wave of invaders stormed out of Central Asia. This time it was the Magyars, cruel and greedy

horsemen who moved across the Danube about the year 900. After ravaging northern Italy, they pressed on to create havoc in the kingdom originally given to Louis. Louis' successors fought valiantly. But not until 955 did the German king Otto the Great defeat the Magyars, who then settled in the lower Danube Valley in what is now Hungary.

The most feared, the most destructive and the most important in this second great wave of barbarian invasions were the Norsemen or Vikings. Germanic peoples from Scandinavia, the

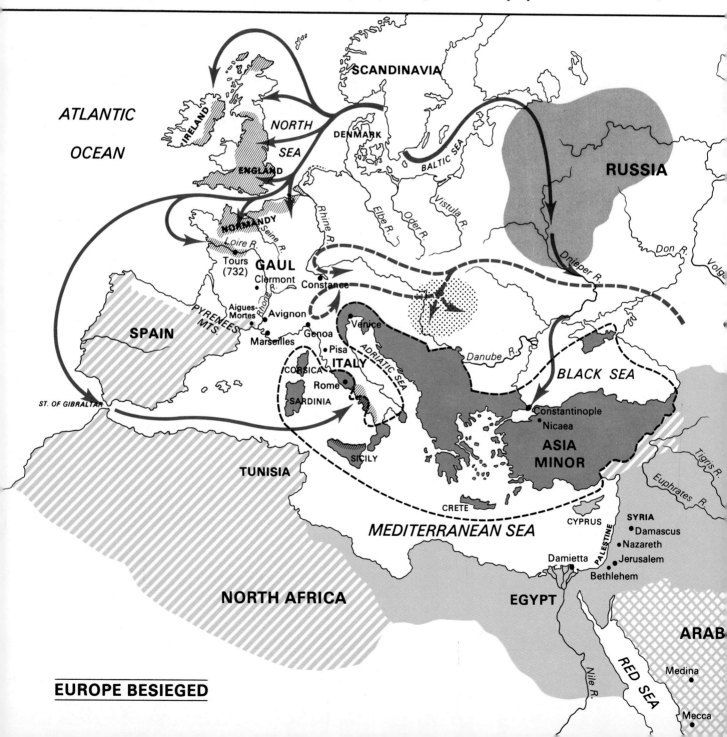

EUROPE BESIEGED

Vikings were drawn by their need for land and their desire for adventure and booty to attack western Europe repeatedly for 200 years. Magnificent sailors and courageous fighters, they struck across the Baltic and moved up the rivers deep into Russia. They plundered the coast of France and the monasteries of Ireland, and drove the inhabitants of Britain inland from the coast. In northern Russia they established a rich trading empire. In France in 911 they forced the Frankish king to grant them territory (which is still called Normandy) along the English Channel. In Britain

This gold and enamel bust shows Charlemagne, who became King of the Franks at twenty-nine and died exhausted at seventy-two. Charlemagne was a brilliant military leader and an even greater organizer and lawmaker. He passed laws dealing with every aspect of life in his kingdom: agriculture, finances, education, religion and morals. He also attempted to encourage and regulate trade. Appalled by the fact that few Churchmen were educated, he brought foreign scholars to his court at Aachen and scoured Europe for books and manuscripts. To set an example for his subjects, and at the same time to improve his own education, he became a pupil in the palace school at Aachen. According to one writer he made a valiant effort to learn to write "... and used to keep tablets under his pillow in order that at leisure hours he might accustom his hand to form the letters; but as he began these efforts so late in life, they met with ill success." In appearance Charlemagne was tall and strong, with a round head and large eyes. This bust was made about 1350 and is not an exact likeness.

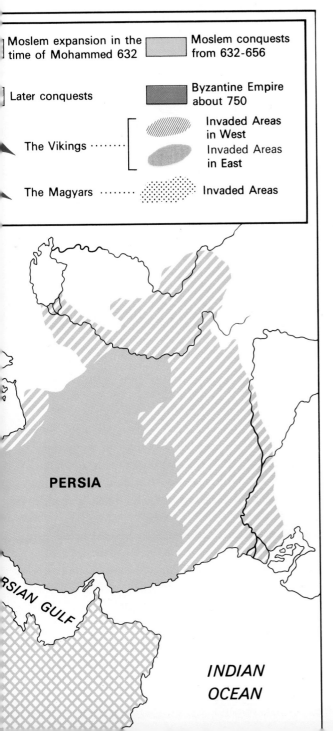

Moslem expansion in the time of Mohammed 632

Moslem conquests from 632-656

Later conquests

Byzantine Empire about 750

The Vikings ⋯⋯

Invaded Areas in West

Invaded Areas in East

The Magyars ⋯⋯

Invaded Areas

PERSIA

PERSIAN GULF

INDIAN OCEAN

The Vikings buried their chieftains in mounds along with their ships and possessions. One of the best preserved vessels is the Oseberg longship, which is about 1000 years old. The vessel was excavated in 1904. Viking ships were built of oak planks which overlapped and were about eighty feet long. Ports on each side for oars were covered with round wooden shields, two for each oar. Painted alternately black and yellow, the shields protected the oarsmen and kept out water when the ship was under sail and heeling. The mast was placed forward of amidships. The square sail was often brightly painted. There was one rudder controlled by a tiller slotted at right angles into the rudder head and located on the right side of the stern. Here we find the origin of the word starboard, which was originally steer board or the steering side. The word port, or left side, was used because crews always tied the ship up in port on the left or rudderless side. It was in such seemingly fragile vessels as this that the Vikings thrust across the wild seas and up unknown rivers, making themselves the most feared of all the invaders.

they conquered large sections of the northeast coast and threatened to seize the entire country. Finally the disunited Anglo-Saxons were organized by Alfred the Great of Wessex who stopped the Viking advance. But Alfred could not defeat the invaders and they were given a large section of land known as the *Danelaw*. Viking invaders later returned to the attack and defeated the English. For many years the island was part of a Scandinavian empire.

By about A.D. 1000, however, the storm had passed. Europe had emerged from what has been called the Dark Ages. The tale seems one of violence and destruction. But at the same time the foundations of a new society had been laid. Europe was ready to begin the slow growth that was to bring her to world leadership.

FEUDALISM

The most important feature of the new society that emerged during the 500 years of almost constant warfare has been called the *feudal* system or *feudalism*. The reason for the description is clear. A *feud*, or a *fief* as it is usually called, was a grant of land made in return for military support. Because of this relationship between the ownership of land and military service, historians came to speak of a feudal society and of feudalism or the feudal system.

The German chiefs or warlords had groups of trusted warriors or *vassals*. These vassals followed their leader in war, and were rewarded by a share in the booty. They lived in the lord's wooden stockade and were fed, clothed and armed by him. But in the early eighth century Charles Martel, duke of the Franks, realized that he needed a much larger and better army than his own followers could provide. He not only had to restore order among the warring Franks themselves, but also to repel Saxons who were invading his eastern borders and Moslems who were attacking from the south.

Charles knew that the best troops were mounted warriors. The introduction of the stirrup into western Europe had given an immense advantage to the man who could fight on horseback. The stirrup made it possible for the soldier to fight with his broadsword or lance without losing his balance and falling off his horse if his blow missed the target. For 500 years the *knight,* as the mounted soldier was called, was to be the major engine of war.

Only a very wealthy man could afford the cost of horse and armour and the weeks of training necessary to fight on horseback. Charles had little money, however, and could not hire an army of knights. Land was almost the only source of wealth. As a result, Charles seized the rich lands of the Church and divided them among his followers or vassals. The income from the land was used by the vassals to outfit themselves as knights. In return for the land, they owed Charles their services in war. The successors of Charles Martel continued the practice, using their own land or conquered lands as fiefs to give to their vassals.

Quite often a vassal was given land that demanded the service not just of himself but of many knights. The vassal simply divided the land (keeping some for himself) among men who became vassals of his and promised him military service. Some of these vassals in turn might further divide the land, until the final vassal might have just one small village or manor, with a few dozen inhabitants.

The feudal system spread rapidly after the death of Charlemagne. As the Moslems, Magyars and Vikings ravaged western Europe, weak men turned to those who were more powerful, gladly becoming their vassals in return for protection. In each area, one noble seemed to emerge as the most powerful and often took what he was not given. These dukes or counts came to rule very large territories. They had their own armies, and even though they might be a vassal of the king, they were often more powerful than he was. On their estates they made their own laws, had their own courts where their vassals sought justice, and collected their own taxes. What had started as a means of defence also became a system of government.

By the year 1000 western Europe was a multitude of feudal estates, such as the great dukedoms of Normandy and Burgundy in France, and Saxony and Bavaria in Germany. Comparing feudal Europe with the great days of the Roman Empire, when one government ruled a third of the known world, many people feel that the world had suffered a serious setback. Actually feudalism was a very important stage of Western history. It enabled western Europe to defend itself for the first time in 600 years. The Romans had not been able to stop the German barbarians. But those same barbarians had organized a system of defence which enabled them finally to stop the attacks of Vikings, Magyars and Moslems.

Moreover, while to our eyes Europe in 1000 would still seem to have been marked by lawlessness, violence and bloodshed, there was in fact more peace and stability than had been known during the previous centuries of invasion and turmoil. Local lords were able to keep peace on their own estates. The great nobles enforced law and order over large territories. Peasants could plow and sow with much greater certainty that they would live to harvest. Merchants, who had almost completely disappeared, would be able once again to trade. In the feudal courts of the great nobles and in the lord's court in the village or manor, vassal and peasant could secure justice. Finally, as time passed, the kings of France and England increased their power and were able to control warfare among the nobles and bring some law and order to a much wider area.

About A.D. 700 when a medieval craftsman carved this figure of a warrior with his lance and shield, the stirrup came into use in western Europe. The stirrup was invented in China where it was in use by the fifth century A.D. It can be seen clearly in the picture on page 32.

The feudal noble

The feudal system was based on a well understood relationship between lords and vassals. The man who granted the fief was the lord or *suzerain;* the man who received it was the vassal. Both lords and vassals belonged to the ruling class of fighting nobles. As a rule, the king was the highest lord, at the top of the feudal order. At the bottom was the knight who held a single manor or less. In between were a host of greater and lesser nobles, ranging from dukes and counts to viscounts and barons. A great lord might hold hundreds of manors. An immense gulf separated all of these members of the feudal order from the mass of labouring peasants.

Under the terms of the feudal relationship, both lords and vassals enjoyed certain rights and were expected to perform a number of duties. In return for his fief, the vassal owed his lord loyalty and military service. The ceremony which accompanied the granting of a fief was full of symbols of mutual loyalty. The new vassal knelt and placed his hands between those of his lord. He took two oaths, one of *homage,* or personal loyalty, and one of *fealty,* in which he promised to keep the faith which he had sworn. In one typical ceremony a vassal said, "I become your man, from this day forward, of life and limb and of earthly worship, and unto you shall be true and faithful." If the lord accepted the homage, he kissed the man and recognized him as a vassal. The vassal then received the symbol of the fief in the form of a rod or a piece of earth. Thereafter, vassal and lord were bound by strong, personal ties of loyalty and support.

In return for his fief the vassal had
to perform many duties. His main
duty was to give military aid to his
lord, to take part personally in his
wars and to provide a number of
fully-equipped mounted knights.
(The number required was based
on the size of the fief.) This
obligation of service was usually
limited to forty days of the year.
By the year 1100 vassals were often
permitted to pay a sum of money
known as *scutage* instead of serving
in the field. To many lords, this
payment of money was preferable
since it could be used to obtain
hired soldiers, who would be
available for longer campaigns. The
vassal's military obligations were
by no means light, for the provision
of one knight would include not
only the man himself but also his
mount, and perhaps a change of
horses, expensive weapons and
armour, servants to look after the
knight and his equipment, and food
to feed both men and animals.

The vassal could also be called
upon for a payment or *aid* for the
ransoming of the lord if he were
captured, for the knighting of his
eldest son or for the marriage of
his eldest daughter. Sometimes he
was also called upon to make a
relief payment when the lord died.
It was customary for the vassal's
son to pay a *relief* to his lord when
he inherited his father's fief.

The feudal pact was not a
one-way street, however, for the
lord also had a number of
obligations to his vassals. In
addition to granting the land in
the first place, he had to protect
the vassal from his enemies. He was
also required to give justice to his
vassals by presiding over a court to
which they could bring their
disputes. In theory, if the lord
failed to provide justice and
protection to his vassals, he broke
the feudal pact and the vassal no
longer owed him allegiance. On the
other hand, if the vassal failed to
live up to his obligations, the lord
could seize the estate. The security
of both vassal and lord depended
upon their recognition and respect
of each other's rights.

The main purpose of the feudal system was to provide fighting men who could ensure protection. The members of the feudal order, the warrior classes, shared a set of customs known as the code of *chivalry,* derived from the French *chevalier,* meaning horseman. During the early Middle Ages, chivalry was a simple code which existed between fighting men to govern their relations with one another. The typical knight was a rough and illiterate strongman. Since his job was to fight, his training was mainly military. At a very early age he learned to ride

and use weapons, and after a period of apprenticeship or training, was allowed to prove his ability in a real battle. If he passed the test, he was knighted in the ceremony of *adoubement,* in which he received the arms and armour of a mature man. As the influence of the Church spread, the ceremony of *dubbing* or knighting became more elaborate and had greater religious meaning. Before being invested with spurs and sword (as is happening in this picture), the knight swore to uphold the true Faith.

Under the code of chivalry, the

knight was expected to be loyal to his lord and devoted to the Church. He was also expected to possess a host of manly and military qualities. He was to be utterly courageous in the face of an enemy, yet treat him with gallantry in defeat. He was to fight fairly, according to the accepted rules, and never seek victory through trickery and cunning. He was expected to be courteous, to be kind to the poor and defenseless, to treat women with respect and be ready at all times to protect them. Above all else, he was to be a man who would never break his word.

In many respects the chivalry of the later medieval period was unreal. At first it had been the code of a ruling class of mounted knights who had to spend much of their time fighting. However, the increasing use of hired soldiers and the introduction of gunpowder made the feudal knight less and less important in society. Feudal fighting became a kind of game, as the nobility tried to display its fighting skills by staging elaborate *tournaments.* Early tournaments had served as war games that kept the knights at a peak of fighting efficiency. Often there was little difference between the games and the real thing, for large bands of

knights engaged in bloody mock battles which destroyed many acres of good farmland and left many a knight wounded or dead. Later tournaments were less a preparation for war than an elaborate pageant. In such tournaments nobles worked desperately to impress one another and to amuse their admiring ladies, whose colours they often wore. Compared with the earlier events, the later *jousts,* or contests between two knights (such as that depicted in the fourteenth-century miniature painting to the right), were rather dull affairs, for the contestants were encased in very heavy armour and used blunted lances.

By the end of the Middle Ages the knight and his mount were so heavily burdened with armour that one can only marvel that they were able to move at all. (This sixteenth-century German knight, for example, wore armour weighing fifty-six pounds, while that of his horse weighed ninety-two pounds.)

The life of a feudal noble was not nearly as glamorous as some romantic literature suggests. If the noble lived to be much over forty, he was more fortunate than most other men of his time. And while his short life was exciting, it was not easy. Early feudal castles were little more than timber forts, protected by moats and drawbridges. Later stone castles, like this grim, cheerless fortress in Spain, were cold, damp and dirty. Open fireplaces provided what heat there was, and in the absence of chimneys, it was probably just as well that the windows lacked glass. It is small wonder that in good weather, the noble spent little time indoors, greatly preferring to hunt or fight.

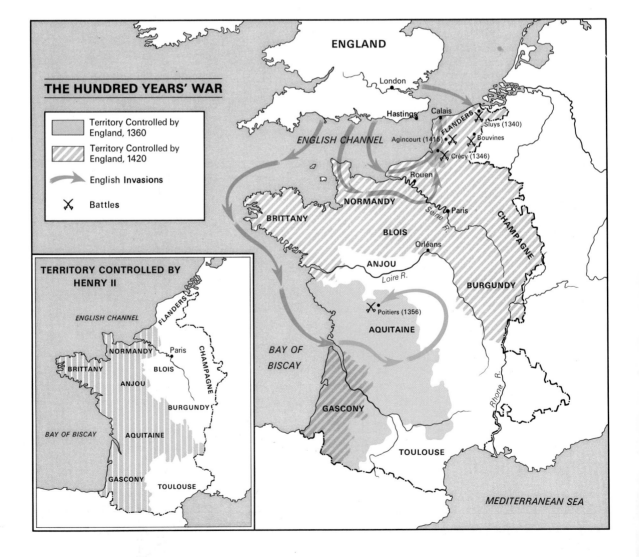

Such activities sharpened the appetite, and the feudal noble enjoyed a plentiful if uninteresting diet. His main foods were meat and fish, cheese, peas, beans, carrots and turnips. Either wine or beer was the main beverage. Fruit was scarce, and sugar and spices available only to the very great. Table etiquette as we understand it was unknown. A knife was the only utensil used, and each guest brought his own. Great hunting dogs lurked about, waiting for their masters to toss them bones and scraps of food. There were no rugs to be soiled, and when filth reached unacceptable limits — not often — the straw covering the floor was easily replaced.

THE HUNDRED YEARS' WAR

- Territory Controlled by England, 1360
- Territory Controlled by England, 1420
- → English Invasions
- ✗ Battles

ENGLAND

London

Hastings

Calais

FLANDERS

Sluys (1340)

Bouvines

ENGLISH CHANNEL

Agincourt (1415)

Crécy (1346)

Rouen

NORMANDY

Seine R.

Paris

CHAMPAGNE

BRITTANY

BLOIS

Orléans

ANJOU

Loire R.

BURGUNDY

Poitiers (1356)

AQUITAINE

BAY OF BISCAY

GASCONY

TOULOUSE

MEDITERRANEAN SEA

TERRITORY CONTROLLED BY HENRY II

ENGLISH CHANNEL

FLANDERS

NORMANDY

Paris

CHAMPAGNE

BRITTANY

BLOIS

ANJOU

BURGUNDY

BAY OF BISCAY

AQUITAINE

GASCONY

TOULOUSE

The medieval monarchies: the emergence of England and France

During the 1000 years since the end of the Dark Ages the nations of modern Europe have gradually emerged from the multitude of feudal states that had arisen in the 500 years following the fall of the Roman Empire. The emergence of these modern nations was by no means complete during the Middle Ages. Indeed, among the larger nations only England and France had developed into states resembling their modern form by the fifteenth century.

ITALY AND GERMANY

For centuries Italy remained divided. Part of the territory was split among city-states like Venice and Genoa; other land was owned by the Pope, while still other regions were ruled by French or German nobles. Not until a century ago was Italy united under one government for the first time since the fall of Rome.

Modern Germany also remained disunited until modern times. The barbarian tribes in what is now Germany had never really accepted the Carolingian kings. As the Empire of Charlemagne fell apart, each of these tribal leaders, using the title of *duke* (meaning army commander), set up his own *duchy* and ruled his territory as a miniature king. Although these great nobles were prepared to elect a king, they were less prepared to accept his rule over them. For several hundred years kings and dukes wrestled for real power in Germany. By the middle of the thirteenth century the great dukes had clearly won. For 600 years Germany remained divided. Finally in the 1860's it was united through the military might of the state of Prussia led by Bismarck.

In Britain and France, on the other hand, the Middle Ages saw the growth of strong feudal kingdoms. In each one the monarch came to control his great vassals and rule over the entire kingdom.

THE ENGLISH MONARCHY

Although there had been a king of England since the time of Alfred the Great, the king's power had never been very great. In 1066, however, William, Duke of Normandy, crossed the Channel at the head of land-hungry and adventure-seeking knights. The Norman invaders soon defeated the Anglo-Saxon foot-soldiers sent against them. William the Conqueror was determined to be a strong king. He kept much of the land for himself, as a *royal domain*. Some Anglo-Saxons, who swore an oath of loyalty, became his vassals and were allowed to keep their land. Much of the country, however, was distributed among his own followers. But William wisely decided that the vassals of his vassals had to swear allegiance to him, and not just to their immediate overlords. In this way, he hoped to prevent his own vassals from having armies which could be used to fight him. William was benefitting from his own experience, for he himself had used his vassals to fight his overlord, the King of France. Overnight William laid the foundations for the most powerful feudal monarchy or kingdom in Europe.

William and the rulers who followed him strengthened the power of the king in many other ways. They attempted to prevent feudal nobles from building castles which they could use as strongholds to increase their power at the expense of the king. They sent royal officials called *sheriffs* to every county in England to collect the revenues owed to the king. The sheriffs also collected the fines at royal courts which the Norman kings established and to which they sent their royal judges. Under Henry II (1154-1189), the king took over responsibility for the criminal law. The king also assumed a great deal of responsibility over civil law, such as cases of disputed land ownership. To enable his subjects to bring these civil cases into court, he developed *writs,* or

The Battle of Hastings: the record of the Bayeux Tapestry

William's army moved down to the beach, and men, horses and equipment quickly moved on board the massive invasion fleet that lay waiting. Seven thousand men crossed the Channel; of these 2000 were mounted knights. While the men came from every part of France, and some from Italy and Sicily, the majority were Norman. The 3000 ships, similar to the Viking ship seen earlier, were propelled by sails and oars. When a favourable wind began to blow on September 27, the fleet put to sea. It anchored offshore until nightfall and crossed the Channel under the cover of darkness. By the morning of September 28 the troops were safely landed, and scouting parties were already looking for the enemy.

The Normans faced no immediate opposition. They therefore moved inland to Hastings and began to build their defences. The English army was in the north fighting another invader, the Norwegian Harold Hardrada, who also claimed the English throne. On September 25 King Harold of England defeated Hardrada. Harold and his Saxon troops then raced southward to meet the Norman invaders. On October 10 the two armies were face to face. The English troops, although they had horses, still fought on foot. Near Hastings the Norman knights launched their first assault on the English position.

The attack was not launched from two sides, as this part of the tapestry suggests. The English shield wall held firm. Lances and spears fill the air, and one English soldier has even thrown his club. A single English archer is also seen in action. One Englishman is wielding a heavy two-handed Danish axe.

Casualties on both sides were heavy. In the scene pictured here, Norman horses have thrown their riders. One Englishman cleaves the head of a horse, while its rider is preparing to strike with his sword. A dismounted Norman has dealt a fatal blow at the neck of his surprised opponent.

At one point, after repelling successive attacks, the English broke ranks to pursue the enemy. The Norman horsemen wheeled and attacked the broken lines. While archers filled the air with arrows, the horsemen broke through the first English lines.

Finally, Normans reached the centre of the English force where Harold and his chief advisers were directing the battle. Until recently it was believed that the man shown with an arrow in his eye was Harold. However, it is now thought that King Harold is the man on the left, whose axe flies from his hands as he goes down from a blow by a Norman knight. The artist suggests that the battle is over as the victors begin to strip the armour from the fallen soldiers.

orders from the king to have a case heard in a royal court. He also developed a jury system in the royal courts for determining right and wrong. As more and more people looked to the king, rather than the local nobles, for protection in maintaining the law, the king's power increased at the expense of his vassals.

This strengthening of royal power, however, depended on the intelligence and character of the king. Before Henry II came to the throne there had been almost twenty years of civil war, for the King during that period had been unable to control the powerful nobles or barons. Under Henry's son John, who reigned from 1199 to 1216, the barons once again rose up in revolt.

John was desperately in need of money for a war against France. However, he had only limited sources of money for his campaign. His income was limited to the revenues from his own lands, the fines of the royal courts, and other sums paid to him by his vassals. To secure additional money, the king had to summon the Great Council (made up of his leading vassals) and secure their consent. In his desperation John had increased fines in the royal courts and had demanded more money from his vassals than he was entitled to without summoning the Great Council. In addition, he often used the royal courts to increase his own income rather than to find out the facts of a case.

Finally, John's defeat by the French showed that he was a hopeless military commander. Furious at having been taxed for what now turned out to be a lost cause, the nobles rose in revolt. In 1215, after months of plotting, they marched against the King. Rather than fight him, however, they forced the reluctant King to sign the *Magna Carta,* or the Great Charter.

In the Magna Carta the nobles forced John to agree to govern according to the rules and regulations that existed between a lord and his vassals. At first sight this would not seem to be sufficient to make the Magna Carta one of the most important documents in history. But behind this statement of the feudal agreement was the idea that the king, like his subjects, had to obey the law. This principle is an essential foundation of modern government in the Western world. It is what distinguishes freedom from tyranny, democracy from dictatorship. Magna Carta emphasized the practice of the German tribes, whereby the lord, whether king or noble, governed through consultation or discussion with his vassals. This consultation in England occurred when the king met the Great Council three times a year. As Magna Carta stated, the king was not allowed to raise any money without the consent of the Great Council, except for that which he received from his own lands or obtained from his vassals as their lord. Later, this restatement of a feudal doctrine was to become the important democratic idea of "no taxation without consent."

During the thirteenth century, the kings of England were constantly in need of money. The nobles of the Great Council, which was sometimes called a *parliament* (from the French word *parler,* to talk), insisted in 1254 that knights or lesser nobles also be summoned to the Council, since they had to pay much of the taxes. A few years later the king tried to increase his support by also inviting representatives of the increasingly wealthy merchants in the towns to attend the Council. By the end of the thirteenth century, King Edward I was using these Parliaments not only to grant taxes but also to approve new laws. Parliament, composed of nobles as well as knights and merchants, had become the instrument through which the king ruled, with the consent of the people.

In 1337 a war began with France which lasted until 1453. During this long struggle (which came to be known as the Hundred Years' War), the king depended on the support of Parliament to raise the money necessary to conduct his campaign. In return for granting money, Parliament constantly increased its powers. Sometimes it forced the king to make changes in the law before granting the taxes. Knights and merchants, who were known as commoners, began to meet separately and became known as the House of Commons, while the nobles became known as the House of Lords.

Medieval war machines

The catapult was designed to shoot darts. The heavy dart was shot by the sudden release of tightly twisted ropes.

The mangonel also used twisted rope to secure the power necessary to lob heavy stones into enemy camps and fortresses.

The release of the box of heavy weights on this trebucket hurled the missile in the sling towards the enemy.

This practice of the king governing with Parliament was medieval England's greatest contribution to Western history. It again confirmed the principle that the king, as well as his subjects, was bound by the law, and that the king should govern with the consent of the people governed. Parliament made the medieval English king both stronger and weaker. It made him stronger because with the support of Parliament he could change the law and raise funds; it made him weaker because he was forced to secure that support. Centuries later, Parliament was to gain all the power, and the king of England was to become little more than a colourful figurehead with no power at all.

The medieval king, however, was still very, very powerful. The peace and order of the kingdom continued to depend on his power and character. Under a weak king the nobles fought among themselves, or fought for the crown itself. From 1422 to 1485 this was the situation in England. Two rival groups of nobles, the Lancastrians and the Yorkists, fought long and hard for the throne. Finally, in 1485, the war came to an end when Henry Tudor, an opponent of the Yorkists, defeated his rivals. King Henry VII quickly put an end to disorder and tried to destroy the power of the nobles. In this he was very successful. By 1485 the Middle Ages and feudalism had largely passed away. England and Western civilization stood on the doorstep of the early modern world.

THE UNIFICATION OF FRANCE

It took the king of France 400 years to unite all the country under one monarch. In England, William the Conqueror had accomplished the same thing in one battle at Hastings. In 987 the great dukes and counts of France had elected Hugh Capet as their king or suzerain. But these vassals were often more powerful than Hugh; they did not treat him or his successors as a ruler with authority over them. For 200 years the Capetian kings slowly built up their power on their own lands. They brought their vassals under control and cleared and opened new lands for settlement. They also encouraged trade and the growth of towns and strengthened their alliance with the Church. By 1180 when Philip II, known as Philip Augustus, came to the throne, the Capetians were ready to meet the great danger that faced them.

The danger came from England. Since William the Conqueror had been a vassal of the King of France, the English kings who followed him were also vassals of the French king. William had also been the ruler of the district of Normandy, and later English kings continued to hold this territory and add more to it. A number of marriages brought the English kings the great lands of Aquitaine, Anjou, Gascony and Brittany. Thus, Henry

Louis IX, who reigned from 1226 to 1270, was one of the greatest kings of France. Only twelve when his father died, Louis was trained by his mother to be a good Christian and a good king. Although he fought to defend France, he disliked war and kept France at peace from 1243 until his death. He supported the weak and poor against the strong and rich. During his reign he freed many serfs on the royal estates, founded hospitals, severely punished nobles who had executed men without a proper trial, and tried to stop private warfare and trial by battle. The tall, handsome king loved good food, luxurious furniture and elegant clothes. But at times he also imitated the life of a monk, wearing a haircloth shirt next to his skin, fasting, and having himself whipped. He often entertained paupers at his dining table, washed the feet of the poor, and even waited on lepers.

King Louis gave so much encouragement to learning, the arts and architecture, that his reign has been called "the Golden Age" of medieval France. Despite his humility and service to others, he never forgot that he was king. He increased royal power at the expense of his vassals and the Church. He allowed his subjects greater rights to appeal from feudal courts to his own courts, and gained control over almost all breaches of the peace. He commanded that his own money be accepted throughout France. Finally, he claimed the right to issue ordinances or laws without the consent of his vassals. Louis was so admired for his Christian rule that many called him Brother Louis. He was made a saint only twenty-seven years after his death.

II, King of England, was the feudal ruler of more than half of France.

Philip Augustus was determined to take these lands from the English king. He encouraged rebellion by Henry II's vassals and even by his sons. When King Richard I (1189-99), the Lionhearted, was away on a Crusade, Philip tried to weaken the English King's control of his French possessions and of the English throne itself. He fought Richard without success, but had better luck with King John, who came to the throne in 1199 when his brother Richard died. Five years later the crafty and able Philip had conquered all the English holdings in northern France. When John attempted to regain them he was badly beaten at the Battle of Bouvines in 1214 and returned home to face the revolt of the barons. Philip's successors continued the war against the English. Finally, after almost thirty years of fighting, the English accepted the Treaty of Paris (1259). By the terms of the Treaty they renounced most of their possessions in France.

To govern their expanding kingdom, the Capetian kings built up the same kind of machinery of government as was developing in England. Royal officials, called *bailiffs*, collected the king's revenues. Other officials closely supervised the work of government in the capital at Paris and in the provinces which had been taken over. Royal judges enforcing laws made by the king increased the power of the monarch at the expense of the nobles. The French king also had his Great Council. By 1300 this was known as the *Estates-General*. It was so named because in it were represented the three "estates" or groups, the nobles, the clergy and the townsmen. But the Estates-General did not develop the power of the English Parliament. The king did not have to call it to raise money or to make laws. He could call for new taxes or change the law more or less on his own authority. Thus, in time the Estates-General disappeared. By the end of the Middle Ages the French king was supreme, and the French people of all classes had much less say in their government than the English. This remained the case until a revolution, which began in 1789, led to the

"We have burned a saint."

Joan of Arc was a peasant girl who could neither read nor write. She was devoted to the saints whose images stood in the little church in her village. She believed she heard their voices telling her to go to the King and lead the French in expelling the English from their country. When she reached the King, who was not only lazy but also afraid of the English, she was examined by a group of Churchmen. These men concluded that she was a simple, honest and virtuous girl. She was then given a horse, a suit of armour and a banner. This fifteenth-century picture of her is probably the best likeness of Joan that we have.

Joan was given a small number of men and permitted to join the French army that was trying to free Orléans. (The accompanying illustration, painted by an artist of the period, shows the city under English attack.) While she knew nothing of military affairs, she somehow gave the French army a new confidence. She refused to let the soldiers swear and tried to persuade them to attend Church. She displayed a reckless courage in battle and was even wounded in the shoulder. There is no doubt that her presence inspired the French troops as they successfully drove away the English army that had besieged Orléans. "Before she came, two hundred Englishmen used to drive five hundred Frenchmen before them," wrote a contemporary French observer. "After her coming, two hundred Frenchmen could chase five hundred Englishmen."

Joan was given much of the credit for the relief of Orléans. In the following years she had command of a few troops. She was determined to drive out the English altogether, rather than to make a peaceful settlement with them as the King and many of his advisers wished to do. The French King himself came to dislike her, and once was supposed to have said, "Let her go hang herself." The English were convinced that she was a witch. When she was captured they were anxious to prove that she was a witch, send her to the stake, and end forever the inspiration she had given to the French army. The Church was also convinced that she was an agent of the devil, for only the clergy were supposed to be able to tell men what God wished them to do. When the English turned Joan over to a Church court, she was found guilty. When she heard the sentence which would send her to burn at the stake, the young girl was tired from her year in prison, homesick and upset because the French King had not really attempted to have her set free. In this weakened condition she confessed that she had lied about the voices. Although her sentence was changed to life imprisonment because she had confessed, she later declared that she had only confessed because she had been afraid. The Church then turned her over to the English, and she was burned at the stake in the Rouen marketplace on May 30, 1431. As he saw the woman consumed by the flames with the name of Jesus on her lips, an English soldier exclaimed, ". . . we have burned a saint." In 1919 Pope Benedict XV, leader of the Church that had sentenced her to be burned as a heretic or a witch, declared that Joan of Arc was a saint.

execution of the king, and later, to the establishment of a more democratic system of government.

Even after the Treaty of Paris in 1259 the English control of some lands in France remained a thorn in the side of the increasingly powerful kings of France. The English in turn always hoped to regain possession of the lost territories. For these and other reasons, war began again in 1337 and lasted with interruptions until 1453. Throughout most of the war the English won the battles. At Sluys in 1340 the English fleet swept the French from the English Channel; at Crécy six years later, English longbowmen slaughtered the cream of the French knights sent against them; at Agincourt in 1415 the famous Henry V led his troops to a mighty victory over the French.

By 1425, however, the tide was turning. In England the presence of a weak king on the throne led to struggles for power among rival groups of nobles. A nation divided could hardly fight a war against a powerful and larger country. In France in 1424 a seventeen-year-old peasant girl was brought before the King. She had travelled 300 miles to see him. God had spoken to her, she said, and had commanded her to help him drive the English from France. The King gave Joan of Arc, as she was called, a small position in the army. Soon she inspired the French troops to greater resistance.

Far more important, however, as causes of the French victory were the activities of the Duke of Burgundy and several Paris merchants. The Duke of Burgundy, long a supporter of the English, turned against his allies and in 1435 made peace with the French King. About the same time the wealthy merchants persuaded the King to call the Estates-General. A large sum of money was provided, which enabled the king to reorganize and enlarge the army. By 1453 the French had driven the disunited English out of all of France except the port of Calais. (See Map, page 210)

While it took almost 500 years, the kings of France had extended their territory from the tiny Ile de France to cover almost all of modern France. The second great Feudal monarchy, by far the largest and most powerful country in the west, had emerged by the end of the Middle Ages.

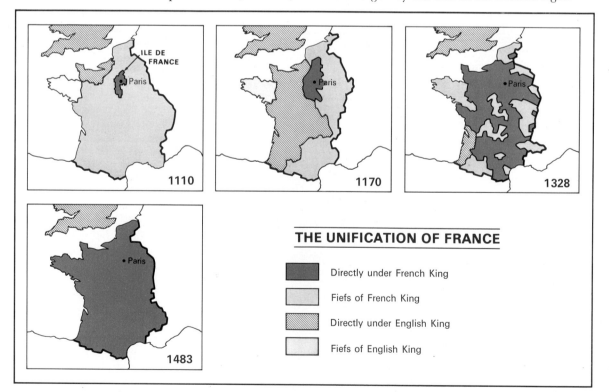

THE UNIFICATION OF FRANCE

- Directly under French King
- Fiefs of French King
- Directly under English King
- Fiefs of English King

The medieval Church

The first barbarian invasions fell upon the Roman world like a heavy storm cloud. In the general darkness, the Church provided a steady beam of light. Throughout the entire Middle Ages, the Church remained the most important organization or institution in western Europe. There was only one Church, and all Christians belonged to it. Its teaching and worship were much the same everywhere. From his birth to his death the Church watched over a man and greatly influenced his life. It baptized him, married him and buried him. The Church educated him, if he were one of the few who were fortunate enough to get an education. If he lived in the country, once a year he marched around the fields with all the people of the parish, praying for a blessing on the crops. If he were a town craftsman, his guild kept a chapel in the cathedral or parish church to which the guild members paraded on their annual festival. The Church was everywhere, doing everything.

ORGANIZATION OF THE CHURCH

The Church was not only the strongest organization in medieval Europe; it also brought people closer together, for the Christian religion was the one thing all Europeans had in common. The Church also promoted learning and culture. It soon developed a well ordered system of government and law based on the example of the Roman Empire and on the experience of early Christians. At the head of the Church was the pope at Rome. Assisting him was a special body called the *Curia*. During the eleventh century, the leading men in the Curia formed a College of Cardinals composed of the most important or "cardinal" priests of the Church. The cardinals advised the pope on matters of Church government, and elected a new pope on the death of the old, just as they do today.

To carry on its affairs effectively, the Church organized western Christendom into provinces which were ruled by archbishops. These provinces

During the twelfth century, Henry II of England determined to claim what he felt were the rights of the Crown. In so doing he came into conflict with the Church. A main cause of the dispute concerned the power of the Church courts, which could try all cases involving the clergy. (See page 222.) Since many people were escaping punishment in the Church courts, Henry tried to arrange an agreement by which a priest who was found guilty in a Church court would be handed over to the king's court for punishment. Thomas à Becket, the Archbishop of Canterbury and head of the Church in England, refused to agree. The struggle between King and Archbishop became very bitter, and Henry is supposed to have said that he would be glad to be rid of the priest. Some of the King's followers took his words literally and murdered Becket in his own cathedral. Henry was forced to confess in public that he was sorry for the part he had played in causing Becket's death.

221

were sub-divided into smaller units known as dioceses, each ruled by a bishop. The diocese was made up of a large number of parishes, and in each parish was a priest. To most of the common people of Europe, the parish priest was the most important figure in the Church organization. He was their spiritual adviser, their teacher and friend. Since the village priest was usually a man of peasant stock with limited education, he remained very close to his parishioners, with whom he lived, worked and prayed.

The Church had its own courts and its own law, which was known as Church law or canon law. The Church courts dealt with all cases involving religion. Since most aspects of medieval life had some connection with religion, the Church courts handled many matters which today are settled in our regular civil courts. For example, Church courts not only tried persons accused of offenses committed on Church property, but also all cases having to do with wills and contracts. Such cases were seen as matters for Church law since the oaths taken in drawing up these documents were religious in nature. Furthermore, all clergy accused of crimes, even those involving theft or murder, had their cases tried in Church courts. Since penalties imposed in the Church courts were more lenient — the death penalty was never imposed — they became very popular. And because they were sometimes the only courts available, they were tremendously important in providing law and order in a violent age.

As the most important institution in Europe, it was natural that the Church should become involved in political matters. In many ways the Church was like a state. Its organization resembled that of a feudal monarchy, with the pope as the suzerain or overlord instead of a king. The pope ruled over the papal states in Italy in the same way that kings ruled over their territories. The Church was certainly richer than any state, with the pope's income estimated to be greater than the combined incomes of all European countries. The Church owned one-fifth of England and one-third of Germany.

It is not surprising that a struggle arose between the pope and the rulers of the various states. The central issue was whether the authority of the Church or the authority of rulers was supreme. The question of who was to appoint Church officials became an important feature of the struggle. During the Middle Ages the Church, increasingly, was drawn into the feudal system. Bishops and abbots held their lands as fiefs from great lords and so became their vassals. Usually these Churchmen received both their lands and Church positions from their feudal overlords, the kings and nobles. As a result the Church and pope tended to lose control over many Church officials who often became more concerned with worldly affairs than with their spiritual duties.

During the eleventh century, Gregory VII, one of the greatest medieval popes, challenged the power of the feudal nobles and kings. Gregory declared that only he could appoint bishops and that he was above all worldly rulers, whether they were princes, kings or emperors. This claim aroused the anger of the young, hot-headed German emperor, Henry IV. Henry ignored Gregory's decrees about the appointment of bishops and refused to recognize the Pope as superior to him. In the test of strength which followed, Gregory won a temporary victory. But the basic question of whether the authority of the Church or of the state was supreme, was far from answered.

The papacy reached its greatest heights of power in the twelfth century under Pope Innocent III. Dedicated and brilliant, Innocent dreamed of creating in Europe a united Christian community ruled by the pope. He fought *heresy* (religious teaching not accepted by the Church) and launched reforms and crusades. He forced his will upon such kings as John of England and Philip Augustus of France. Under Innocent, the medieval Church reached its highest point as a force in Western civilization. Beneath the surface, however, there were signs that the Church in the end would lose its position of leadership in Europe. The attempts by the Church to gain political power and the failure of the Crusades caused widespread discontent. More important in the long run was the fact that many vigorous European states were rapidly growing in power.

Although the Church did become involved in politics, it worked tirelessly throughout the entire Middle Ages to improve conditions for all members of society. Most Churchmen tried, often with little success, to reduce the suffering caused by feudal warfare by preaching the *Peace of God* and the *Truce of God*. By the Peace of God, nobles agreed not to injure priests, monks, peasants, merchants and women, or their property. The Truce of God forbade fighting on the principal holy days of the Church, including Sundays, or during times for plowing, sowing and reaping. The Church also supported the ideals of chivalry—courtesy, charity, loyalty, purity, temperance, courage and justice. These ideals or beliefs were accepted, if not always practised, by all who became knights. The Church also tried to enforce the idea of the "just price." By insisting that the cost of all goods should be based only on the value of the material itself and the labour put on it, the Church opposed the idea of profit. It was also against the lending of money at interest.

At the climax of the bitter conflict between King and Pope, Gregory excommunicated Henry IV, declared his throne vacant and released all his subjects from allegiance to him. Faced with the possible revolt of his vassals, the hot-headed King journeyed to Canossa in northern Italy in the depth of winter to beg the Pope's forgiveness. Here we see Henry kneeling before the Abbot High of Cluny and the Countess Matilda of Tuscany, requesting them to speak with Pope Gregory on his behalf. Eventually the Pope forgave Henry who recovered his throne.

223

THE MONASTERY

The Church's main concern was with religion and the salvation of men's souls. Many early Christians had tried to escape the temptations of an evil world by fleeing from it and taking up a life of solitude and hardship. In this way they hoped to find God, and salvation for their souls. The first monks, as they were called, usually lived alone as hermits or in small groups in the desert, in caves, on islands or on isolated hilltops. Living in a monastery, a monk might not only find God but also friends and security, a chance to study and to learn skills and crafts. During the last centuries of the Roman Empire, however, the early Christian monasteries had tended to decline. A major cause was the lack of rules to control the way in which the monks should live. Without such rules, a number of monks lived very un-Christian lives, doing whatever they pleased.

The man who revived the monasteries was St. Benedict, who lived from A.D. 480 to 543. The illustration below, like those which follow, is from a book on the life of Benedict which was done by monks almost 1000 years ago. Here Benedict is seen with his teacher in Rome, where he had gone to study as a youth. But Benedict was so shocked by the sinfulness and brutality of life in Rome that he fled to the hills where he joined other hermits in the caves.

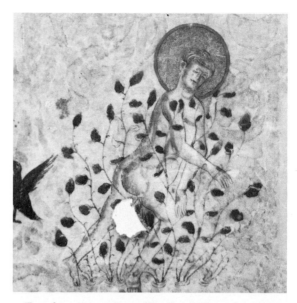

For three years Benedict lived alone in a cave, spending his time at work and prayer. A monk from a neighbouring monastery let down food in a basket. But even though he lived in such isolation, Benedict still found it difficult to avoid temptation. One day he apparently threw himself into a thorn bush to overcome his temptations.

Gradually reports of his devotion and wisdom spread. Much to his surprise, monks from a neighbouring settlement came to him, and, as this illustration shows, begged him to become their leader.

But it soon became clear that many monks did not want to live under the strict discipline that St. Benedict had imposed upon himself. Following an attempt to poison him, Benedict returned to his cave.

Benedict did not live alone for very long. Other monks continued to press him to take over the leadership of their monasteries. He was soon head of twelve monasteries. Forced to leave his first site by a jealous priest, he moved to Monte Cassino, between Rome and Naples, where he built a monastery with stones from an old pagan temple. Destroyed during the Second World War, the famous monastery has now been rebuilt.

Benedict placed each monastery under a set of strict rules, which became known as the Benedictine Rule. The monks who followed it were known as Benedictines. Monks who refused to live up to the Rule were expelled from the monastery. In this illustration, a monk, who apparently has been led astray by the devil, is being driven away. St. Benedict demanded that the monks take the three basic vows of poverty, chastity or purity, and obedience. He also insisted that they work hard—"idleness is an enemy of the soul"—and allowed them to leave the monastery only on the most urgent matters. Upon their return they were never to mention the world outside.

St. Benedict was reported to have had miracu-

lous powers to heal the sick. But during Benedict's time the people of Italy had an even more serious problem than disease. They were treated cruelly by the barbarian Goths, who had conquered much of the peninsula. Around Monte Cassino the Goth Zalla was determined to take everything he could find from the farmers. One farmer admitted under torture that he had given his gold to St. Benedict. Zalla then tied the farmer to his horse and rode to the monastery, where he found Benedict reading a book. As Zalla demanded the gold, the rope which tied the farmer to the horse fell away. Apparently Zalla was so amazed that he leaped from his horse and threw himself at Benedict's feet.

Before his death Benedict and his monasteries had become well known throughout the Christian world and had established a guide for monastic living. So famous was he that Totila, King of the Goths, paid a visit to Monte Cassino. Soon after this visit Benedict died, according to this illustration drawn 500 years later by monks at Monte Cassino, on the arms of his followers.

225

The Rule of St. Benedict was successful because it offered a demanding but reasonable way to salvation and a useful way of life. St. Benedict provided for an eight-hour day: eight hours for work, eight hours for sleep and eight hours for devotion, reading, meditation and meals. A monk's life under the Rule was a simple one, as these rare photographs of life inside a modern Trappist monastery reveal. Their clothing consisted of long, loose robes of coarse material, with hoods to cover their heads. They had two meals a day in the monastery and neither the food nor utensils were luxurious. Eggs, fish or fowl, bread and vegetables and a little fruit made up their main diet. There was no meat. The monks ate in complete silence or listened to one of the brothers who read aloud from some holy book.

The church was the most important of several buildings which made up the monastery. Each day long before sunrise the monks began their devotions. Seven times during the day the chapel bell summoned them to the church to sing psalms and to pray.

The influence of St. Benedict has never died. His famous Rule soon became the model for monasteries throughout western Europe. Even today, as monks serve God in such isolated monasteries as St. Michel d'Aiguille in France and Mouse Island monastery in Corfu, they observe rules laid down almost 1500 years ago.

Not long after midnight the bell sounded again and the monks rose from their hard cots and went to the church to chant the mass.

Sick monks enjoyed the best medical care that was available during the Middle Ages, for the monasteries had the only hospitals, while their brother monks were the only physicians. And should they die, they knew that even while they awaited burial, their fellows would silently pray for their souls. In the photograph above, a Trappist monk prays for a dead brother.

On the south side of the monastery church was the cloister which comprised four long, sheltered walks forming a square. Here the monks could walk or pause in silent meditation. All the monastery buildings were grouped around the cloister. As well as the church, there were dormitories where the monks slept on hard cots, special cells where they studied and thought, the refectory where they ate, and the chapter house where they discussed monastery business. Other buildings that were part of the monastery included a kitchen, bakery, brewery, workshops, storehouses and a hospital.

It is rather strange that the monks, who renounced the outside world, should have contributed so much to it. More than any other force, the monasteries helped to civilize the Middle Ages. To a cruel and warlike society, the monasteries were a constant example of a peaceful and well ordered life. The monks stressed the value of physical work. As this medieval illustration and

the modern photograph show, from early times to the present they worked hard in the fields. Their importance to Europe's economic and social development was immense. They cut down forests and cleared and farmed vast areas of land. Their farms were the best in medieval Europe. They also did much to care for the poor and the sick, providing them with food, clothing and medical care. And in an age when inns were few and thieves numerous, many a weary traveller had reason to bless the kindly monks who welcomed them into their monasteries where they could find rest, refreshment and safety.

The monks also made valuable contributions to such practical arts as cooking (the Benedictine Rule required all monks to pray for the cooks), glass-blowing, masonry and weaving. Monasteries were also the main centres of learning and art. The monks conducted schools like the one shown in this twelfth-century illustration by a Canterbury monk. The scene shows a writing lesson in progress.

The monks also kept libraries and copied manuscripts. In the Spanish manuscript illumination below the monks are doing such work in one room of a typical monastery building. Here monks painstakingly and artistically copied and created manuscripts, and sometimes broke the spirit of their vow of silence by exchanging notes written in the margins of the manuscripts.

The monastic orders also sent out missionaries to Ireland, England and eastern Europe. Monks like St. Patrick, St. Augustine and St. Columban gladly risked their lives to preach the word of God.

DECAY AND REFORM

At its best, life was peaceful and well-ordered in a monastery. The monks, sheltered from the world, lived Christian lives of self-sacrifice and quiet industry. Sometimes, however, neither the monks nor monasteries lived up to their high ideals. Although a monk could own nothing as an individual, a monastery, by holding possessions in the name of the Church, could amass much wealth. Wealth came through the work of the monks and the gifts of rich or generous men. But as wealth increased, many monks became lazy and sinful. Wealth was not the only cause of decline. During the Viking and Moslem invasions, many monasteries came under the control of local strongmen. These feudal kings and nobles often came to regard the monasteries as pieces of property to be used to increase their own wealth and power, rather than as centres of religious life.

The decline of the monasteries was only one sign of a general weakness in the entire Church during the later Dark Ages. Many local bishops and Churchmen went their own way, scarcely recognizing the authority of the pope and paying little attention to their spiritual duties. Many of the popes themselves did not deserve recognition. During this unhappy time, many of the clergy did not learn to read and write; many married and had children despite their vows of chastity. Official Church teachings were not clearly known, and as a result Christian beliefs were often mixed with superstitions. But as often happened with the Church, weakness led to reform. Between 1000 and 1300 the Church underwent an amazing revival.

The reform movement was inspired by the Benedictine monastery at Cluny in France. The Cluniac monks worked to free the Church from control by kings and nobles. They vigorously opposed the growing tendency of clergy to marry. Their ideas had a great effect on Gregory VII, who became pope in 1073. Gregory ordered the clergy to concentrate on their religious tasks, give up politics and warfare, free themselves from control by feudal nobles and kings, and leave their wives and children. The monastery of Cluny became widely known for its enthusiasm, simplicity and purity, and many ancient monasteries joined with it under leaders named by the Abbot of Cluny. As time passed, however, the Cluniacs lost much of their desire for reform and succumbed to the evils of wealth, good food, tournaments, hunting and politics.

The Cistercians were the next order to take up the cause of reform. Originating in France, the Cistercians completely rejected the outside world, building their abbeys in the most lonely places. The greatest of the Cistercians was St. Bernard, a simple man who taught that the greatest thing in the world was the love of God. He fought against evil wherever he saw it and bitterly attacked the wealth of the Church. "The Church gilds its stones, and leaves its children naked. With the silver of the wretched it charms the eyes of the rich."

With the growth of trade and towns, the Church had to change to meet the needs of the townspeople. The old monastic orders with their emphasis on living away from the world could not meet such needs. Monks would have to live with the people and move among them. During the thirteenth century two new monastic orders, the Franciscans and the Dominicans, concentrated on serving the growing number of townsmen. Their members were friars (from the Latin *frater,* a brother) who lived their lives on the roads and in the villages and towns as travelling preachers.

St. Francis of Assisi, the founder of the Franciscans, was the most beloved of all the friars and one of the most remarkable men of the Middle Ages. The son of a prosperous merchant, he gave up his sinful life and determined to live in poverty. His aim was to help all men, and to live as nearly as possible as Jesus had lived on earth. St. Francis wandered barefoot from town to town, caring for the sick, begging from the rich, giving to the poor, and constantly preaching the love of God. Unlike the earlier orders of monks, he and his followers devoted their lives to the salvation of others, not just themselves.

Although this thirteenth-century Basilica of St. Francis at Assisi is a magnificent building, the Franciscans were remarkably successful in following the simple beliefs of their founder. Within ten years after he had established his order, St. Francis had attracted 5000 Little Brothers of the Poor, as the Franciscans were sometimes called.

Where the Franciscans spoke to the hearts of men, the Dominicans appealed to their minds. They were particularly concerned with the growing number of heresies within the Church. Heresy was not new and had been a problem throughout the early life of the Church. But the new heresies of the thirteenth century seemed particularly dangerous because they were directed against a Church which was not living up to its own ideals and teachings. Because of these weaknesses, the new doctrines preached by the heretics, and their demands for major reforms, attracted many supporters. Many Churchmen feared that if the heresies were not suppressed, the Church would split up into hundreds of quarrelling religious groups, each viewing Christianity in its own way. The Dominicans were in the forefront of the movement to wipe out heresy in the thirteenth century. They relied partly upon preaching, but they also prosecuted heretics in special courts and even led armed crusades against them.

The Church also fought heresy through a special court known as the *Inquisition,* which was created in 1233. Feared throughout medieval times, the Inquisition considered as guilty those who were accused of heresy. It also refused to allow them to obtain legal advice or to cross-examine their accusers. Torture was often used to secure confessions from those who would not "confess" their guilt in any other way. Convicted heretics were often turned over to the civil authorities for punishment — usually burning at the stake.

Churchmen often defended the Inquisition by arguing that a heretic had no chance of salvation unless he repented. Thus torture was justified in order to save the heretic and prevent him from spreading his ideas among the faithful. Furthermore, the use of torture was commonly used in the civil courts to get people to confess; the Inquisition did not introduce it. Horrible as it was, the Inquisition was a product of the times. The inquisitors usually were sincere in feeling that they were serving society and being merciful to the heretic.

230

One of the most important contributions of the Church was to encourage the development of universities. By the twelfth century there was a clearly recognized need for better trained men in both the Church and government. The Church provided most of the professors, and many of the students looked forward upon graduation to careers in the Church. Medieval universities were a far cry from those of today. Often there were neither classrooms nor equipment; teachers and students met wherever it was most convenient. The main subjects on the curriculum were theology, law, medicine and arts.

Despite some limitations, medieval universities encouraged sound scholarship. New and exciting ideas flourished. Although most university teachers were clergymen, it was in the universities that criticism of the Church began. One of the most

Student life

Like some modern students, a few of those attending this lecture at Bologna University were not exactly carried away by the words of their professor. As is still the case today, there seems to be a fair sprinkling of more mature students.

The students in the upper picture (right) are obviously more serious about their studies than those in the centre. A medieval criticism of Oxford undergraduates was that they "sleep all day and roam about all night." Certainly many medieval students led boisterous lives, quarrelling and gambling, as well as studying. Student rowdyism was somewhat more serious than pulling down goalposts after football games. In 1314, two large bands of students met on Oxford's High Street "with swords, bucklers, bows, arrows and other arms, and there they fought together" leaving many dead and wounded when they went off. One Oxford law made the penalty for night-walking twice that for shooting an arrow at a teacher with the intent to wound him. No doubt after a day of study and a session of "night-walking" even this sparsely-furnished student's room and narrow bed would look very inviting.

famous scholars of the twelfth century was Peter Abelard. Although he was a sincere Christian, Abelard shocked many Churchmen and scholars by raising doubts about some of the teachings of the Church. Abelard believed that the best way to reach the truth was to doubt and to question. "By doubting we are led to enquire; by enquiry, we perceive the truth," he said. He was convinced that a person's religious faith would be deeper if it were based on understanding and reason, as well as on beliefs. Abelard's emphasis on questioning and doubting had an unsettling effect upon an age in which men relied for truth upon the writings of old authorities.

The most influential scholar of the age was a Dominican, St. Thomas Aquinas. In his famous book, *Summation of Theology*, he outlined and explained Christian beliefs and answered the arguments of doubters and unbelievers. Aquinas believed that man could understand God's will either by reason or by faith. However, if the conclusions reached by faith or belief differed from those reached by reason, man should rely upon faith because human reason was open to error.

Medieval Churchmen were concerned with more than religious teaching and learning. They built upon the ideas and knowledge of Arabia and Greece, which came into Europe through southern Italy and Spain. In this way they added to the limited scientific knowledge of medieval Europe. In fact, the first real scientist of the West was a Franciscan monk, Roger Bacon. He wrote, "There are four principal stumbling blocks to comprehending truth, which hinder well-nigh every scholar: the example of frail and unworthy authority, long-established custom, the sense of the ignorant crowd, and the hiding of one's ignorance under the show of wisdom." Bacon stressed that men should reach their conclusions by observing and experimenting, rather than by relying upon what some supposed authority had written. This approach, which scientists still use, led to such new inventions as a blast furnace, eye glasses, and the mariner's compass. But although Bacon's modern scientific methods stirred the minds of some scholars, many medieval men remained superstitious and believed in magic.

The Church also inspired much of the literature of medieval Europe. Most writing was done by Churchmen and most of it was in Latin. Biographies of the lives of the saints were extremely popular. The hymns of the Church are among the finest medieval poems. But with the expansion of schools and increased security and prosperity, many nobles and townsmen also learned to read and write. As a result, there was the beginning of literature in what is called the *vernacular*, that is, the language of everyday speech, rather than Latin. In the towns, actors performed plays which dealt either with stories from the Bible or with fables. The latter were always used to stress a moral, such as "honesty is the best policy." The most popular forms of vernacular literature, however, were the epic poems or songs of heroic deeds. One of the best known of the written epics from the medieval period is the *Chanson de Roland*, the Song of Roland. In the epic, Roland is pictured as a courageous and charming medieval knight who protected the rear of Charlemagne's army when it was retreating before the Moslems in the eighth century. Another very famous and popular subject was the legend of King Arthur and the Knights of the Round Table. Many of these poems were sung by troubadours or minstrels to entertain at banquets in feudal castles or at fairs in the towns.

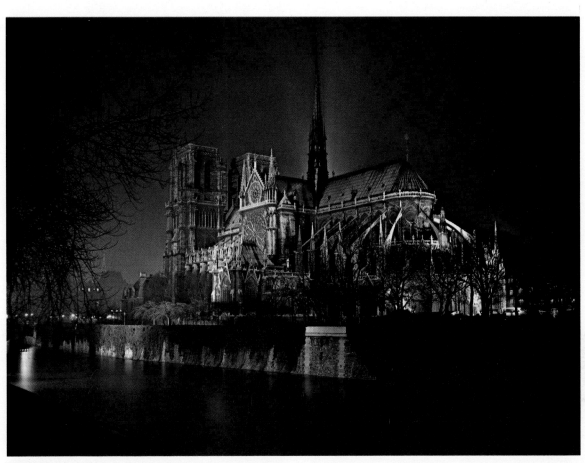

The Cathedral of Notre Dame, Paris

TRIUMPHS IN STONE AND GLASS

The Church not only took the lead in learning and knowledge; it also stimulated architecture, the greatest of medieval arts. Churches and cathedrals such as those at Chartres and Notre Dame in France were the finest building achievements of the age. In the late twelfth and thirteenth centuries, the Romanesque style of architecture, with its thick walls, heavy roofs and rather squat appearance, gave way to a new style of architecture known as Gothic. Later generations at first used the term scornfully to suggest their contempt for the achievements of the medieval barbarians. Nothing could be more unsuitable. One need only glance at the great Gothic cathedrals to appreciate the creative skill of medieval man.

One of the most impressive features of Gothic cathedrals is their soaring height; as one writer said, they seemed to "defy gravity to glorify God." Such lofty structures were possible because of the pointed arch, which permitted the weight of a vaulted ceiling to be distributed to the foundations through pillars. In this way a stone skeleton could be built. Walls could then be built between pillars, and since these walls did not have to bear the full weight of the roof, they could be much lighter than those of a Romanesque cathedral. Furthermore, they could be pierced by as many large windows as the builders wanted. One writer has described a typical Gothic church as a "soaring glass house held together by a skeletal framework of stone." The use of *flying buttresses,* seen

233

A medieval illustration shows cathedral
builders at work. Other contemporary
drawings show men using primitive
winches and pulleys to raise the stones.
Here a man in a treadmill provides the
power necessary to lift stones and mortar.

The interior of Rheims Cathedral

on the outside walls of both of these cathedrals
(pp. 233, 235), provided further support for the
roof and thus made it possible to build even
higher structures with more windows.

Since cathedrals often took several centuries to
complete, they often show great changes in design. The two spires on Chartres provide a good
example of such changes. The shorter one was
completed in the twelfth century and gives the
impression of rather massive simplicity; the one
on the left (as you face the Church) was completed in the highly decorated later Gothic style
of the sixteenth century.

The interior of a Gothic cathedral tended to
be rather simple in comparison with the exterior.
Sculpture was the chief form of decoration. It was
often used to illustrate stories from the Bible,
incidents from Christ's life or teachings of the
Church. There was also intricate carving on wood-
work and altars and sometimes frescoes or wall
paintings, and tapestries. Although this interior
of Rheims seems very simple in its structure, it is
anything but dull or gloomy. Filled with marvel-
lous stained glass, the cathedral is bathed in
magical light suggesting the spiritual qualities
man should try to achieve.

The spires of Chartres dominate the Beauce countryside. Chartres is a small town, fifty miles southwest of Paris. The Virgin was supposed to have visited Chartres, and the town became a shrine. The first church was burned down in 1020, and a second burned to the ground a century later. But the Bishop and the townsmen were determined to build yet another, more magnificent building on the sacred site. The Bishop aroused such devotion for the task that, according to an observer of his day, "kings, princes, mighty men of the world, puffed up with honours and riches, men and women of noble birth, bound bridles upon their proud and swollen necks, and submitted themselves to wagons which, after the fashion of brute beasts, they dragged with loads of wine, corn, oil, lime, stones, beams, and other things necessary to sustain life or build churches. . . . Moreover, as they draw the wagons we may see this miracle, that although sometimes a thousand men and women . . . are bound in the traces . . . yet they go forward in such silence that no voice, no murmur, is heard. . . ."

The Cathedral had just been completed, however, when another fire destroyed the town and gutted the church. For a while the people of Chartres thought of abandoning the town, but soon they turned again to the task. Men came from all over Europe to work with the labourers and craftsmen; funds were collected in every cathedral, and Chartres became again, as it is today, a goal for the pilgrim.

The magnificent stained-glass windows, like these from Chartres showing the coronation of Charlemagne and the Crucifixion of Christ, were not painted but were made up of many pieces of stained glass. In this art the medieval craftsmen have never been surpassed. The windows caught the rays of the sun and bathed the interior with warm and gay colours. They also served the same purpose as the carving and sculpture; that is they gave people who could not read a picture of biblical incidents and of some of the important events in the history of the Church. The medieval cathedrals were meant to be used and enjoyed by ordinary people. They were not just centres of worship, for they also served as schools, libraries and community centres. Many generations of townsmen had built them and naturally were proud of their achievement, which they regarded as community property.

If Chartres cathedral is the finest Gothic building in the world, the most complete and most typical, in the opinion of many scholars, is the great abbey at Mont St. Michel in Normandy, France. (See page 195.) Located on a tiny island joined to the mainland, the great structure was begun in the eleventh century just before Duke William conquered England. It was really a fortress and town as well as a monastery. It has been said that no other building captures so perfectly the spirit of the Middle Ages.

The breath-taking beauty of the Gothic cathedral is one of the great triumphs in history.

Charlemagne

The Crucifixion

236

Moslem horsemen deal a fatal blow to a Crusader.

Moslem and Crusader

The Crusades were a series of wars which lasted for about 200 years, from the eleventh to the thirteenth century. One of the greatest adventures of the Middle Ages, they have often been pictured as battles between mighty Christian warriors in shining armour and heathen Turks. Such a picture is not wholly accurate. There were daring deeds on the burning sands. But the Crusades were also the story of Moslems being stabbed to death in the shadow of the Church of the Holy Sepulchre, of blood-spattered Christian knights sacking the Christian city of Constantinople while they sang praises to God, and of thousands of doomed children crowding into ships to cross the Mediterranean and win the Holy Land from the Moslems.

MOSLEM CIVILIZATION

Who were these Moslems? They were a desert people whose story is one of the most astonishing in history. The first Moslems lived as nomads in Arabia, a land of burning deserts. Their story began in the seventh century with a self-educated Arab orphan boy named Mohammed. Mohammed became a caravan guard and then a trader. On his travels across Arabia he met Jews and Christians who told him of their belief in one God. Mohammed, who was deeply religious, was impressed. He spent much of his time alone, thinking and fasting. Often he fell into trances, when he believed that the Angel Gabriel spoke to him in the name of Allah, who Mohammed believed was the God of all people. Finally he became convinced that

In the year 711 a small force of 12,000 Moslems crossed the eight-and-a-half-mile Strait from North Africa to begin the conquest of the Visigoth kingdom in Spain. There was little opposition, and within seven years most of Spain had become a Moslem province. The conquerors were far more tolerant and generous than most people in the ancient and medieval world. Christians and Jews were allowed to practice their own religions. There were no slaughters. The vanquished were forced to pay heavy taxes, however, and as this thirteenth-century drawing shows, many were herded off to slavery along with their livestock. By the time this drawing was made, parts of Spain had been reconquered, but it was not until the fifteenth century that the Moslems were completely expelled.

Allah had chosen him to be his prophet. He began preaching his religion of one God to the pagan Arabs, who believed in some 360 gods. His religion was called Islam, meaning surrender to Allah.

Mohammed was laughed at, mistreated and driven from Mecca, the main city of Arabia. In 622, with a few followers, he fled to the town of Medina, where he had more success. (His journey is called the *Hegira,* which means literally "the breaking of former ties." Moslems, as the followers of Mohammed and Islam are called, date their calendar from the Hegira.) The Hegira was a momentous event. Islam spread like a prairie grass fire. Within eight years Mohammed returned to Mecca in triumph. When he died in 632, Islam

238

had inspired and united the desert people of Arabia.

The sacred book of Islam is the *Koran*. Moslems regard its teachings as the revelations of Allah to Mohammed. The Koran, which has not been changed since the seventh century, was written to be recited and chanted. Its main teaching was simple. "There is no God but Allah; God is one and omnipotent [all powerful]; Mohammed is his prophet." Islam has no priests or ministers. By good conduct and the proper worship of Allah the Moslem could achieve salvation and enter into a heaven described by Mohammed as a Garden of Paradise, cool and full of delicious food. Hell was pictured as a desert with only boiling water to drink.

The Koran stressed that all Moslems were equal. "Know ye that every Moslem is a brother to every other Moslem and that ye are now one brotherhood." It also clearly set out the duties of the faithful: prayer, alms giving, fasting and a pilgrimage to Mecca. The Moslem was to give to the poor, to pray five times a day, to fast between sunrise and sunset during the holy month of *Ramadan,* and to go to Mecca at least once in his lifetime. Islam forbade the worship of idols, wine-drinking, gambling and the eating of pork.

Islam not only united the Arabs, but also gave them a reason to spread their faith. The Arabs had always been good fighters. Their war-like spirit was increased by the belief that if they died while fighting for Islam, they were certain to enter Paradise. Other factors help explain their success in expanding their territory. They desperately needed land. Their neighbours in Persia and the Byzantine Empire were weak. Furthermore, the Moslems promised equality to peoples who accepted Islam. They were also tolerant of Jews and Christians. As a result, there was less opposition to their rule than might have been the case otherwise. For all of these reasons the Arabs were able to burst east, west and north of their desert homeland.

These daring Arabs did not stop until they had crossed the distant Pyrenees in Europe and the inland Caspian Sea on the edge of the Russian steppes. After conquering Syria, Palestine and Egypt from the Byzantine Empire, the Moslems swept across North Africa and up into Spain. Moslem armies even pushed over the Pyrenees to move into France. In 732, however, exactly one hundred years after the death of Mohammed, the Frankish leader Charles Martel checked the Arab advance at the Battle of Tours.

The peoples in the Moslem Empire enjoyed prosperity and security. The Arabs traded with China, central Russia, Africa and western Europe. They also encouraged agriculture and manufacturing, especially of silk and linen cloth, pottery, enamels and fine metal-work. Their capital city, Mecca, was surpassed only by Constantinople as the greatest city in the world, with magnificent palaces, mosques, schools and public gardens.

The Arabs also did much as teachers and cultural leaders of the Western world in the Middle Ages. They made Spain one of the most civilized of European countries. In architecture the Moslems improved the dome and the use of arches. In literature they gave the West the poem, *The Rubaiyat of Omar Khayyam.* Perhaps their best known work is *Tales from the Arabian Nights* with its wonderful stories of Sinbad the Sailor, Ali Baba and the Forty Thieves, and Aladdin and his Magic Lamp.

Their work in mathematics and medicine was especially valuable to western Europe. Avicenna, one of the greatest Arab physicians, wrote more than 200 books on diseases. Two Moslem studies on the eye were used until the eighteenth century. At a time in Europe when barbers acted as surgeons, and doctors used charms to cast out demons, Moslem physicians were performing skilful operations. Moslem mathematicians developed algebra by the use of Arabic numerals and zero. Up to this time, men had used clumsy Roman numerals in calculation. Moslem scientists made many advances in astronomy, giving us such terms as *zenith* and *nadir,* and naming many of the stars. Moslem learning and scholarship continued to have influence long after the Arab Empire had declined. Islam today is still one of the most influential religions in the world.

BACKGROUND OF THE CRUSADES

The expansion of Moslem power, like the later invasions of the Vikings, was a serious threat to western Europe. The victory of Charles Martel at the Battle of Tours checked the Moslem advance, but it did not remove the threat. Many centuries were to pass before the Christian West felt strong enough to challenge the invader both in Europe and in the East. In the meantime, Christian Europeans could do little more than grieve that the centres of Christianity, Bethlehem and Jerusalem, were in the hands of the Moslems.

Despite Moslem control over these centres, Christians from the West could make pilgrimages to the East. For many years the Arabs who controlled Palestine did little to interfere with Christian pilgrims. In fact, they often treated them with kindness and generosity. By the eleventh century, pilgrimages had become very popular. Thousands of pilgrims made the difficult journey to the Holy Land, either as a form of penance or to show their devotion to the Christian faith. But just as pilgrimages reached a peak of popularity, the dangers involved greatly increased. The reason was simple. In the eleventh century a new and more aggressive group of Moslems, the Seljuk Turks, gained control of the Holy Land. They discouraged pilgrims and treated many Christians harshly. They also threatened to overthrow the Byzantine Empire, which for 700 years had protected Europe from invasions by Asian armies. In desperation the Byzantine emperor asked Pope Urban II for help to drive back the Turks.

This plea for assistance came at just the right moment. Stories of Turkish cruelties against pil-

An early sixteenth-century mapmaker drew the Mediterranean world as he imagined it during the time of the Crusades. The walled city of Aigues-Mortes, from which King Louis IX departed on his Crusade, Athens, Rome, Constantinople and Jerusalem can be found in something like their correct place. However, other cities on the map are in locations that must amaze anyone who knows anything about geography.

konstantinople · ermenie · romme · sirie · iherusalem · egipte · cipre · akre · sizalle · thunes · mallorie · flum de nile · damiete · babiloinne

241

As this fifteenth-century drawing reveals, much of the ordinary work at the Council of Clermont was done inside. But when the time came for Urban II, seen above preaching, to make his appeal for the Crusade, he moved to a large platform outside. Since he had been touring northern Italy and southern France for six months to secure support, there was a huge crowd—bishops, nobles and knights, ordinary people and pilgrims. In part of his speech, Urban made a direct appeal to the pride of the Franks: "Oh, race of Franks, race from across the mountains, race chosen and beloved by God . . . let the deeds of your ancestors move you and incite your minds to manly achievements." He also reminded the medieval noble and knight of their sinfulness: "You, girt about with the badge of knighthood, are arrogant with great pride; you rage against your brothers and cut each other to pieces. . . . You, the oppressors of children, plunderers of widows; you, guilty of homicide, of sacrilege, robbers of another's rights. . . . If, forsooth, you wish to be mindful of your souls, either lay down the girdle of such knighthood or advance boldly, as knights of Christ, and rush as quickly as you can to the defence of the Eastern Church." At once, wrote an eyewitness, "some of the nobility, falling down at the knees of the Pope, consecrated themselves and their property to the service of God."

grims had angered Christian Europe. Moreover, the West was now in a position to take action. By about A.D. 1000 Europe had largely recovered from 400 years of upheaval caused by one invasion after another. Increasing law and order had encouraged new economic activity which had made Europe prosperous and strong. Signs of this new strength could be seen in the reconquest of Sardinia from the Moslems and in great victories by European knights over Moslems in Spain. Thus it was that when Pope Urban II called for a crusade against the Turks, he aroused great enthusiasm. It was really Pope Urban who set the Crusades under way. On a cold November day in 1095 he spoke in the open air to a great throng at Clermont in southern France. He appealed to many different motives — faith, ambition, greed and love of adventure.

> .... Even now the Turks are torturing Christians, binding them and filling them with arrows, or making them kneel. . . . This land which you inhabit is too narrow for your large population; nor does it abound in wealth; and it furnishes scarcely food enough for its civilization. Hence it is that you kill and devour one another, that you wage war. . . . Enter upon the road to the Holy Sepulchre.... That land which, as the Scripture says, "floweth with milk and honey" . . . is fruitful above others . . . may you deem it a beautiful thing to die for Christ in that city in which He died for us. . . . The possessions of the enemy, too, will be yours, since you will make spoil of their treasures. . . . If those who set out thither should lose their lives their sins will be remitted. . . . He that doth not take his cross and follow after me is not worthy of me!

The crowd replied to this heady, exciting speech with shouts of "God wills it." This became the battlecry of the Crusades. As Urban's speech suggests, men had many reasons for going on a crusade. Religion was important. Many knights felt that by freeing the holy places from the infidel they would serve God. Many believed their sins would be forgiven if they went on a crusade.

There were strong economic reasons. Urban promised to suspend taxes and cancel debts for those who joined the Holy Pilgrimage. Ambitious knights and barons often sought new land and opportunities in the East. The Italian cities such as Venice, Pisa and Genoa hoped to increase their own trade by breaking Moslem control of the eastern Mediterranean. And there were always the adventurous and restless who turned to the Crusades as something new and exciting. For all of these reasons—religious, economic and political—men went on the Crusades.

THE FIRST CRUSADE

Within a year of Urban's speech, the first crusading army assembled at Clermont. Months before this, a peasant army, more enthusiastic than sensible, had set out for Constantinople. Led by a fanatical monk, Peter the Hermit, and a poor knight, Walter the Penniless, this civilian mob had arrived in Constantinople and had crossed into Asia Minor. Few were ever to see their homes again, for they were almost completely wiped out by the Turks at Nicaea.

The first battle took place at Nicaea, where the Peasant Crusade had met its end. No sooner had the Crusaders pitched camp than the Turkish cavalry attacked. The Crusaders grabbed the closest weapons and mounted the closest horses. Many were without armour or saddles. The Turks soon found they were facing men far different from the peasants they had destroyed earlier. The heavier horses of the Crusaders ran down the lighter Turkish animals, and the heavy Western longswords slashed through the thin shields and steel-mesh armour of the Turks. When the Turks withdrew behind the heavy walls of the fortress at Nicaea, the Crusaders used their slings to toss into the fortress a few heads taken from the battlefield.

The army of Crusaders assembled at Clermont was much more powerful, however, for it was led by the great feudal lords, Godfrey of Lorraine, Robert of Normandy, and Bohemond, a prince from southern Italy. The army moved across Europe and the Mediterranean to Constantinople. Then they fought their way overland to Jerusalem, surviving attacks by the Turks, blistering heat and shortages of food and water. Flagging spirits were restored when a priest, Peter Bartholomew, claimed to have found the spear which had pierced the side of Christ. When the Christians marched out to battle, the lance was carried aloft as a sacred standard. When some knights claimed that the lance was a forgery, Bartholomew underwent the ordeal of fire to prove his good faith. He ran through a gauntlet of burning faggots and emerged apparently safe. On the following day, however, Bartholomew died of burns or an overstrained heart. The Crusaders abandoned the lance.

In June 1099, after a campaign of three years,

A fourteenth-century artist tried to illustrate the way in which the Crusaders finally were able to overcome the sturdy walls of the city of Jerusalem and defeat the small Moslem garrison. The picture at left shows the Crusaders' army approaching the city. Led by Godfrey of Bouillon, one group of the Crusaders built a large tower which they slowly moved towards the walls (above). As soon as it came close enough, the Moslems hurled flaming balls of wood and straw into it. Some Crusaders fought the fire, while others continued to push the tower closer to the wall. The Crusaders answered the Moslem missiles by shooting flaming arrows into the wooden scaffolding on top of the defenders' walls. When the tower reached the wall, Duke Godfrey ordered his men to cut the ropes that held a small drawbridge, and the bridge fell across to the flaming wall. Followed by his men, Godfrey raced through the smoke and held the wall. The Crusaders flooded across the bridge and along the walls. Soon they had fought their way into the streets of the city.

the Christian armies, their numbers reduced from 30,000 to 12,000, gathered outside the walls of Jerusalem. After a frontal attack failed, they constructed a huge battering-ram and two large siege towers. The Moslem garrison, which numbered about 1000, held out for forty days, but the Crusaders finally fought their way over the walls and into the city. A priest who was an eyewitness described the conquest of the city.

> Wonderful things were to be seen. Numbers of the Saracens were beheaded . . . others were shot with arrows, or forced to jump from the towers; others were tortured for several days and then burned in flames. In the streets were seen piles of heads and hands and feet. One rode about everywhere amid the corpses of men and horses.

Historians agree that almost the entire Moslem population of the city, estimated at between 40,000 and 70,000 were killed in what is usually regarded as one of the great crimes in history. After the slaughter the victorious Christians flocked to the Church of the Holy Sepulchre within the city. Here they embraced one another, wept

with joy and sang praises to God for their victory.

The Christians now tried to hold the land they had conquered. They established four kingdoms along the Mediterranean coast of the Holy Land. In these insecure kingdoms the Europeans were only a small minority ruling over the native Moslems. They therefore created a permanent fighting force made up of two orders of military monks known as the Templars and Hospitalers. The Templars were originally a group of humble knights who protected pilgrims, while the Hospitalers at first helped sick pilgrims and maintained a hospital in Jerusalem. Both orders pledged themselves to everlasting war against the hated infidels. However, they soon came to hate one another as much as they hated their Moslem enemy.

The capture of Jerusalem and the conquest of parts of the Holy Land did not end the Crusades. The Christians had trouble defending their long, narrow kingdoms, despite the efforts of the Templars and Hospitalers. The Moslems still held important strongholds in the mountains and seaports. Finally a new Turkish tribe replaced the

Seljuks in power. Christian holdings in the Holy Land were attacked and important forts and cities were captured.

To meet this challenge, European Christians launched the Second Crusade. The great monk, St. Bernard, pleaded for volunteers, promising, "The Christian who slays the unbeliever in the Holy War is sure of his reward, the more sure if he himself be slain." Although it was led by two European kings, the Second Crusade failed miserably. The movement was at a standstill when in 1187 Saladin, the brilliant Moslem leader, recaptured Jerusalem. The event so aroused Europe that within three years the famous Third Crusade had been organized.

The greatest rulers of Europe, Richard the Lionhearted of England, Philip Augustus of France and Frederick Barbarossa of Germany personally led the Crusade. But Barbarossa was drowned in Asia Minor, and Richard and Philip quarrelled so bitterly that the latter went home to France. This left Richard, the gallant and courageous, if somewhat childish King of England, against Saladin. They were worthy opponents. Saladin was more than just a great warrior. He was well educated, just and merciful. When he had recaptured Jerusalem he had allowed few acts of violence or insults toward any Christian. When Richard became seriously ill, his chivalrous Moslem opponent sent his own personal physician to the Christian camp, as well as some appetizing fruit. After victories for both sides, Richard and Saladin finally signed a three-year truce. The Christians kept some coastal areas, but Jerusalem remained in the hands of the Moslems. Both Moslem and Christian pilgrims, however, could visit the Holy City in peace and safety.

In fact the Moslems had won, for the Christians had failed to gain their objective. Saladin's moderation and patience had overcome Richard's courage and military skill. In many ways the Moslem sultan was the most admirable figure of the Crusades. Shortly before he died he left instructions to his son.

> My son, I commend thee to the most high God. . . . Do his will for that way lies peace. Abstain from shedding blood . . . for blood that is spilt never sleeps. Seek to win the hearts of thy people, and watch over their prosperity; for it is to secure their happiness that thou art appointed by God and me. Try to gain the hearts of thy ministers, nobles and emirs. If I have become great, it is because I have won men's hearts by kindness and gentleness.

Once having captured Jerusalem and a strip along the eastern shore of the Mediterranean, the Christians had to defend their conquests. They created feudal kingdoms and divided the land among their followers. Since their numbers were always small, they relied for their defence on a number of magnificent castles. These castles were modelled after those the Crusaders had seen in the East, rather than on the weaker and much more primitive castles in Europe. Although some stone was being used in western Europe at the time, the fortifications were built largely of stone and wood. In the East, however, the castles were massive buildings made of stone. (Nicaea, for example, had been built by the Romans and had stone walls six feet thick.) The Crusaders located these huge stone castles along the routes used by the trading caravans and at other strategic places. The most famous castle was the Krak des Chevaliers, seen here. It was never taken by the enemy.

The Third Crusade was the last great effort to destroy Moslem power. Crusading enthusiasm diminished as western Europeans turned to other interests. There were later Crusades, but they were often badly organized or undertaken to promote narrow, selfish interests. The Fourth Crusade of 1202, for example, was launched and financed by greedy Italian merchants. It was not directed against the Moslems but against Constantinople, the great trade rival of the Italian cities. The Crusaders sacked the great city, burning, stealing and killing. Since the Venetians had often been to Constantinople as merchants, they were quickly able to seize the most valuable treasures. Pope Innocent III lamented, "These defenders of Christ, who should have turned their

247

In 1229, a sixth crusade led by the brilliant Frederick II of Germany won back for the Christians Nazareth, Bethlehem and Jerusalem. But fifteen years later the Moslems once again recaptured Jerusalem. Stirred by this event, King Louis of France took up the cross and led an expedition which set out in 1248. In this illustration from a medieval manuscript, King Louis is seen on his way to Damietta in Egypt. Shortly after they captured the city, the Crusaders were surrounded by the Turks and forced to surrender. After paying a heavy ransom, they were allowed to leave for Palestine, where their only accomplishment was to strengthen a few of the remaining Christian ports. In 1254, it was clear that the Crusade had failed. King Louis, who embodied the highest ideals of Christian knighthood and feudal monarchy, returned disappointed to France. (See map, page 240.)

swords only against the infidels, have bathed [them] in Christian blood."

The scandal of the Fourth Crusade almost destroyed the original spirit of the crusading movement. It also shamed and puzzled Christians. Some foolish people concluded that innocent children might succeed against the Moslems, where strong men had failed. This feeling led to the unbelievable Children's Crusade. In 1212 a German youth named Nicholas announced that God had called on him to lead a crusade of children to the Holy Land. Although adults condemned Nicholas, some 30,000 children, averaging twelve years of age, followed him across Germany and over the Alps into Italy. Many died of hunger; some stragglers were eaten by wolves. The survivors reached Genoa, but happily there were no ships to carry them to Palestine. When they appealed to Pope Innocent III, he gently told them to go home.

More terrible was the fate of the children who listened to Stephen, a twelve-year-old shepherd boy in France. Some 20,000 followed him to the port of Marseilles in southern France. Stephen had promised them that the Mediterranean Sea would divide to let them march to Palestine. It did not. Two shipowners, however, offered to take them to Palestine without charge. The children, singing hymns of triumph, crowded into seven ships. Two of the ships were lost off Sardinia and all on board perished. The other children were taken to Tunisia or Egypt in Africa, where they were sold as slaves. So ended the Children's Crusade.

Europe's sense of shame and sorrow led to further efforts. More Crusades went forth, but the movement was dying. The Crusades did not end in violence. They simply ceased as men turned to other interests in Europe. The Crusades had not achieved their first aims. The Moslems still controlled the Holy Land. Perhaps the task had been impossible from the start. To hold the East, colonists were needed. Europeans made pilgrimages to the Holy Land, but very few people remained there. Nor could men maintain the intense religious enthusiasm of the First Crusade. The revival of trade in Europe and new opportunities in the growing cities provided an outlet for adventurous Europeans. Then too, Christians learned that it was safer and more profitable to trade with the Moslems than to fight with them.

The Crusades had an enormous effect on western Europe. By bringing Europeans into direct contact with the East, the Crusades broadened their outlook. European Christians met a new civilization and a different religion. Those who lived in the Holy Land with the Moslems learned that they were not children of Satan, but intelligent and moral human beings. As a result, some Christians became more tolerant.

Although they did not achieve their goals, the Crusades influenced almost every feature of medieval life, from trade to health habits. They quickened the commercial and cultural developments of the thirteenth century. After the Crusades, oriental goods came into Europe by way of Venice and Genoa and other ports, in quantities unknown since the days of imperial Rome. Silks, sugar, spices (pepper, ginger, cloves, cinnamon), rare in the eleventh century, became more common by the thirteenth. And ladies now used glass mirrors from the East instead of polished metal disks.

In spite of their cruelty and violence, the Crusades *did* express medieval man's faith and ideals. As the Crusades died, so did much of the medieval world, a world of brutality and chivalry, blind faith and savage prejudice.

Village and town

The 300 years after the end of the Dark Ages saw a remarkable economic growth which was to make western Europe the richest and most powerful part of the world. At the centre of the economic revival was the rapid expansion of trade and commerce, and the growth of towns. But the new activity in trade and commerce after the end of the Dark Ages would have been impossible without improvements in agricultural methods, which in turn increased farm production. This in turn would not have been possible without the increase in law and order brought about by the feudal system.

THE MEDIEVAL VILLAGE

In the eleventh century a Bishop described society as being composed of "the nobles who do the fighting, the clergy who do the praying, and the others who do the work." The "others," most of them peasants, made up about ninety per cent of the population of medieval Europe. The peasants were the unsung heroes of the Middle Ages. It was their back-breaking work that supported the monarchs, the nobles and knights, and the clergy. Their home was the medieval village, sometimes called a manor. Each village was made up of a cluster of small huts where the peasants lived. The centre of the village was the house of the lord who owned the village (or that of his overseer if the lord did not himself live in the village) and the village church. There was also a blacksmith's shop and a mill, usually owned by the lord, where the peasants ground their grain into flour.

For centuries after the barbarian invasions, it was all the new inhabitants of western Europe could do to grow enough food to feed themselves. But the soil was rich and the climate good. Since they had heavy iron plows, they were able to cultivate the heavy soil of northern Europe. The heavy plow did not merely scratch the surface as had the plows of earlier peoples like the Egyptians, who lived where the soil was light. It dug a deep furrow and turned the soil. To do this, con-

This fifteenth-century picture shows peasants at work, while the lord of the manor is apparently making some comment on their progress. The medieval peasant not only had to cultivate the lord's farmlands; he had a number of other duties as well. The village herdsman looked after the lord's cattle and swine. The villagers had to fix his fences, repair his house, maintain the moat, and look after the roads. All in all, the peasant worked about three days a week for the lord, perhaps more often at seeding and harvest time. He also gave the lord some of his own crops. Often he had to use the lord's mill, winepress and ovens, and give him a share of his crop. The peasant usually paid in cheese for using the pasture, and in pigs for using the wasteland; for fishing in the lord's stream he gave the largest fish he caught. He also had to pay a fine if his daughter married outside the village or if his son became a monk or a priest, for the lord had then lost some of the labour force in the village. When the peasant died, his best, if not his only, cow was given to the lord, and his second-best animal to the Church. The Church also collected one-tenth of the peasant's crop each year.

250

siderable power was required. At first, eight oxen appear to have been needed, but by about 1100 four seem to have been enough. This reduction was made possible by improvements in the collars and harness. Later, the development of the horse collar and the horseshoe made possible the use of horse-power, which was twice as effective as ox-power.

These improvements in equipment or technology not only made the land more productive; they also explain why each peasant did not have his own small farm but worked strips in large fields shared by all the villagers. Since no peasant could afford a team of oxen, the job of plowing had to be shared. Furthermore, the longer the strip to be plowed without a turn, the better. As a result, strip farming in large fields was usual in most of western Europe. While the peasant's total holdings varied in size, thirty acres appears to have been normal, and was apparently enough to support a family.

Not all the village land was divided among the peasants or available for their use. In each of the three fields, about one-third of the strips were reserved for the lord. They were farmed by the peasants of the village, however, in return for their own strips. The village farmlands lay beyond the tiny settlement. About A.D. 800, the practice of dividing all the land of the manor into three fields began. By 1000 the three-field system was common in most of northwestern Europe. The three fields, in each of which a peasant would have one or more strips, were cultivated in rotation: one section would be sown with oats or barley in the spring, the second with wheat or rye in the fall, and the third would not be cultivated but would lie fallow. This was a great improvement over the two-field system, for it increased by one-third the acreage under cultivation.

Each village also had woodland, meadows and pastures. There were also wastelands, usually undrained marshes and swamps. Each villager had the right to use these lands for his wood, his cows and his pigs. Since hay from the meadow had to feed the plow teams over the winter, there was little left for the other animals, and most that

were not needed for breeding were killed every winter. The animals that survived the winter by remaining on the common pasture were apparently not the most appetizing, for one medieval writer declared that if he had to choose between the meat and the hide, he would eat the hide. The pig was by far the most important animal for food because he could look after himself, rooting around in the forest and wastelands.

By A.D. 1000 most medieval peasants were not free men. But neither were they slaves who could be bought and sold as in ancient Egypt, Greece and Rome. The majority were unfree men called *serfs*. The serf could not leave the land; nor could he marry the tenant of another lord without permission. If the manor or village was sold, so were the villagers, for the serf went with the land and neither he nor his land could be sold separately.

Although his lot was an unfortunate one in many ways, the serf could look forward to better things. Through hard work he could increase his holdings and even build up a surplus with which he could buy his freedom. There was swampland to be drained as the village expanded, and new fields or even new villages to be established. Some lords would offer serfs their freedom if they would agree to leave their village and open up new lands. Beyond the village, too, lay the growing towns. There a man could become free by escaping and living for a year and a day. But generally the peasants' life did not change very quickly, and few ever travelled more than a few miles from home.

By 1000, the medieval serfs, using the heavy plow and the three-field system, had increased the supply of agricultural produce. The lords could sell the surplus at a profit. They could then invest in trade or use their funds to buy new lands. A surplus of food made possible an increase in the population. More people were therefore available for trade, commerce and industry. An increased supply of food could also be used to feed a town population for the first time since the Romans had drawn on the rich granaries of Egypt and the Middle East to feed the people of their great cities.

A Peasant's Week*

The sun rose early, for it was late June, but not much earlier than the peasants of the village of Belcombe, in the year 1320. As the light strengthened, bit by bit the village became visible and the confused medley, in which here a roof and there a bit of wall stood out, began to arrange itself as a narrow street with flimsy houses dotted about in little groups. In the centre of it all the stone-built church loomed up high and very new-looking above everything about it, and made the peasants' houses appear small and insignificant. . . . Most of them [far less attractive than those in the 1515 painting opposite] had a rudely constructed shed or lean-to at the back of the house, and running away from this stretched another enclosed piece of ground. This was mainly broken up and planted with vegetables, and both here and in the rough grass beyond there were a few apple and cherry trees. At the bottom of the garden where it ran down to the stream the pigs had their styes, and any villager fortunate enough to own a cow tethered it there in among the rankly growing grass. Smaller houses had meagre plots about them, with sparse room for cabbage or onion, and only rarely a pig or a few fowls.

They soon passed by the church and came out into open country, for no hedges or fences were to be seen. One large tract, however, had clearly been cultivated recently, for as they passed they saw how it was divided into narrow plots, each with grassy raised strips dividing it from its neighbours. Now, however, this field was fallow, and, early as it was, one of their fellows was there before them, and was guarding the sheep which were quietly feeding on such sparse vegetation as was to be found, for the first ploughing had already taken place, and next month any weeds the sheep might leave would all be ploughed in.

Within most of these houses men were stirring, and before long began to appear at their cottage doors, taking a look at the sky before they ate a brief meal . . . a lump of bread and a draught of ale. Then they came out again, fetched their scythes and rakes from the sheds, and started off down the street, so that for a few minutes the noisy chatter and greetings of neighbours broke the silence.

A little farther on they . . . turned from the main path to follow a track which led to a piece of meadow land. This, unlike the fallow, was enclosed on three sides with a hedge, whilst a little stream formed its other boundary. On entering the field the peasants broke up in little groups, some going to one and some to another part of the meadow, for amongst the long grass there were little pegs and twigs marking off one portion of the field from another. By this time the sun was well up and the dew was drying rapidly as they prepared for work. The wide blade of the scythe was sharpened with the whetstone, and then they turned, and with rhythmic movement began to mow the grass in wide sweeping swathes.

In one corner of the field John Wilde and his two sons, Richard and Roger, kept to their task for some time without pause. The younger son moved steadily across the strip, turning the hay which

*This imaginative re-living of a few days in the life of a fourteenth-century English peasant has been adapted from pp. 4-25 of H. S. Bennett's, *Life on the English Manor,* Cambridge University Press, 1960. By permission of the publishers. The pictures are from medieval manuscripts.

had been cut on the previous morning, while his brother Richard worked on side by side with his father at the mowing. Save for a pause when the scythes were re-sharpened they worked without resting and with but little to say, for there was much to do and time was short, since this was Sunday, and ere long they would have to leave their work for Mass. . . .

During their absence the house had not been untended, and after a while the good wife Agnes and her daughter Alice appeared from a room which led out of the main living room. Alice ran out in the garden close, and soon the clucking of the hens was heard, and a little later she returned and set down on the wooden bench inside the door a rough earthen-ware jar of milk which she had just taken from the cow.

Meanwhile, her mother had brushed up the embers and piled together the kindling and a few logs, and already a fire was burning cleanly, and over it hung a large metal pot of water. Then she and her daughter went into the small inner room, which was cleaner and less sooty than its neighbour, and pulled back the thick coverlets and remade the only two beds that stood there. Once this was done, the rough earthen floors of both rooms were swept out with a brush of large twigs, and then the trestle-table

was put in its place near the side of the room. Some bread and a little ale satisfied Agnes' hunger, while Alice took a drink

of the milk she had just brought in. All being done, they turned to prepare for Mass. . . .

The next morning saw another early start, for John knew well the Lord Prior's officers would be on the look-out for late-comers [In this account the village was owned by a monastery; here the Prior was the second-in-command and responsible for managing the monastery's lands.]. . . . So John roused up the two boys, and Alice as well, for on these days every one, save the housewife, had to appear, and help with the lord's hay. As they started they soon met many neighbours: it was a far larger party

than that of yesterday, all making their way to the lord's great meadow (for on this manor all the Prior's pasture was in one immense field) which lay in the little valley to the west of the village, and through the midst of which the streamlet flowed so sweetly. Soon after they arrived they had been divided up into groups, and placed in different parts of the field by the reeve and the hayward [the Prior's officials], who bustled about from place to place to see that all was well and that work was beginning in good earnest.

254

. . . As the sun rose higher and higher the blades swung to and fro, while up and down the field moved a man, with a stave in his hand, whose duty it was to oversee the workers. John looked at him as he passed, recalling his own early days, and how often he and the father of this man who now stood over him had worked together in this very meadow, for they had been partners, or "marrows," as the country people termed it, and so did whatever was possible to help one another. But, in his old age, his friend had bought his freedom at a great price, for he had paid to the Lord Prior six marks [pieces] of silver, the savings of a lifetime, and as much as the yearly income of Sir William, the vicar, himself. Now, therefore, his son was free of everything except a few small services from time to time, of which this was one.

The workers paused to sharpen their scythes, or for a momentary rest, . . . or while some careless fellow, who was working in a lazy or incompetent fashion, was soundly berated by the hayward. At other moments, again, there was a most welcome respite, for this was fortunately a "wet boon," and old Alice atte Mere, who had only a tiny cot on the edge of the village, held it [in return for] . . . carrying ale to the workers at these boons. Hence, she was continuously going to and fro from the manor house for reinforcements of ale which the thirsty labourers seemed to consume almost as soon as it was doled out to them. . . . Steadily the work went on till well-nigh noon, when at last the hayward's horn was heard. John straightened himself, and made for the shade with his companions. There they threw themselves down, and soon the manor servants appeared, some carrying great loaves and cheeses, while others brought the ever-welcome barrels of ale. John and his family were given four of the loaves for themselves, and as they cut them open they saw that these were the good wheaten loaves, which so seldom came their way. They ate ravenously of these and of the cheese after their six hours in the open air, and called again and again for ale, of which there was no stint. . . .

Steadily the work went on, and from time to time the now tiring mowers looked at the sky, and watched the slow course of the sun over the big trees which bordered the field. The girls and women busied themselves in raking and turning the first cut hay, while the officials were moving busily from place to place trying to keep the workers at their tasks. At last the long-awaited sound of the hayward's horn was heard, and in a few minutes the field was deserted, and old and young were making their way and chattering together as they went towards the manor house. The toil of the day was over, and all that remained was the good evening meal that the Lord Prior always gave them as a reward for their labours. . . . Each group tackled the portion set down before them with eagerness, and with many a call to a friend here and a joke with a neighbour at another table, the meal wore on. Ale flowed liberally, and there was "cheese at call" for those who were still hungry.

When some of the women showed signs of wishing to leave, the hayward blew his horn for silence, and the reeve announced that if the weather remained fine there would be two more boons on the Wednesday and the following Monday, and by then he hoped all the hay would be cut and carried into the great manor courtyard. Little by little the company dispersed, most of them ready enough to get home and do whatever was necessary about the house before they went to bed. John and his family walked back together, and saw as they passed their own meadow that Agnes had been at work during the day. The hay that was dry had been raked up into small cocks, and she had turned most of that which had only been cut the previous morning.

Much of their time in the next few days was spent by the peasants either on the lord's hayfield or on their own. John had but little more to cut on his allotted portion, and all was done by the Wednesday evening. The following Friday he and his boys spent the afternoon in loading it onto a wagon they borrowed from a friend. Roget the ox pulled it home, and they stored it away in the little shed behind the house.

What little time John and his sons had from the haymaking seemed to go all too rapidly in a variety of tasks. The work which he had promised to do in the east field with his neighbours took up the Thursday afternoon, and besides this they were hard at work on an "assart" or clearing they were making near the edge of the great wood. The prior had granted this to John only the previous autumn; and, although it was but three acres in extent, the work of grubbing up [digging]

the furze and briars and cleaning the land so that they could sow it this coming autumn seemed endless. Richard spent all the time he could at this, for he hoped one day to make this plot the site of a home for himself, since he was now fully grown and eager to marry Johanna, the daughter of William Sutton, an old friend of his father.

The other two days of work on the lord's meadow passed much like the first, except that there was no ale provided at the second boon, for it was a "dry-reap," but they had to work only till midday. The last boon, however, surpassed all the rest, for not only was there ale again, but other pleasures as well. As the last load was carried from the field the hayward loosed a sheep in their midst. All watched this poor frightened beast with interest, for if it remained quietly grazing they could claim it for a feast of their own, but if it wandered out of the field they lost it, and it remained the lord's property. As they looked on, restraining the children from noise or sudden movement, the sheep gazed around and then began to eat what it could find. . . .

[The next day John went to the Manor Court.] John left the Court with his sons who soon joined their own friends and set off homewards. He, however, made a roundabout circuit so as to pass by the great west field, for he was anxious to see how things were coming on, for the whole week past had been so taken up with haymaking and work elsewhere that he had had no time even to do an hour's work there. As he came round by the field his eye rapidly moved from strip to strip and he saw there was much to be done. St. John's Day was already past, so they must set to work at once at the weeding, he thought, and he determined to spend the rest of the day at this. For a few minutes before turning homeward to his midday meal he sat down and looked across the great field at the village as it straggled over the neighbouring slope — a familiar sight, but dearer to him than any other place on earth. There stood the church, clean and white in the midday sun, and there a few hundred yards to the right his own little house and its narrow close which, with his land in the common fields, represented all he had in the world.

It seemed little enough, yet, he reflected, things might be worse. The last winter had been hard, and the death of his only cow had made life even harder. Now, however, his twenty-four half-acre pieces were all ploughed and planted with crops which promised well, but everyone knew that twelve acres was none too much, if more than the barest existence was hoped for. Last year the crops had been poor, and for several months food had been scarce, so that many of his neighbours had been half starved, and nearly everyone in the village was forced to live on victuals lacking in flavour or variety. The oats had been their salvation: with oatcake and porridge, and with the bread they had made from a mixed corn of barley and rye they had been able to hold off the worst pangs of hunger; but for weeks on end no meat or flesh, except an occasional chicken or something snared by night in the Prior's woods, had come their way. Since then . . . summer had come and the hay crop had been a good one, and hope sprang up once again. . . .

John reflected sadly as to the end of all this, but what was to be done to stay it he could not tell. Life was so strange and in his fifty odd years he had seen ups and downs in the village. Some he had played with as a boy had stolen away by night, and had been heard of no more; some, like his wife's brother, had become priests, and were now important people; some, like his own brother, had lost their grip on life, and had become a byword in the village. But there it was, and each must abide his fate. As Sir William [the priest] had often told them, they were in the hand of God, and He and His holy angels would protect them all their days. Then, as he rose to go, the sound of the midday bell rang out clear over the fields. He crossed himself, and after repeating an *Ave,* went quickly to his own home.

THE MEDIEVAL TOWN

Trade and commerce had almost completely disappeared during the turmoil of the invasions. Towns had either vanished or shrunk in size. By A.D. 1000, however, there were many signs that trade and commerce was reviving and that old towns were growing or new ones were being formed. There were several reasons for the revival of trade. Feudalism brought increased law and order. Since their crops and flocks were no longer being destroyed by invaders or warring nobles, the people in many areas found that they could produce more goods than they needed for their own use. Some parts of Europe were particularly well suited for the large-scale production of special products which could be sold in other areas not suited to their production. For example, in Flanders, or what is now Belgium, Flemish weavers had become expert in making woollen cloth. This cloth soon became popular in many parts of Europe. Britain, on the other hand, found that she could produce a surplus of raw wool. Since Flemish weavers needed raw wool to weave into cloth, there grew up a flourishing trade between Britain and Flanders. French wines, German timber and iron, and Scandinavian furs were also in demand in other parts of Europe. Slowly, by land, sea and river, merchants began carrying these products of the new society in the west from one area to another.

Throughout Europe, towns and small cities grew rapidly to handle this local trade. Feudal nobles had created some towns, often on the sites of old Roman cities which had declined or been destroyed. These towns were little more than walled fortresses, with the townsmen serving as a permanent garrison. Since these strongholds provided more security than unwalled villages, it was natural for them to become centres of trade and commerce. Often towns sprung up near a feudal castle or a cathedral. Since travel by land was difficult, they were usually located on a river or by a good harbour. As European merchants travelled from town to town, there developed a number of definite trade routes. Among the best

The town of Carcassonne in southwestern France is the best existing example of a medieval walled town. Although it was rebuilt during the nineteenth century, its general appearance today is probably very similar to the way it looked centuries ago. Most of the inner wall was built during the eleventh and twelfth centuries, but parts date as far back as the sixth. The outer wall, built during the late thirteenth century, shows how medieval towns expanded to contain a growing population. By 1304, Carcassonne had a population of about 9500. In many respects it was not a typical medieval town, for there were only forty-two merchants. There were, however, a number of professional groups which included sixty-three notaries, fifteen advocates, nine doctors, nine priests, and 250 other members of the clergy. The city also contained forty-three noble households.

known and most important was the route from Italy to Flanders. Throughout western and southern Europe, by 1100, there seemed to be a town with a few hundred or a few thousand people every twenty or thirty miles along the route.

259

As the population of these towns grew, many people had to settle outside the original town wall, which often had been rebuilt on the foundations of old Roman walls. As a result, the walls had to be extended to contain the new settlement. Time and again during the Middle Ages, this expansion was repeated, so that many medieval cities had rings of encircling walls. Often, the merchants' marketplace became the centre of the new quarter of the town, and eventually the centre of the entire town. As time passed, the towns tried to buy their freedom from the feudal lord or king, who owned the land. Most of the towns concerned with this trade within Europe were small. There were some large cities, however, like London, Marseilles and Venice, which had grown because of their participation in overseas trade.

The small cities in Italy had played an important part in stimulating this distant trade. The city of Venice, for example, had been founded in 570 by people trying to escape from the barbarians. Since their coastal city had no agricultural land, the Venetians were forced to

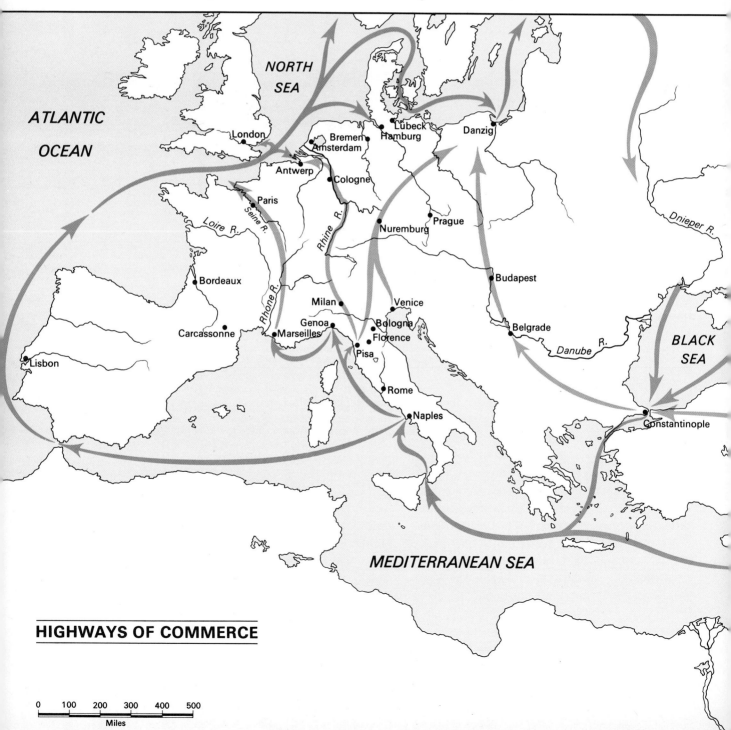

HIGHWAYS OF COMMERCE

0 100 200 300 400 500
Miles

make their living on the sea. Gradually, Venetian sailors began to trade along the Mediterranean coasts and revived trade in the whole Mediterranean region. By the year 1000, the cities of Venice, Genoa and Pisa had built fleets strong enough to defeat the Moslems and make the Mediterranean safe for their commerce. Thus, the merchants of the Italian cities became the "middlemen" in the trade between east and west.

During the eleventh century the Crusades stimulated the development of trade with the Near East. The Italian cities played a leading role in supplying the ships and equipment for the Crusading armies. Finally, when the Crusaders captured eastern cities, the way was opened for much greater trade between the eastern Mediterranean and Europe. Since these eastern cities had developed a trade along caravan routes with China, Chinese goods were soon to be seen in the castles of medieval kings and nobles. Before the Middle Ages drew to a close, western traders were **visiting the fabulous court of the mongol rulers, Genghis and Kublai Khan.**

Most of the thousands of new European towns

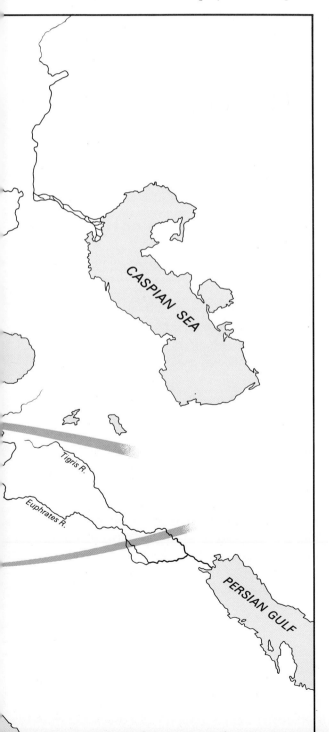

Although Paris was founded in Roman times, it expanded greatly during the Middle Ages. Located on the River Seine, it was favourably situated for trade. In this view from a fifteenth-century illuminated manuscript, we see part of the island of the city, the protecting walls, the courts of justice and the royal chapel. On the left bank of the river, where the peasants are seen cutting and raking hay, thousands of modern Parisians pursue a busy, urban life.

261

created in the Middle Ages took no direct part in the distant trade and remained small. Paris, with 100,000 people by 1200 and more than 200,000 a hundred years later, was one exception. And the rich Italian cities, Venice, Milan and Florence, could boast of populations of 100,000, while the population of London was about half that. Most medieval towns, however, contained about 5000 people. Although northern Italy, like ancient Greece, was almost completely composed of city-states, only about ten per cent of medieval people were townsmen. In England, France and Germany, cities were the exception, isolated little islands of urban life amid a great sea of villages, manors, forests, swamps and wasteland.

The centre of the medieval town or city was the church. So important was the church in the lives of the people that its construction usually involved the entire community. Often it took several hundred years to complete such magnificent cathedrals as Chartres or Notre Dame. The church was more than a place of worship. It was also a kind of community centre in which the people took great pride and in which they gathered for most events. The church served as a dining hall for a festival or as a theatre for a play.

The town marketplace was usually located near the church. Because the church was the centre of town, it was natural that, when possible, the marketplace should grow up as close to it as possible. Sometimes the market was simply a widened street or a number of widened streets. In other cities it was a square, with stores and stalls and workshops opening off it, and with a large central plaza where festivals, pageants and plays could be held. It was here that the citizens gathered to watch the punishment and execution of criminals and heretics.

The highlight of town life was the fair or the market. Most towns had market days once or twice a week. Then the farmers came to town and exchanged their goods with those of the townsmen. The larger cities had great international fairs several times a year. During the week of the fair the city would attract merchants from all over Europe. Many merchants moved from fair to

The illustration above shows market day in a medieval village. In this medieval illustration, the dominant figure is the priest, seen blessing the proceedings, surrounded by the little booths or stalls of the merchants. In the foreground, a peasant peacefully watches his flock grazing.

fair during the good travelling months, carrying the produce of east and west, north and south. In the stalls and booths could be seen British wool, Flemish and Italian textiles, armour and jewelry, religious objects for the churches and cathedrals, and even spices and silks from Asia. Minstrels and entertainers were always on hand to entertain the throngs. When the fair was over, the stalls and booths came down, the merchants departed for the next fair on the route, and the town settled down to its normal life.

Until about 1250 the most important fairs in Europe were those held in the Duchy of Champagne in France. Not only was Champagne on the main trade route between Italy and Flanders, but the counts of Champagne realized how profitable

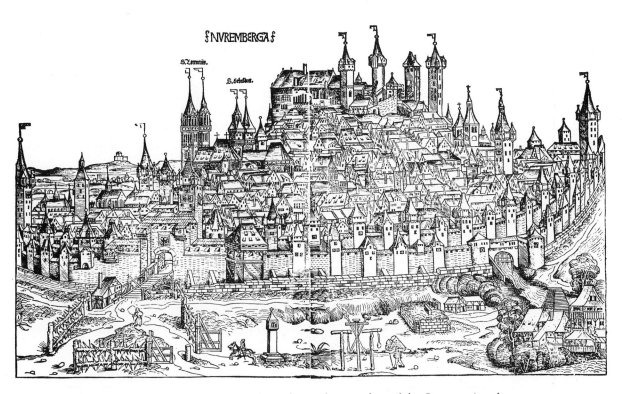

S. NVREMBERGA. S

S. Lorentis.

S. Sebaldus.

This woodcut of the German city of
Nuremberg in the fifteenth century shows
the protecting moat and turreted walls,
as well as two gates to provide entrances
to the city. Atop the hill, overlooking the
city, stands the imperial castle. Traders and
artisans lived crowded together in the
many-storeyed houses and carried on their
affairs in the city's narrow streets. The
illustration suggests the growth, vitality and
variety of the late medieval city.

fairs could be. As a result they held a number of
fairs—usually six a year. The counts rented
booths and stalls to the merchants, made sure
there were money-lenders and money-changers
and guaranteed protection to the merchants during the fair. They also forced their own vassals to
ensure merchants a safe passage on the way to the
fairs and persuaded other nobles to do the same.
Buyers and sellers from all over Europe attended
the fairs. The buyers took back goods to sell at
their local fairs or markets, or even at another
international fair closer to home.

By 1250 the fairs of Champagne were losing
their dominant position. The counts of Champagne had been wise enough to know that if the
taxes on the merchants or the rents for stalls
were too high, the merchants would not come.
But when the King of France took control of
Champagne, he rapidly increased taxes and rents.
More important, a number of young and vigorous cities—Lübeck, Bremen, Cologne, Hamburg,
Danzig — had grown up in northern Germany.
These cities banded together in the thirteenth
century to form the *Hanseatic League* to strength-
en their trade. This League of trading towns drew
up rules for cooperation among themselves, and
persuaded other cities to grant their traders favourable treatment. They also built permanent
warehouses in such cities as London, and maintained warships for protection against pirates.
By the late Middle Ages they had an army strong
enough to protect themselves. With their army
they were also able to force feudal nobles and
even kings to grant them favourable trading
terms. As the German cities came to dominate the
trade routes of northern Europe, the route from

263

Italy to the north moved east. This meant that Champagne was no longer on the main trade route. Soon after the close of the Middle Ages, the discovery of sea routes to the Far East and the Americas shifted the main trading centres to the ports on the Atlantic. The German and Italian cities then fell rapidly into second place behind such centres as Amsterdam and London.

The streets in medieval towns and cities were little more than alleys. Usually between six and ten feet wide, they were built for pedestrians. Many of them would not even permit the passage of a small cart. Such streets can still be followed by the tourist in the older sections of many European cities, twisting and turning and frequently leading to a dead end. By 1200 Paris had begun to pave its main streets, and by 1400 paved streets were common in most of the major European cities.

Along the streets were the homes and shops of the medieval townsmen. Indeed shops and homes were often not separate, for artisans and shopkeepers lived and worked in their homes. At first the houses were two-, sometimes three-storeys high. But as the city population grew and as land became more expensive, they often stretched up to five or six storeys, with the upper storeys dangling precariously over the street. Houses were not built within a yard, but in a solid block along the street. Often there were gardens or courts in the rear. In fact, many townsmen had small gardens and kept pigs or chickens. But once again, as property became more expensive, the gardens gave way to new buildings. The pig, however, remained the most effective garbage collector throughout the Middle Ages. Since litter and refuse were usually just dumped in the street to be cleaned up perhaps once a week, the pig was a most valuable member of the community.

The houses and shops were built of whatever materials were handy. Sometimes they were built of stone or brick, but frequently of little more than mud. Fire was a constant hazard because of open hearths in the middle of the floors, fireplaces with poor chimneys (sometimes made of wood), and highly inflammable thatched roofs.

Life in a medieval town

A merchant watches while medieval craftsmen dye his bolts of cloth in a huge vat.

Glass blowers, like those shown in this drawing from Bohemia, needed special training. The illustration shows the phases of glass-making.

Using his simple tools, a cabinetmaker
works on a chest.

An armourer puts the finishing touches
on a piece for a suit of armour.

A medieval craftsman fashions a spur.

A shoemaker plies his trade.

A guild master judges the work of a
carpenter and a stonemason.

Town and countryside were not very distinct
in medieval Europe.

Life in the Middle Ages was not all work
as this tavern scene reveals.

The fashionable dress of these medieval
townsmen suggests the growing wealth
and importance of the middle-class merchant
in medieval society. The picture also
provides a good illustration of street life
in the town.

Bucket brigades were not very effective; thus many cities passed laws demanding fireproof roofing. Nevertheless, large parts of many medieval towns burned down more than once within one man's lifetime. The homes were small. Those of more prosperous townsmen had a number of bedrooms, but poorer families were often confined to the same room. Until the end of the Middle Ages, glass was too expensive for use in any but public buildings or the homes of the very rich. The windows had shutters, with oilcloth or paper covering.

Merchants engaged in trade were only one group of townsmen. Four-fifths of the inhabitants were involved in the production of goods. In the fourteenth century, a city like Florence, for example, had 1500 merchants and 30,000 workers in the 200 textile shops. Florence also had 1500 nobles, eight to ten thousand children, 110 churches, eighty money-changers and sixty doctors.

The lives of merchants and artisans or workers were controlled to a large extent by their membership in a *guild*. The guild was not unlike a modern trade union. There was a merchant guild which regulated the conditions of trade in the city. There were also guilds of bakers, butchers, weavers and dye-makers. Indeed, every commercial or manufacturing enterprise had its guild. The guild decided on the hours and conditions of work, and set prices for anything that was sold. An artisan who sold his goods at a higher price, or who sold goods of a poor quality would be fined and forced to spend some time in the stocks in the marketplace.

The guild also regulated the numbers that could be engaged in any trade. A young boy would be apprenticed to a master craftsman, working in his house for from two to seven years and learning the trade or business from him. He then became a *journeyman,* remaining in the household, but working for wages. When he had completely mastered the craft, he could present his *masterpiece,* an example of his work. If it was acceptable, he would become a master craftsman. He would then be permitted to set up his own

shop. Many artisans could not save enough money to establish their own businesses and remained in someone else's employ throughout their lives. Like some modern unions the guilds also provided special services for their members. They cared for the widows and children of members who died. Often they established schools for children of their members.

In time, the guilds became a barrier to further economic development. Often they became monopolies, that is, they controlled all of one trade and refused to allow others to engage in it. Frequently they opposed the introduction of new methods or ideas. But for most of the Middle Ages they played an important role in organizing the new economic and social life of the medieval townsman.

Like all land, most towns were part of the feudal system and were originally owned by kings or nobles. But the towns could not fit into the feudal system and function properly as trading centres at the same time. A merchant could not carry on his business satisfactorily if he might be summoned to serve as a knight when his lord went to war. An artisan could hardly live by the same rules and regulations that were acceptable for the village peasant. What the townsman needed was freedom: freedom to work, to own and sell his own property, to establish courts to settle the problems that came up in trade and commerce, to move about as he wished.

Thus every town struggled to be free and to secure personal freedom for its citizens. Some towns, particularly in Italy, were strong enough to revolt and become independent city-states. In most places, however, the townsmen bought a *charter* from the king or lord. The charter would declare that the residents of the towns were personally free. They then became a new class of people, who were neither nobles nor serfs, but a new group known as *burghers* or the *bourgeoisie,* from the word *burgh* meaning town. This class was to have a tremendous influence on European history. The charter permitted the town to develop its own form of government. By and large it could regulate its own affairs. The governing body in most towns was a council, made up largely of the wealthier merchants, or of nobles who had moved to the city. Often there were serious conflicts between rival groups of nobles and merchants within the town as they fought to control the council. Sometimes the struggles were between the wealthy, who governed, and the poor, who had little voice in government. Over the next few centuries it was to be in the towns that the pressure for greater democracy appeared. And it was to be the bourgeoisie (sometimes called the middle class) who pressed the nobility and the kings to share with them power within the country.

Politically then, the medieval town was an organization that helped to weaken the feudal system and to bring the medieval world closer to the modern. The same was true economically.

The feudal world was based on land and military service; the town came to be based on money or *capital,* and was the home of capitalism. The peasant (unless he escaped to the town) and the noble were born to their rank and position in life. The townsman, on the other hand, was a free man. Hard work or luck could bring him fame and fortune. And long before the Middle Ages had ended, the manufacturers, the merchants and the bankers of the medieval towns rivalled feudal nobles, princes and even kings in wealth. Better educated than the feudal nobles, they increasingly became officials in government. The feudal noble had done much to create the world of the Middle Ages out of the wreckage of the Roman world. The townsman was to do even more to shape the early modern world out of the Middle Ages.

Towards a new world: 1300-1450

No age in history comes to a sudden end, like the city of Pompeii when Vesuvius erupted, with another ready to take its place immediately. Even the "fall" of Rome took several centuries. And it was centuries after the final collapse of the Roman Empire before medieval European civilization came into being. So it was with the passing of the Middle Ages. Looking back, we can see that by 1300 there were signs that the medieval world was changing. The signs multiplied throughout the fourteenth century. By 1450 the Middle Ages had largely passed in western Europe, though many features of medieval life have lingered on, almost to the present in some areas. By 1450 we can begin to speak of the early modern world.

The 300 years before 1300 were years of great expansion. Wherever we look — at agriculture, population, trade and industry, towns—there are clear signs of growth and prosperity during this period. Europe also expanded its frontiers. Through trade, new lands were opened beyond the old borders. Conversion to Christianity brought Hungarians, Poles and Scandinavians into the civilization of the West. The Church was reformed and took on a new and more vigorous life. Europeans not only created new towns and cities; they also established schools and universities and built magnificent monasteries and cathedrals. They expanded their horizons in literature, art and architecture, and music.

About 1300 this expansion came to an end. Europe entered a time of troubles, during which much of the old way of life slowly changed. The following 150 years saw wars, unrest among the people, terrible divisions within the Church, famine and plagues, and a population that first

The Mongols were a group of tribes from Central Asia who were united during the twelfth and thirteenth centuries under a great ruler, Genghis Khan. Under a number of able leaders they ranged far and wide in an amazing march of conquest. They defeated the Turks, captured Palestine and conquered Northern China. By 1241, they had swept through what are now Poland and Hungary and devastated the whole of Silesia. It seemed that nothing could prevent them from overrunning all of the divided and weak lands of central and western Europe. Fortunately for the West, however, the death of their leader forced them to return to Mongolia to elect a new khan. This miniature painting, showing the Mongols attacking a fortified town in 1241, suggests something of their ferocity. Of a similar incident, one historian has written, "Princes, bishops, nuns and children were slain with savage cruelty. It is impossible to describe the barbarities that prolonged the death of the unfortunate inhabitants. None remained to weep or to tell the tale of disaster."

ceased to grow and then fell sharply. Geographic expansion also ended. In the northeast, the Russians in 1242 stopped the advance of the Teutonic knights. Soon afterwards, the Mongols threatened Europe itself. In the east, Jerusalem again fell to the Moslems in 1244, and by 1291 all the territories won by the Crusaders in the Holy Land had been lost. In Spain the Moslems also halted the Christian reconquest in 1263, and held their foothold in Europe for another two centuries.

A CHANGING SOCIETY

When European medieval society entered a time of difficulty about 1300, it was already undergoing a gradual change. This change was due in large part to the increasing use of money. As long as most people lived in a village or manor, there was little need for money. The village was largely self-sufficient, producing almost all the foods and goods it needed. Goods which had to be secured outside the village were few in number and could usually be bought and sold locally by exchanging one product for another. But the development of trade, commerce and town life brought with it a rapid increase in the use of money. The village and the feudal system had been based on service or duties, not on payments of money. The peasant worked the lord's fields and provided him with farm products in return for the right to live on his land. But as money came into increasing use in the economic life of medieval Europe, it replaced service and duties as the measure of what a peasant owed his lord, or a noble his king. Thus,

money had a great effect on all features of economic, social and political life.

Very early the medieval kings found it preferable to hire troops rather than to rely completely on the services of their vassals to fight their wars. Many vassals preferred to pay scutage for a least part of the military obligations they owed the king or their lord. As money became more common, this practice increased. This change in the relationship between lord and vassal occurred at

At the Battle of Crécy in 1346, (below left) the great range and power of the English longbow was shown. As the French knights advanced against the English lines, they were met by a hail of death-dealing arrows The heavy armour of the French knights provided little protection, for the arrows of the English yeomen pierced all but the heaviest plate. By the day's end, the field was littered with the cream of the French army, many of them dead or wounded and others, their horses shot out from under them, lying helpless in their armour. The French dead were one sign that the dominance of the mounted knight was passing. The cannon in the illustration (below) of the siege of a walled town was another. Gunpowder was brought to medieval Europe from China and was used during the later campaigns of the Hundred Years' War. At this time cannon were not very effective, but later improvements in firearms and artillery were finally to spell the doom of both the feudal knight and his castle, for neither could withstand the new weapons.

a time when the feudal knight ceased to be as important as he once was on the battlefield. When troops of English longbowmen slaughtered the French knights at Crécy in 1346 and later at Agincourt in 1415, a new day had dawned in warfare. The use of gunpowder and the development of the cannon further lessened the value of the mounted knight. And just as the noble became less important in war, he also became less important in government. Kings and princes preferred to rely on educated men from the new middle class as their advisers and civil servants. The nobles also remained as advisers to the king, but their influence became less and less.

Money changed the way of life on the manor in several ways. Lords had to secure a surplus from the manor to pay for their military obligations, and to buy the elegant clothes, manufactured goods and rare foods offered by medieval traders. Some landlords tried to concentrate on the production of crops for sale. Many were also prepared to sell or rent their lands for cash, or to sell the serf his freedom. All of them tried in one way or another to secure more money from the peasants. In this way they helped to bring on serious peasant unrest, and even rebellion, in the fourteenth century.

The towns also became increasingly dependent upon money. Long-distance trade required large sums of money or *capital,* as did the large-scale industries of the Italian cities, the German mines and the Flemish factories. Huge banking firms developed in Italy to finance trade and industry and to lend huge sums to kings and princes. While the Church opposed the lending of money at interest, rates of over 200 per cent on risky loans were not uncommon. The increasing importance of money also changed the guild system. The old, personal relationship of master, journeyman and apprentice often gave way to a relationship based on cash wages. Cities became the homes of wealthy men or *capitalists* who had made a fortune in trade, industry or agriculture. In the cities, as in the feudal castles and tiny villages, relationships between people became more impersonal and materialistic; that is, they were based not on personal loyal-

ties, duties and respect, but on money. The payment of wages in money was not new, but until this time it had not been the only, or most important, reward for work. With the establishment of money as the main basis of all work, the Western world was entering the modern age. It was also entering the age of *capitalism* in which large sums of money are necessary to engage in trade, industry and agriculture.

Surprisingly, all these economic changes in medieval life were hastened by a slowing down of economic growth that began about 1300. Instead of increasing, the population began to level off. Then in 1347, western Europe was struck by the Black Death. A bubonic plague carried by fleas on black rats, the Black Death came to Europe from the Near East. How it had first reached the eastern Mediterranean is unknown, but very likely the dread disease had come from China in the trading caravans that travelled the long overland route. At any rate, in 1347 Genoese trading ships carried the rats and the plague from the eastern Mediterranean to Genoa. From there it spread to other Italian cities. Other ships brought it to Marseilles in southern France. Highly infectious and incurable, the plague spread quickly in the crowded and unsanitary cities and towns, and then spread into the countryside. For three years it raged, surprisingly hitting hardest among the young and vigorous. The loss of life was immense. Some cities were almost wiped out, while many lost more than half their population. Estimates of losses in western Europe as a whole range from twenty to thirty-five per cent of the population. By 1350 the Black Death had been checked, but for more than a century afterwards there were minor epidemics.

The effects of the plague can easily be imagined. As the population fell, production of goods decreased and trade declined. Without markets in which to sell, merchants became bankrupt. Manufacturers and merchants could not repay their loans, and many bankers had to close their doors. On the other hand, the shortage of workers in town and country led to increased wages. The peasants found they could force their lords to sell

The horror of the Black Death, so called because of the dark patches on the skin in the early stages of the disease, can be well understood from this eyewitness report: "The pestilence seized especially the young and strong, commonly sparing the elderly and feeble. Scarcely any one ventured to touch the sick, and healthy persons shunned the precious possessions of the dead as infectious. People perfectly well one day were found dead on the next. . . ." So deadly was the disease that burial parties such as the one illustrated above were a very common sight throughout medieval Europe.

Although the disaster of the Black Death caused many Europeans to lose their faith and form strange religions to worship Satan, many more turned to God as they always had in times of trouble. Just as St. Gregory (seen in this painting) asked God for deliverance from evil, many medieval Europeans at the time of the plague would heartfully echo the familiar response of the Litany, "O Lord, deliver us!"

them their freedom. Free peasants moved openly into the towns, where wages were high, while serfs fled there secretly.

Naturally the landlords did everything they could to maintain their own position and prosperity. But their efforts to keep wages down made the peasants discontented. In England the breaking-point came when in 1378, 1379 and 1380 the King and Parliament introduced a poll tax (a tax to be paid by everyone, no matter how rich or poor) to raise money for the war against France. Although the tax was small, the poor English peasants were outraged. Led by Wat Tyler, an ex-soldier, they broke into an open rebellion in 1381. After burning manor records to destroy the evidence of their serfdom, they marched on London. Sympathizers inside the city opened the gates and the rebels ran wild, burning mansions, destroying government records, opening prisons and even beheading unpopular officials. The Londoners joined in the orgy of destruction, burning and looting.

The fourteen-year-old King, Richard II, met Tyler outside London and agreed to all his demands for the abolition of serfdom, the equality of all men and the division of Church lands among the people. But during the discussion one of the King's knights killed Tyler. In the confusion which followed, the King's soldiers surrounded the peasants and forced them to disband. Elsewhere in England, other fierce revolts broke out. Soon the government and landlords organized their forces, put down the rebels throughout England and executed many of their leaders. One of those executed was John Ball, a priest who had joined Tyler. Ball had roused the peasants by bitterly contrasting the conditions of the rich and the poor in England. "If we all came of the same mother and father, how can they say or prove that they are better than we, if it not be that they make us gain for them by our toil what they spend in their pride?" he asked. Such questions were on many minds.

In France an even more significant rebellion broke out in 1357 and 1358. The English had captured the King of France in 1356 during the Hun-dred Years' War, and they demanded a huge ransom for his release. To raise the money the King's son increased the taxes. These taxes sparked a revolt in Paris and a savage rebellion among the desperate, hungry and disease-ridden peasants of southwestern France. As in England, the peasants burned the manor houses and often murdered at sight their lords or his officials. But the French government soon regained control and cruelly put down the rebellion.

There was unrest not only in London and Paris, but in many other cities throughout Europe. In the last half of the fourteenth century there were numerous strikes, as the town workers tried to break the power of the wealthy merchants and the guilds to secure better wages and working conditions.

Both peasants and townsmen lost their struggle, for they were weak and disorganized. But although they had been defeated, their protests could not be completely ignored. No poll tax was levied again in medieval England. Serfdom was gradually ending in much of Europe. The power of guilds was declining. Moreover, the workers of town and country had found new allies, not only in each other but in some members of the Church who were beginning to be concerned about man's life in this world, as well as his preparations for the next.

THE DECLINE OF THE CHURCH

As the Middle Ages drew to a close, the Church declined in power and influence. The Church and the state again came into sharp conflict, but this time the Church was no match for the growing power of the feudal monarchies. Many Christians came to criticize the life of the pope and other leading Churchmen, who seemed to place wealth and power ahead of religious duties and spiritual leadership. Many people lost their respect and admiration for the Church when in 1409 three people claimed to be the pope. A large number of Christians also came to question some features of Church doctrine or beliefs, and began a movement which, after the close of the Middle Ages, led to the rise of Protestantism and a split within what had previously been a united Christian community.

The struggle between the Church and state began when the kings of France and England taxed the immensely rich lands of the Church. While churches in England and France had always sent enormous sums of money to Rome, they had never been taxed by the state. In 1296 Pope Boniface VIII issued a statement or bull, called *Clericos Laicos,* threatening to expel from the Church any ruler who dared to tax the clergy, or any Churchman who paid such taxes. Edward I of England replied that if the clergy did not pay he would seize their property. Philip the Fair of France refused to permit French churches to send gold or jewels to Rome. Faced with this determined opposition from both kings, the Pope changed his position. He declared that the monarchs could tax for purposes of defence in case of "dire need," leaving it to the state to determine what was "dire need."

Six years later, however, Pope Boniface issued another statement declaring that ". . . it is altogether necessary for every human being to be subject to the Roman pontiff [pope]." Philip replied by sending troops to arrest him. Boniface, an old man of eighty-six, died within a few weeks of his capture. Philip then used all his influence to secure the selection of a French pope who, when elected by the cardinals, decided to live in Avignon in France rather than in Rome.

The popes lived in Avignon until 1378. The splendour of their court was greater than that of any king. But many Europeans regarded the pope as little more than a captive of the king of France, and they no longer expected him to be their spiritual leader. Abuses in the Church mounted. Important positions in the Church were bought and sold. Officials in the Church gained positions for their relatives. A donation of money could usually buy an "indulgence" or pardon. The indulgence promised the purchaser an escape from punishment after death.

In 1378 a scandalous situation developed within the Church. The French group of cardinals elected one pope, who remained at Avignon. The other cardinals elected a different pope, who lived at Rome. In an attempt to end what was called the *Great Schism* or split, the cardinals met in 1409, deposed both popes, and elected a third. But neither of the previous popes accepted the decision. There were now three popes, each claiming to hold the keys of Saint Peter. By 1418, when the cardinals were finally able to agree on one pope, there were a great many Christians who began to

The almost constant warfare, as well as the terrible suffering brought by the plague, caused many Europeans to become fascinated with all kinds of strange and revolting practices. Among the most popular books of the time were the many that dealt with the "art of dying." A common theme in painting was the Danse Macabre, *the dance of death. In this French version of the dance, two corpses lead a noble and a bishop to the grave.*

question the authority of the Church and its claim to their support.

Troubled Christians tried to correct the worst abuses and weaknesses in the Church. Some declared that the Church was *all* Christians, and not just the clergy, as was often maintained. They held that a council representing all Christians could force the clergy, even the pope, to change their ways. One such reformer, the Englishman John Wycliffe, went further. He taught that the Church, with its priests, bishops and pope, was not necessary for salvation. Ordinary people, he said, could obtain salvation by reading the Bible themselves and following God's word. To make the Bible more readily available he translated it into English. Wycliffe's views were branded as heresy, but he won many followers in England, particularly among the poor. These followers were called *Lollards*. His views also influenced John Huss, a religious reformer in Germany, who eventually was burned at the stake as a heretic.

General Councils or meetings also made repeated attempts to reform the Church. One such Council held at Constance finally ended the Great Schism. The single Pope who was then elected agreed to reform the Church. But once in office, he dissolved the Council, ignored his promises and declared that the pope was supreme. Further Councils were held, and the tug of war between pope and Council continued. Although the pope generally won, the failure of the Church to reform itself meant that the criticism continued. Less than a century later, the criticism led to the movement which split Christendom into the Roman Catholic and Protestant faiths.

POETS AND PAINTERS

Signs that the Middle Ages was drawing to its close could be seen in the work of poets and painters of the fourteenth century. These men who worked with pen and brush were the forerunners of what we call the *Renaissance*. The word renaissance means re-birth, and is used to describe the brilliant flowering or development of Western art and literature in the fifteenth century. These were developments that marked the dawn of the modern world. In the poems and paintings of these men we can see a concern for humanity, that

John Huss (shown here being taken to the stake) was a Bohemian (Czech) religious reformer who lived from 1369 to 1415. Like many other Christians at the time, he was disturbed by evils within the Church. He denounced the luxurious and immoral lives of many high Churchmen, and on one occasion, contrasted Christ riding a donkey with the Pope riding a stallion with the people crowding to kiss his feet. Huss also condemned the misuse of indulgences, and defended some students of the University of Prague who had burned the papal bull of indulgence. At the Council of Constance, he was accused of teaching doctrines not in keeping with those of the Church. Although he denied the charges, he was condemned to be burned at the stake as a heretic. While at the stake, he recited the Litany, "O Christ, thou Son of the living God, have mercy upon me." After he had been burned, the earth around the spot was dug up so that none of his followers could recover his ashes as relics.

is, a concern for man as man. It is the same spirit that we noted in the art and literature of ancient Greece. Indeed, the Greek writings played an important part in the Renaissance. These writers and artists were laymen, not priests or monks, and they were concerned with life in this world, not in the next. Moreover, they wrote not in Latin, the language of the Church, but in the language of the people.

Standing like a giant at the head of this new movement was Dante Alighieri, who was born in 1265 and died in 1321. Dante, the son of a lawyer in Florence, was a member of a political group which was struggling for power in the city, and an opponent of the wealth and political power of the pope. Although he was a master of the Latin classics of ancient Rome, he wrote in his native Italian rather than in Latin. In his great masterpiece, the *Divine Comedy,* Dante is concerned with salvation. But he is also constantly inquiring into the nature of man and life. A central figure in the *Divine Comedy* is the Roman poet, Virgil, who stands for reason and freedom of thought.

This German woodcut of Venice in the fifteenth century gives a good idea of the appearance of the second richest and strongest of the Italian city-states. There were no protecting walls, no castles or fortified homes. Like many other Italian city-states, its wealth came mainly from trading, and the city could boast more than 3000 ships and 36,000 sailors. It was no wonder that the new culture should have developed in such Italian cities as Venice, Florence and Genoa, for in all of them were men of immense wealth. Many of these wealthy men became patrons or supporters of the arts, using their money to aid and encourage poets and artists of all kinds. The cities governed themselves, and although there was corruption in politics and strife among different groups within the cities, there was, at the same time, a sense of freedom in which new ideas could grow. It was in these cities, too, that the great classical books from Greece and Rome first made their appearance.

An even greater change from medieval writing can be seen in the work of Francesco Petrarch, born in 1304. Petrarch, who was a great admirer of the Greeks and Romans, collected and copied ancient manuscripts. Much of his writing was in Latin, but some was in Italian. His poems to his beloved Laura did not express the courtly love of the age of chivalry, but the real personal love he felt for her. They expressed his interest in man and the joy he felt for life in the real world. This concern with life in the real world rather than the next one is a feature of the modern age.

The work of Giovanni Boccaccio, a contemporary of Petrarch's was concerned only with everyday matters. His famous *Decameron* is a collection of tales told by ten people who have fled from plague-ridden Florence to the safety of a country villa. The stories ridicule the age of chivalry, criticize Churchmen and deal with people in their daily lives.

A similar theme was used by the Englishman, Geoffrey Chaucer, born in 1340. Chaucer was a civil servant who held important positions in the government. His *Canterbury Tales* is a collection of stories told by a band of pilgrims on their way to the shrine at Canterbury. Each pilgrim—a knight, a squire, a clerk, a monk, a sailor, a miller

This detail from The Massacre of the Innocents, *which Giotto painted for the Arena Chapel in Padua, reveals the immense power of his work. A real concern for the drama of the situation (such as was seldom seen in earlier medieval painting) is revealed as Herod's soldiers strike out at the child. Each face has its own particular expression, and the artist has captured the brutality and the suffering of the event. The bodies of dead children, which form the base, increase our sense of horror.*

and others—tells his own story. The stories give us an accurate and colourful picture of medieval life, and provide an opportunity for Chaucer to question, criticize, and poke fun at his society. Like many others, he was an open critic of the wealth and worldliness of the clergy; in one of his *Tales* he described the monk as follows:

> Full many a deyntee hors hadde he in stable
> And when he rood, men might his brydel her
> Ginglen in a whistling wynd as clear.

But the poor village priests stood much higher.

> But Cristes lore, and his apostles twelve
> He taught, but first he folwed it himseleve.

These extracts from the *Canterbury Tales* provide an excellent example of the English language as it had developed by the close of the Middle Ages. Latin was still the language of the Church and of written government records. Although French had become the language of the aristocracy after the Norman Conquest, the Anglo-Saxon inhabitants had continued to use their Germanic speech. However, a new language gradually emerged, with a German base, but strongly influenced by French and Danish. Many of our most common words—work, house, sing—are German; others—happy, ugly, get—are Danish; while yet others—beef (*boeuf*) and pork (*porc*)—are French. By the end of the Middle Ages, this new English language was not only the language of ordinary conversation, but of government and the law courts as well. In France, Italy and Germany a similar development took place in the development of languages. Only Italy and England, however, produced men of the stature of Chaucer, Boccaccio, Petrarch and Dante. Each of these men, writing in his own language, made lasting and magnificent contributions to Western civilization.

The movement towards a new age in painting can be seen in the work of Giotto di Bandone, born in Florence around 1266. Giotto was opposed to the view that poverty was good for the soul, and made a fortune from the paintings that were purchased by rich businessmen and the Church. Like most medieval artists, Giotto painted religious scenes. But his paintings were not like the rigid and lifeless works of earlier artists, such as can be seen on pp. 244 and 273, for example. He tried to reveal the faces of the people he painted, the human feelings of fear, sorrow or happiness he believed they had. He paid more attention than earlier artists to the form of the body, and to movement, although artists, like physicians, still knew very little about the way the body was built or worked.

Thus in painting as in literature, there was a growing concern for the individual human being and for humanity, although the subject matter was still largely religious.

EPILOGUE

Giotto and Dante, Petrarch and Chaucer, were the heralds of a new age. So too were the national monarchies of England and France, a divided and restless Church, and rich capitalists and striking workers. Historians cannot agree on when the Middle Ages ended and the early modern era began. But during the fourteenth century the change was clearly under way. And by the middle of the fifteenth century the Western world belonged more to the early modern period and less to the medieval. By 1450, the Western world was on the eve of the Renaissance, and the discovery of the Americas and a sea route to Asia. The rise of Protestantism, the final end of feudalism, battles between France, England and Germany and newer nations such as Spain, Portugal and Holland for the mastery of Europe and the world —all these were about to come. But that is another story.

ACKNOWLEDGEMENTS

The authors and publishers wish to express their appreciation to the following individuals for providing special and valuable assistance in the preparation of this book: Mr. W. G. G. Saywell, Department of East Asian Studies, University of Toronto, for writing the chapter, "The men of Han"; Professor Gary Smith, The College of Education, University of Toronto, for much of the research for the unit, "Rome: A State in Arms"; and Professor A. H. C. Ward, Department of East Asian Studies, University of Toronto, for the samples of Chinese calligraphy.

For their outstanding assistance in photo research and in making illustrations readily available, special thanks is also extended to René Faille, (*Photographie Giraudon*); Jim Fox and the staff of Magnum Photos Inc.; Mrs. Muriel O'Neil (American Heritage Publishing Company); Charles Rado and the staff of Rapho-Guillumette Pictures; Walter Shostal; and Homer A. Thompson, Field Director, Excavations of the Athenian Agora, The Institute of Advanced Study, Princeton.

Grateful acknowledgement is made to the following museums, agencies and individuals for providing the illustrative material reproduced on the pages listed:

Alison Frantz, 81, 83, 119

Courtesy of The American Museum of Natural History, 3, 5 (both), 7, 8, 9 (both), 10, 11 (top), 12, 13, 16, 18 (top)

American School of Classical Studies at Athens, 106, 108 (all), 109, 123 (bottom), 132 (top)

Art Museum, Princeton University, 133 (right)

Art Reference Bureau: Alinari, 143, 148, 165 (bottom), 179, 182; Anderson, 153, 157; Bruckmann, 120-1 (bottom)

Photograph Ashmolean Museum, Oxford, 97 (bottom)

The Bettmann Archive, 18 (bottom), 25 (top), 56, 76, 91 (bottom), 95 (top), 137 (right), 145, 147, 168, 188, 205, 208, 223, 231 (left), 255 (bottom), 270, 271 (left), 276

Bibliothèque Nationale, 190 (bottom, transparency courtesy of American Heritage Publishing Co.), 192 (left), 208 (top), 219 (top), 237, 243, 244, 245, 248, 262

Bibliothèque Royale de Belgique, 227 (bottom), 271 (right), 267

Bildarchiv Foto Marburg, 70, 150

Black Star: Beal, 87; 171, 178 (bottom)

Bodleian Library, Oxford, 134, 184, 189 (all), 193, 253 (left, permission courtesy Corpus Christi College; bottom right), 254, 256 (all)

Bradley Smith, 238

The British Museum, 14, 19, 90, 98, 99 (both), 102, 105 (top), 115 (top), 128 (both), 130 (top), 206, 210, 255 (top), 264 (both), 266 (upper left and right)

British Travel Association, 156

Caisse Nationale des Monuments Historiques, Archives Photographiques, Paris, 185, 275

Cincinnati Art Museum, 40-1 (all)

Culver Pictures, Inc., 110, 136

Deutschen Archaeologischen Institut, 151, 154, 155, 176 (top)

European Art Colour Slide Company, 135, 235 (right)

Freelance Photographers Guild, 59, 60-1, 64, 68, 75 (top)

French Government Tourist Office, 11 (bottom), 226 (top), 234 (right), 259

Giraudon, 161, 180, 181, 218, 219 (bottom), 226 (bottom left), 242, 261, 273 (top), cover illustration

Greek National Tourist Organization, 126 (top), 131 (bottom), 132

Hebrew University of Jerusalem (Beth Alpha Synagogue), 23

Hirmer Fotoarchiv München, 124 (top), 133 (bottom)

Italian Government Travel Office, 152, 164 (bottom), 170, 171 (top), 178 (right), 187 (top), 209 (bottom), 227 (lower left), 230

Magnum Photo Library, 27, 62, 63; Erwitt, 66; Haas, 72 (all), 73 (left); 86 (top), 111, 120 (top), 129, 130 (bottom), 163, 191; Kertesz, 226 (right top and bottom), 227 (top left and right)

The Mansell Collection, 165 (top), 174 (all), 175 (top and bottom)

The Metropolitan Museum of Art, New York, 65 (right), 91 (top, Fletcher Fund, 1956), 95 (bottom, Rogers Fund, 1941), 100 (top, Purchase, 1947 Joseph Pulitzer Bequest), 101 (top, Rogers Fund, 1921; bottom, Walter C. Baker Gift Fund, 1956), 103 (bottom, Rogers Fund, 1917), 105 (right, Rogers Fund, 1941), 117 (bottom, Rogers Fund, 1906), 124 (middle, Rogers Fund, 1941), 131 (top, Rogers Fund, 1907), 207 (Gift of Bashford Dean, 1923), 209 (top), 241 (Gift of J. Pierpont-Morgan, 1917), 273 (Cloister Collection, 1954), 277 (Rogers Fund, 1919)

Courtesy, Museum of Fine Arts, Boston, 34, 36, 48, 50-1 (all), 52-3, 54, 55, 100 (bottom), 103 (top)

Museum Sparta: Courtesy American Heritage Publishing Company, 117 (left)

Courtesy of the Oriental Institute, University of Chicago, 21 (all), 115 (bottom), 116 (bottom)

Phaidon Press, 212-13 (all, photographs courtesy Victoria & Albert Museum)

Philip Gendreau, 22, 25 (bottom), 28, 29, 80, 82, 118, 126 (bottom), 137 (left), 159, 162, 171 (middle left and bottom)

Pierpont Morgan Library, 217, 221, 228 (right), 231 (right three, from the University Library of Freiburg-in-Breisgau), 234 (left), 250, 252, 253 (top), 254 (right), 257 (bottom), 258 (top), 266 (bottom left)

Radio Times Hulton Picture Library, 24, 190 (top)

Rapho-Guillumette, 67, 97 (top), 114, 167, 172, 176 (bottom), 178 (top left), 197; Belzeaux-Zodiaque, 235 (left), 236; Brihat, 187 (bottom); Cash, 186; Goldman, 233; Silberstein, 138; Johnson, 236 (right); Von Matt, 140, 142, 164 (top), 192 (right), 224-5 (all), 228 (top)

Royal Ontario Museum, University of Toronto, 30, 32, 33, 35, 45, 49, 96

Scala, 278

Shostal, 69, 71, 74, 78-9, 86 (bottom), 92-3, 122 (top), 123 (top), 125, 127, 131 (centre), 194, 195 (both), 203, 246

Staatliche Museen, Berlin, 89, 104-5, 122 (bottom)

Stadbibliothek Nürnberg, 263 (photo courtesy The Metropolitan Museum of Art, New York), 265 (all)

Trinity College Library, Cambridge, 228 (bottom left), 254 (bottom left), 257 (top), 258 (bottom)

United Arab Republic, 75 (bottom)

Universitetets Oldsaksamling, Oslo, (in collection of Historical Services), 204

Vatican Museum, 175 (centre)

Wadsworth Athaneum, Hartford, Conn., 112

West Point Museum Collections, 215 (all)

William Rockhill Nelson Gallery of Art, Kansas City, Mo., 38, 42, 43, 47

Every effort has been made to acknowledge correctly the source of illustrations reproduced in this book. The publishers welcome any information which will enable them to rectify, in subsequent editions, any errors or omissions which may have been made in giving a credit line.

PRONUNCIATION GUIDE

STRESSED SYLLABLES ARE IN CAPITALS

acropolis (uh.KROP.uh.lis)
Aegean (i.JEE.uhn)
Aeneas (i.NEE.uhs)
Aeneid (i.NEE.id)
Aeschylus (EES.ki.luhs)
Agamemnon (a.guh.MEM.non)
agora (A.guh.ruh)
Amenhotep (a.men.HOH.tep)
Amon (AY.muhn)
Amorite (AM.uhr.yt)
Antioch (AN.tee.ok)
Aphrodite (a.fruh.DY.tee)
Appian (A. pee. uhn)
archaeology (ar.kee.O.luh.jee)
Ares (A.reez)
Aristophanes (a.ris.TOF.uh.neez)
Artemis (AR.tuh.mis)
Assisi (a.SEE.zee)
Assyria (a.SEE.ree.uh)
Athena (a.THEE.na)
Attica (A.ti.kuh)
Augustine (AW.guhs.teen)

Bithynia (bi.THI.nee.uh)
Bohemond (BOH.huh.mond)
Bologna (buh.LOH.nuh)
brontosaurus (bron.tuh.SOH.ruhs)
Buddha (BOO.duh)

Canaan (KAY.nuhn)
Cannae (KAN.y)
Canossa (kuh.NO.suh)
Capetian (kuh.PEE.shun)
Carcassonne (kar.ka.SOHN)
Carthage (KAR.thij)
Cato (KAY.toh)
Cecrops (SEE.krops)
Celt (SELT)
Chaldea (kal.DEE.uh)
Charlemagne (SHAR.luh.mayn)
Chartres (SHAR.truh)
Charybdis (kuhr.IB.dis)
chevalier (shuh.val.YAY)
Cilicia (si.LI.see.uh)
Cistercians (sis.TUR.shuhnz)
Claudius (KLO.dee.uhs)
Cleisthenes (KLEIS.thi.neez)
Clermont (kler.MOHN)
Clovis (KLOH.vis)
Cluny (KLOO.nee)
Colosseum (ko.luh.SEE.uhm)
Columba (ko.LUHM.ba)
Confucius (kuhn.FYOO.shuhs)
Constantine (KON.stuhn.teen)
Corfu (KOHR.foo)
Corpus Iuris Civi.lis)
   (KOHR.puhs YOO.ris si.VI.lis)
Crete (KREET)
Croesus (KREE.suhs)
Cro-Magnon (kroh - MAG.non)
Cyclops (SY.klops)
Cyrus (SY.ruhs)

Dacia (DAY.shuh)
Dante Alighieri (DAHN.tay a.leeg.YAY.ree)
Decameron (di.KA.muhr.uhn)
Delphi (DEL.fee)
Demeter (di.MEE.tuhr)
Democritus (di.MOK.ri.tuhs)
Diocletian (DY.uh.KLEE.shuhn)
Dionysius (dy.uh.NEE.shuhs)

Epidaurus (e.pee.DOH.ruhs)
ephor (E.fuhr)
equites (E.kwi.teez)
Erechtheus (ee.REK.thuhs)

Etruscan (i.TRUH.skuhn)
Euphrates (yoo.FRAY.teez)
Euripides (yoo.RI.pi.deez)

fealty (FEE.al.tee)
feudalism (FYOO.duh.li.zm)
fief (FEEF)
Forum (FOH.ruhm)

Galatia (ga.LAY.shuh)
Giotto (JAWT.to)
Gizeh (GEE.zuh)
Gracchi (GRA.kee)

Hammurabi (ham.moor.A.bee)
Hegira (he.JEE.ruh)
helot (HEL.ot)
Hephaestus (hee.FE.stuhs)
Herodotus (he.RAW.duh.tuhs)
Hesiod (HEE.see.uhd)
hieroglyphic (hy.ruh.GLI.fik)
Hippocrates (hi.PAW.kruh.teez)
Hittite (HI.tyt)
hominid (HO.mi.nid)
hoplite (HOP.lyt)
Hyksos (HIK.sos)

Ikhnaton (ik.NAH.tuhn)
Iscariot (is.KA.ree.uht)
Isis (EI.sis)
Islam (IS.luhm)
Issus (I.suhs)

Judaea (joo.DEE.uh)

Knossos (NAW.suhs)
Koran (KOHR.an)
Kublai Khan (Koo.bly KAHN)

Lacedaemon (la.suh. DEE.muhn)
Laertes (lay.UR.teez)
Lagash (LAY.gash)
Leonidas (lee.OH.ni.duhs)
Lepidus (LE.pi.duhs)
Lubeck (LOO.bek)

Magyars (MAG.yahrz)
Manchu (MAN.choo)
maniple (MAN.i.pl)
Marathon (MAR.uh.thown)
Marius (MA.ree.uhs)
Menander (mi.NAN.duhr)
Menelaus (me.nuh.LAY.uhss)
Mesopotamia (me.suh.puh.TAY.mee.uh)
Messana (muh.SA.nuh)
Miletus (my.LEE.tuhs)
Miltiades (mil.TY.uh.deez)
Minos (MY.nos)
Minotaur (MI.nuh.tohr)
Mohammed (moh.HA.mid)
Mohenjo-Daro (moh.HEN.joh - DAH.roh)
Moslem (MOZ.luhm)
Mycenae (my.SEE.nee)

Neanderthal (nee.AN.duhr.tahl)
Neolithic (nee.oh.LI.thik)
Nicaea (ny.SEE.uh)
Ninevah (NI.ne.vuh)

oligarchy (O.li.gahr.kee)
Osiris (oh.SY.ris)
ostracon (O.stra.kawn)

palaeontologist (pay.lee.awn.TAWL.oh.jist)
Paleolithic (pay.lee.oh.LI.thik)
parthenon (PAR.the.nohn)
patrician (pa.TRI.shun)
Peisistratus (py.SIS.truh.tuhs)
Peloponnesian (pe.luh.puh.NEE.zhuhn)
Penelope (pe.NE.luh.pee)
Pericles (PE.ri.kleez)
Persephone (puhr.SE.fuh.nee)

Persepolis (puhr.SE.puh.lis)
Petrarch (PE.trahrk)
pharaoh (FAH.roh)
Pharsalus (FAHR.sah.luhs)
Phoenicia (fih.NEE.shuh)
Pindar (PIN.dar)
Piraeus (py.REE.uhs)
Plataea (pla.TEE.uh)
Plautus (PLOH.tuhs)
plebian (pli.BEE.uhn)
Pontius Pilate (PON.shuhs PY.luht)
Pompeii (pom.PAY)
Poseidon (poh.SY.duhn)
praetorian (pray.TOH.ree.uhn)
Priam (PRY.uhm)
propylaea (pro.pi.LAY.a)
pterodactyl (ter.o.DAK.til)
Ptolemy (TO.le.mee)
Punic (PYOO.nik)
Pythagoras (pi.THA.guh.ruhs)

Ramadan (ra.ma.DAN)
Ramses (RAM.seez)
Re (RAY)
Remus (REE.muhs)
Rheims (REEMZ)
Roland (ROH.land)
Romulus (ROM.u.luhs)

Saladin (SA.luh.din)
Salamis (SA.luh.mis)
Schliemann (SHLEE.mahn)
scutage (SKYOO.tij)
Scylla (SI.luh)
Segovia (se.GOH.vyah)
Seleucus (se.LOO.shuhs)
Sinai (SY.ny)
Sluys (SLWEE)
Sophocles (SO.fuhk.leez)
Spartacus (SPAHR.tik.uhs)
Sulla (SUH.luh)
Sumer (SOO.muhr)
Sumeria (soo.MEER.ia)
Susa (SOO.zuh)
suzerain (SOO.zuh.ruhn)

Teutonic (too.TO.nik)
Thales (THAY.leez)
Thebes (THEEBZ)
Theodosius (thee.uh.DOH.shuhs)
Thermopylae (thuhr.MO.pi.lie)
Thrace (THRAYS)
Thucydides (thoo.SI.di.deez)
Tiglathpilesar (ti.glath.puh.LEE.zuhr)
Tigris (TY.gris)
Titus (TY.tuhs)
Totila (TOH.ti.luh)
Torah (TOH.ruh)
Tours (TOOR)
Trajan (TRAY.juhn)
Trasimeno (trah.zee.MAY.noh)
Triumvirate (try.UHM.vir.it)
Tyne (TYN)

Vandals (VAN.duhlz)
Varro (VA.roh)
Via Sacra (VEE.uh SA.kra)
vizier (VI.zier)
Vulgate (VUHL.gayt)

Wycliffe (WI.klif)

Xanthippus (zan.TI.puhs)
Xerxes (ZOORK.seez)

Yahweh (YAH.we)
Yangtze (YANG.see)

Zama (ZAY.muh)
Zeus (ZOOS)
ziggurat (ZI.goo.rat)

INDEX

NOTE: If a page reference is in italics, the information is contained in the illustration, caption or map only. Ruling dates are given for kings and popes; life dates for all others.

Aachen, 201, 202
Abelard, Peter (1079-1142), 232
Abraham (c. 1800 B.C.), 23
Abu Simbel, 57
Acropolis, 84, 91, 96, 106, 125, 126
Adrianople, battle of (378), 197, 198-9
Adriatic Sea, 88, 148-9, 198-9, 201, 202-3
Aegean Sea, 81, 82, 83, 84, 85, 86, 87, 88, 89, 94, 148-9
Aeschylus (525-456 B.C.), 132
Agamemnon, of Troy, 81
Age of the Heroes. See Greece, Mycenean period
Age of Pericles, 109, 111
Age of Tyrants. See Greece
Agincourt, battle of (1415), 210, 220, 272
Agora, 84, 96, 97, 106, 108, 109
Agriculture
    Egyptian, 28, 59
    Greek, 82, 98
    Medieval Europe, 196, 198-9, 202, 205, 216, 228, 233-6, 250, 270
    Moslem Empire, 239
    Near Eastern, 16, 19
    Neolithic, 10-12, 13, 15-16, 28
    Roman Empire, 156, 163-4, 166
    Roman Republic, 141, 150, 151
Aigues-Mortes, 202-3, 240
Akkadian Empire, 16-17, 20
Alexander, the Great (356-323 B.C.), 26, 29, 92-5, 136, 139
Alexandria, 57, 93, 94, 148-9, 167
Alfred, the Great (871-899), 204, 211
Alphabet. See Writing, Near Eastern
Alps, 148, 148-9, 162, 249
Amenhotep IV. See Ikhnaton
Amorites, 20
Amos (c. 750 B.C.), 24
Amsterdam, 260-1, 264
Ananias, 190
Angles, 197
Anglo-Saxons, 200, 201, 204, 211, 212, 279
Anjou, 210, 216
Antigonus, of Macedonia (382?-301 B.C.), 95
Antioch, 148-9, 167
Antony, Mark. See Mark Antony
Antwerp, 260-1
Appian Way, 164, 191
Aquinas, St. Thomas (1225-1274), 232
Aquitaine, 201, 210, 216
Arabia, 31, 57, 167, 198, 202-3, 232, 237, 239.
    See also Moslem Empire
Aral Sea, 94
Arcadia, 85
Architecture. See Art and Architecture
Argolis, 85
Argos, 85
Aristophanes (450-385 B.C.), 133
Aristotle (384-322 B.C.), 93, 103, 134, 136
Armenia, 148-9, 155
Art and Architecture
    Chinese, 32, 36, 38, 42, 48-9, 54
    Egyptian, 28, 29, 56, 60-2, 71-5

Greek, 78, 82, 83, 95, 112, 121, 125-7
Medieval Europe, 196, 233, 270, 276-7, 278, 279
Moslem Empire, 239
Near Eastern, 19, 20
Paleolithic, 10
Roman Empire, 155, 166, 178, 180, 181-3
Roman Republic, 141
Asia, 15, 152, 262
Asia Minor, 16-17, 20, 29, 88, 198-9, 202-3, 243
    and Greeks, 81, 83, 84, 89, 90, 92-4, 115
    and Persians, 116, 119
    and Romans, 148, 149
Assur, 16-17
Assyria, 16-17, 18, 20, 22, 23, 24, 25
Asurbanipal, of Assyria (668-631 B.C.), 18
Athens, 78, 84, 85, 88, 94, 95, 96-111, 198-9, 240. See also Greece
    culture, 90, 91, 100, 104, 125-7, 137
    education, 103-5
    government, 88, 90, 100, 106-11
    growth of empire, 89-90, 98, 110
    law, 107-9
    and Persian Wars, 89, 98, 115-16, 118
    slaves in, 100, 101
    social and economic conditions, 96, 97, 98, 100-1, 103, 110
    struggle for reforms, 110-11
    trade, 98, 100
    wars with Sparta, 90-1, 92, 109
Attica, 84, 85, 89, 98, 110, 118
Attila, the Hun (406-453), 197
Augustine, St. (354-430), 228
Augustus (27 B.C.-A.D. 14), 158, 164, 168, 181
    reform of army, 154, 160
    reform of government, 154-5, 159-60, 161
Avignon Papacy, 275

Babylon, 16-17, 20, 93, 94
Babylonian Captivity, 22, 25
Babylonian Empire (first), 20, 24
Babylonian Empire (second), 20-2, 77
Balearic Is., 198-9
Ball, John (d.1381), 274
Baltic Sea, 148-9, 198-9, 201, 202-3
Barbarian invasions. See Barbarians (Germanic); Huns; Magyar invasions; Viking invasions
Barbarians (Germanic)
    agriculture, 198-9
    effects of invasions, 198-9, 250, 259
    government, 199-200, 214
    law, 200
    invasions of, 157, 158, 163, 193, 197-8, 198-9, 221, 225
Barcelona, 198-9
Bavaria, 201, 205
Beauce, 235
Becket, Thomas à (1117-1170), 221
Belgium, 197
Belgrade, 260-1
Benedict, St. (480-543), 224-6
Bernard, St. (1090-1153), 229, 247
Bethlehem, 148-9, 184, 202-3, 240
Bible, the, 187. See also ·New Testament; Old Testament
Bismarck (1815-1898), 211
Bithynia, 148-9, 152
Black Death, 272-4

Black Sea, 15, 87, 88, 94, 152, 196, 198-202-3, 260-1
Blois, 210
Boccaccio, Giovanni, 278, 279
Boeotia, 85
Bohemia, 201, 264
Boniface VIII, Pope (1294-1303), 275
Bordeaux, 260-1
Bosphorus, Strait of, 88
Bouvines, battle of (1214), 210, 218
Bremen, 260-1, 263
Britain. See England
Brittany, 210, 216
Bronze Age, 81
Budapest, 260-1
Buddhism, 44-6, 49
Burgundy, 201, 205, 210
Byzantine Empire, 148-9, 158, 162, 197-8, 200, 201, 202-3, 239, 240
Byzantium, 32, 148-9. See also Constantinopl

Caesar, Julius (102?-44 B.C.), 152, 153-4, 159, 166, 168, 181
Calais, 210, 220
Canaan. See Palestine
Cannae, battle of (216 B.C.), 148, 148-9
Canossa, 223, 260-1
Capetian, Hugh (987-996), 216
Capetians, 205, 216-20, 263, 274
Capua, 164
Carcassonne, 259, 260-1
Carolingians, 200-2, 211
Carthage, 22, 88, 146-8, 149, 150, 152, 197, 198-9. See also Punic Wars
Caspian Sea, 15, 16-17, 94, 148-9, 155, 159, 202-3, 239
Cathay. See China
Catiline (c. 108-62 B.C.), 181
Cato (234-149 B.C.), 179
Caucasus Mts., 94, 148-9
Cecrops, of Athens, 126
Celts, 143, 200
Central Asia, 50, 196, 270
Chalcidice, 85
Chalcis, 85
Chaldeans, 16-17, 20-2
Champagne, Duchy of, 210, 262-3, 264
Charlemagne (771-814), 200-1, 203, 205, 211, 236
Chartres, 233, 235, 261
Chaucer, Geoffrey (1340-1400), 278, 279
Ch'en dynasty, 34, 36
Children's Crusade, 249
Ch'in dynasty, 31, 37, 52
China, 15, 30-55, 198, 270
    art and architecture, 32, 36, 38, 42, 48-9, 54
    Ch'en dynasty, 34, 36
    Ch'in dynasty, 31, 37, 52
    Chou dynasty, 30-1
    education, 39, 40, 41, 43, 47
    government, 31, 37-40
    Han Empire, 32, 35, 37, 38, 39, 40, 44, 46, 47, 48-50, 52, 55
    law, 42-3
    literature and learning, 32, 38, 46-8
    Manchu dynasty, 33, 40, 55
    Ming dynasty, 33
    Mongols, 32-3, 40, 55, 270, 271
    philosophy, 35-7
    religion, 43-6

science and technology, 49-50
Shang dynasty, 30, 48, 49
social organization, 40-3
Sung dynasty, 32, *48*
T'ang dynasty, 32, *38*
trade, 32, 52, 167, 239, 261, 272
writing, 31, 46
Christianity, 22, 184-194. *See also* Church,
the; Eastern Church
  becomes state religion, 192
  contributions of, 192, 194
  life of Christ, 184-9
  organization of, 162, 193-4
  persecution of, 155, 177, 191-2
  spread of, 46, 158, 183, 190, 192, 194
  teachings of, 187, 191, 194
Christians. *See* Christianity
Church, the, 221-36, 274-6. *See also* Christianity; Eastern Church
  in Dark Ages
    and culture and learning, 221, 228
    decline of, 229
    and economy and society, 221, 228
    and feudalism, 223
    monasteries, 224-8
    organization of, *197*, 221-2
    struggle with kings, *221*, 222-3
  1000-1300
    and architecture, 233-6
    and learning, 231-2
    and literature, 232
    reform movements, 229-30, 270
  after 1300
    Avignon Papacy, 275
    Great Schism, 274, 275, 276
    growth of abuses, 270, 274
    reformers, 275
Cilicia, *148-9*
Cistercians, 229
Cleisthenes, 111
Cleopatra (69-30 B.C.), *153*
Clermont, Council of, *202-3*, 242, 243
Clovis (468-511), 200
Cluny, 223, 229
College of Cardinals, 221
Cologne, *260-1*, 263
Colosseum, Roman, 168, 173, *177*, 178
Columba, St. (521-597), 228
Commerce. *See* Economy; Trade
Confucius (551-479 B.C.), *35*, 37, 44
Confucianism, 35-44 *passim*
Constance, Council of, *210*, 276
Constantine, Emperor (305-337), 157-9, 192
Constantinople, 158, 172, 193, 198, *201*,
202-3, 239, *260-1*
  and Crusades, 237, *240*, 243, 244, 247
Corinth, *85*, *88*, 92, *148-9*
Corpus Iuris Civilis, 163
Corsica, *88*, 146, *148-9*, 149, *198-9*, 201, *202-3*
Crassus (53 B.C.), 152-3
Crécy, battle of (1346), *210*, 220, 271, 272
Crete, 80, 81-2, 83, *85*, *88*, *94*, *198-9*, *202-3*
Croesus, of Lydia (560-c. 540 B.C.), 133
Cro-Magnon Man, 6, *8*, *15*
Crusades, 222, 237, 240-9, 261
Culture. *See* Agriculture; Art and Architec-
  ture; Economy; Government; Law;
  Literature and Learning; Philosophy;
  Population; Religion; Science and Tech-
  nology; Social Organization; Trade;
  Writing

Cuneiform. *See* Writing, Near Eastern
Cyprus, *16-17*, *57*, *88*, *94*, *198-9*, *202-3*
Cyrus, of Persia (c. 549-529 B.C.), 22

Dacia, *141*, *148-9*, 155
Damascus, *57*, *148-9*, 190
Damietta, *202-3*, 248
Danelaw, 204
Dante, Alighieri (1265-1321), 277, 279
Danube R., *88*, *94*, *141*, *148-9*, 154, *155*, *164*,
  196, *198-9*, *202-3*, 203, *260-1*
Danzig, *260-1*, 263
Dardanelles, 81, *85*, 87, *116*
Darius, of Persia (521-485 B.C.), 88-9, 115,
  116, 119
Dark Ages (A.D. 400-1000), 196-204. *See also*
  Church, the; Feudalism; Medieval Europe
Dark Ages, Greek, 84, 110, 111
David (c. 1012-c. 972 B.C.), 23, 26
Dead Sea, *16-17*
Delian League, 90
Delos, *85*, *88*, *116*
Delphi, *85*, *116*
Democracy, 79, 88, 90, 91, 100, 196, 200, 269
  development of, 110-11
  government under, 106-9
Democritus (c. 460-c. 370 B.C.), 137
Diocletian, Emperor (284-305), 157, 158
Dnieper R., *198-9*, *202-3*
Dniester R., *198-9*
Dominicans, 229, 230
Don R., *202-3*
Dorians, 83-4, 111
Dragon Throne, 32

East Asia, 35
Eastern Church, the, *162*, 193, 242
Eastern Roman Empire. *See* Byzantine
  Empire
East Goths, 197
Ebro R., *198-9*
Ecbatana, *94*
Economy. *See also* Trade
  Egyptian, 29, 60, 63
  Greek, 97, 98, 100
  Medieval Europe, *202*, 205, 221, 228, 243,
    250, 251, 264-72 *passim*
  Neolithic, 10-13
  Roman Empire, 156, 163, 164, 167, 170,
    174-5
  Roman Republic, 141, 149-50
Education
  Athenian, 103-5
  Chinese, 39, 40, 41, 43, *47*
  Egyptian, *76*
  Medieval Europe, *202*, 221, 228, 243, 250,
    251
  Spartan, 113
Edward I, of England (1272-1307), 214
Egypt, *15*, *16-17*, 20, *24*, 26, 27-9, 56-77, 88,
  93, *94*, 95, *148-9*, 185, *202-3*, 239, 249
  agriculture, 28, 59
  art and architecture, 28, 29, 56, 60-2, 71-5
  economy, 29, 60, 63
  education, *76*
  expansion of, 29, 58
  government, 28, 29, 58
  law, 29
  literature and learning, 76-7
  Middle Kingdom, 28-9, 74
  New Kingdom, 27, 28, 29, 58, 63, 74

Old Kingdom, 28, 71
  religion, 29, 58, 66-70, 71
  and Rome, 146, 152, 159, 163, 166
  science and technology, 29, 77
  slavery in, 63, 64, 71, 251
  social organization, 58, 59, 63-5
  trade, 28, 29, 63, 98
  writing, 27, 28, 29, 76
Elbe R., *198-9*, 201, *202-3*
Eleusis, *85*
Engineering. *See* Science and Technology
England, *148-9*, *198-9*, *202-3*, *210*, 211-16. *See*
  also Medieval Europe
  under Anglo-Saxons, 200, 204
  barbarian invasions, 197, 198
  civil war, 216
  common law, 211-14, 215
  growth of Parliament, 214-15
  growth of royal power, 205, 211-14
  Hundred Years' War, *210*, 214, 218-19, 220,
    274
  literature and learning, 278, 279
  Magna Carta, 214
  Norman invasions, 211, 212-13
  peasant rebellion (1381), 274
  under Rome, 152, 155, 159, *163*, *164*, 166,
    172, 196
  social organization, 274
  trade, 98, 259, 262
  Viking invasions, 203-4
  wars with France, 214, 216-18, 220
English Channel, 203, *210*
Estates-General, 218
Etruscans, 141, 144
Euboea, *85*
Euphrates R., 15, 16, *16-17*, 19, 33, *94*, *148-9*,
  154, *156-7*, *202-3*
Euripedes (480-406 B.C.), 132
Europe. *See* Medieval Europe
Eurotas R., *85*, 111

Fabius (?-c. 203 B.C.), 148
Far East, 167, 264
Fertile Crescent, 16, *16-17*, 17-26, 27, 28
Feudalism
  decline of, 268-9, 271-9
  effects of, 205-8, 250, 259
  growth of, 204-5
  life under, 209-10, 211, 214, 216
  relationships of, 204, 206-7, 208, 271-2
First Crusade, 243-6, 249
Flanders, *210*, 259, 262
Florence, *260-1*, 262, 268, 277
Forum, Roman, *166*, 168
Fourth Crusade, 247, 249
France, *210*, 216-26. *See also* Medieval Europe
  art, *216*
  barbarian invasions, 197, 198, 200
  under Capetians
    government, 218-20, 274
    growth of royal power, 205, 216-20, 263
    Hundred Years' War, *210*, 214, 218-19,
      220, 274
    other wars with England, 214, 216-18,
      220
  under Carolingians, 200-2, 211
    Treaty of Verdun, 201
  early Frankish kingdom, 200
  law, *216*, 218
  literature and learning, *216*, 279

283

Moslem invasions, 202
peasant rebellions, 274
social organization, 274
trade, 216, 259, 262
Viking invasions, 203
Francis, St. (1182?-1226), 229-30
Franciscans, 229-30
Franks, 196, 197, 198, 200
Frederick II (1220-1250), 248
Frederick Barbarossa (1155-1190), 247

Galatia, *148-9, 154*
Gallic War (58-51 B.C.), *152*, 153, 154
Gard R., *148-9, 172*
Gascony, *210*, 216
Gaugamela, *94*
Gaul, *148-9*, 166, *198-9, 202-3*
    barbarians in, 157, 158, 197, 198, 200
    and Rome, 141-3, 149, 152, 153, 154, *163*
Genghis Khan (1206-1227), 32, 261, *270*
Genoa, *202-3*, 211, 249, *260-1*, 272, 277
Germany, *148-9, 155*, 196, 198, 211, 249
Gibraltar, Strait of, *198-9, 202-3*
Giotto di Bandone (1266-1337), 279
Gizeh, *16-17*, 56, *57*, 71
Goths, 196, 197, 198
Government
    Chinese, 31, 33, 37-40
    Egyptian, 28, 29, 58
    Greek, 79, 83, 84, 88, 90, 91, 100, 106-9,
        110-11, 113
    Indian, 33
    Medieval Europe, 196, 199-200, 214, 268-9,
        271, 272, 277
    Near Eastern, 16, 18, 20
    Neolithic, 13
    Persian, 22
    Roman Empire, 154-5, 159-61, 163, 164,
        166, 180, 200
    Roman Republic, 144-6, *148*, 149-54, 159-
        60, 181
Gracchus, Gaius (153-121 B.C.), 151-2
Gracchus, Tiberius (163-133 B.C.), 151
Granicus R., *94*
Great Charter. *See* Magna Carta
Greater Greece, 87, *88*
Great Pyramid, 56
Great Schism, 274, 275, 276
Great Wall, of China, 31, 55
Greece, 78-137, 139, *148-9*, 197, *198-9*. *See also*
    Athens; Sparta
    Age of Tyrants, 88
    agriculture, 82, 98
    and Alexander the Great, 92-3, 94, 139
    art and architecture, 78, 82, 83, 95, 112,
        121, 125-7
    colonization by, 83, 84-7, 99
    Cretan period, 81-2
    Dark Ages, 84, 110, 111
    Dorian invasions, 83-4, 111
    economy, 97, 98, 100
    government, 79, 83, 84, 88, 90, 91, 100,
        106-9, 110-11, 113
    law, 79, 95, 107-9
    legacy of, 78-9, 121, 196, 232, 277, 278
    literature and learning, 78, 81, 83, 104, 121,
        125, 128-33
    Mycenean period, 82-3, 84
    Peloponnesian Wars, 90-1, 92, 95, 109
    Persian Wars, 88-90, 98, 114-19, 121, 126

philosophy, 79, 134-6
population, 84, 87, 98
religion, 86, 120-4, 125, 131
rise of city-states, 84, 87, 110
and Rome, *143*, 149, 180, 181-3
science and technology, 78, 137
slavery in, 100, 101, 103, 145, 251
social organization, 84, 87, 96-7, 100-5, 111,
    112-13
trade, 81-2, 83, 84, 87, 98, 100
writing, 80-1
Gregory VII, Pope (1073-1085), 222, *223*, 229
Gregory the Great, Pope (590-604), 197
Guilds, 268, 271, 272, 274

Hadrian, Emperor (117-138), *156*
Hadrian's Wall, *148-9, 156*, 159, 196, *198-9*
Hamburg, *260-1*, 263
Hammurabi, of Amorites (c. 1750 B.C.), 20,
    22
Han Empire, *31, 32*, 35-55 *passim*
Han Kao Tsu. *See* Liu Pang
Hannibal (247-183 B.C.), 147-8
Hanseatic League, 263
Harappa, *15*, 33
Harold Hardrada (1046-1066), 212
Harold, of England (1066), 212, 213, 232
Hastings, battle of (1066), *210*, 212-13, 216
Hebrews, 22, 23-6, 70
Hellas. *See* Greece
Hellespont, *85, 116. See also* Dardanelles
Henry II, of England (1154-1189), 211-14,
    216-18, *221*
Henry V, of England (1413-1422), 220
Henry VII, of England. *See* Henry Tudor
Henry IV, of Germany (1069-1106), 222, *223*
Henry Tudor (1485-1509), 216
Heptarchy, 200
Herod, the Great (37-4 B.C.), 185, 278
Herodotus (484?-425? B.C.), 89, 103, 115,
    116, 117, 133
Hesiod, 103
Hierakonpolis, *57*
Hieroglyphics. *See* Writing, Egyptian
Hippocrates (460?-377? B.C.), 137
Hittites, 20, 22
Holland, 197, 279
Homer (c. 800 B.C.), 80-1, 83, 104, 128, 129,
    130, 131, 181
Hosea (750 B.C.), 24
House of Commons, 214
House of Lords, 214
Hsüan Ti, Emperor (557-589), *36*
Hundred Years' War (1337-1473), *210*, 214,
    218-19, 220, *271*, 274
Huns, 196-7
Huss, John (1369-1415), 276
Hyksos, *27*, 29

Ice Age, 6
Ideographs. *See* Writing, Chinese
Ikhnaton (c. 1375-c. 1358 B.C.), 70
Illyria, *85*
Illyricum, *148-9*
India, *15, 31, 32, 33*, 44, 55, 88, 94, 167, 198
Indus R., *15, 33, 94*
Innocent III, Pope (1198-1216), 222, 249
Inquisition, 230
Ionia, 84, *85, 88*, 93, 115
Ireland, *201, 202-3*, 203

Isaac, *23*
Islam, 22, 198, 238-9. *See also* Moslem Empire
Israel, 23, 24, 26
Italy, 98, *148-9, 197, 198-9, 201, 202-3*, 211,
    232. *See also* Rome

Japan, *31, 32*
Japan, Sea of, 31
Jarmo, 10, *16-17*
Java Man, *8, 15*
Jericho, 10, *57*
Jerusalem, *16-17*, 22, 23, 25, 26, *57, 148-9*, 182,
    190, *202-3, 240*, 243
    and Crusades, 244, 245, 246, 247, 248, 271
Jesus, 184-9. *See also* Christianity
Jews, 237, *238*, 239
Joan of Arc (1412-1431), 218-19, 220
John the Baptist, 186
John, of England (1199-1216), 214, 222
Jordan R., *16-17*, 23, *148-9*, 186
Joseph, 185
Joseph of Arimathea, 189
Judaea, *148-9, 154*, 184, 185
Judah, 23, 26
Judaism, 22, 23, 26. *See also* Hebrews
Judas Iscariot, 187, 188
Justinian, Emperor (527-565), 162, *163*, 198
Jutes, 197

Khan, Genghis. *See* Genghis Khan
Khufu, Pharaoh (c. 2600 B.C.), 56, 71
Knossos, 80, 81, 82, *85*
Koran, the, 239
Korea, *31*
Kublai Khan (1260-1294), 32, *33*, 261

Lagash, *16-17*, 19
Lancastrians, 216
Law
    Chinese, 42-3
    Egyptian, 29
    Greek, 79, 95, 107-9
    Medieval Europe, 196, 200, *202*, 205, *216*,
        218, 243, 250, 259
    Near Eastern, *22*
    Roman Empire, 139, 159, 160, 161-3, 188,
        189
    Roman Republic, 146, 162
League of Corinth, 92, 95
Legalism, 37
Leonidas, of Sparta (c. 491-480 B.C.), 89, 117
Lepidas (c. 13 B.C.), 154
Lesbos, *85*
Lisbon, *148-9, 260-1*
Literature and Learning. *See also* Education
    Chinese, 32, 38, 46-8
    Egyptian, 76-7
    Greek, 78, 81, 83, 104, 121, 125, 128-33
    Indian, 33
    Medieval Europe, 196, *216*, 228, 232, 270,
        276-9
    Moslem Empire, 239
    Near Eastern, 19
    Roman Empire, 139, 164-5, 180-1
    Roman Republic, 141
Liu Kuan-tao (c. 1300), *47*
Liu Pang (c. 206 B.C.), 31-2, *52*
Loire R., *198-9, 201, 202-3, 260-1*
Lombards, *197*, 198
Lombardy, 201

London, 198-9, 210, 260-1, 262, 263, 264, 274
Lost Ten Tribes, 24
Lothair, 201
Louis IX, of France (1226-1270), *216*, 240, 248
Louis, the German, 201
Lübeck, *260-1*, 263
Luxor, *57*
Lydia, *16-17*

Macedon. *See* Macedonia
Macedonia, 23, *85*, 89, 92-5, *94*, *116*, 146, 148, *148-9*, 149, 152, *198-9*
Magna Carta (1215), 214
Magyar invasions, 202-3, 205
Main R., *148-9*, 155
Manchu dynasty, 33, 40, 55
Manchuria, *31*, 33
Mandate of Heaven, 37-9
Marius (c. 155-86 B.C.), *151*, 173
Mark Antony (c. 83-30 B.C.), 154, *166*, 181
Mao Tse-Tung (1893-   ), *47*
Marathon, battle of (490 B.C.), *85*, 89, *90*, 98, 114-15, *116*
Marco Polo (1254?-1324?), 33
Marseilles, 87, *201*, 202, *202-3*, *260-1*, 272
Martel, Charles (688?-741), 198, 200, 204-5, 239, 240
Mary, Mother of Jesus, 185
Maspilia, *88*
Mathematics. *See* Science and Technology
Mecca, *202-3*, 238, 239
Medes, 20
Medieval Europe
   agriculture, 196, 198-9, *202*, 205, *216*, 228, 233-6, 250, 270
   art and architecture, 196, 233, 270, 276-7, *278*, 279
   barbarian invasions, 196-200, 202-4, 205, 221, 225, 229, 240, 250, 259
   role of Church, 221-36, 274-6
   and Crusades, 222, 237, 240-9, 261
   economy, *202*, 205, 221, 228, 243, 250, 251, 264-72 *passim*
   education, *202*, 221, 228, 231-2, 268, 270
   emergence of England and France, 205, 211-22
   feudalism, 204-10, 211, 214, 216, 250, 259, 268-9, 271-9
   government, 196, 199-200, 214, 268-9, 271, 272, 277
   law, 196, 200, *202*, 205, *216*, 218, 243, 250, 259
   literature and learning, 196, *216*, 228, 232, 270, 276-9
   and Moslem Empire, 198, 200-5 *passim*, 229, 232, 238-49, 271
   population, 251, 260, 262, 264, 270-1, 272
   religion, *202*, 273, 279. *See also* Church, the
   slaves in, 196, 251
   social organization, 228, 250, 251, 267, 268-9, 271-2, 274
   science and technology, 196, 232
   trade, 216, 229, 250, 259-64, 268, 270, 271, 272
   warfare, 204-5, 207, 211-20, 223, 237-49, 261, *270*, 271, 272, 274
   village and town, 250-69, 272-4
Medina, *202-3*, 238
Melos, *85*

Memphis, *16-17*, 28, *57*, *94*
Menander (342?-291? B.C.), 133
Menes, of Egypt, 28
Mesopotamia, 15-22 *passim*, 23, 76, *148-9*
Messana, 146, *148-9*
Messenia, *85*, 112
Middle Ages. *See* Medieval Europe
Middle East, 94, 196, 251
Middle Kingdom, Egyptian, 28-9, 74
Milan, *260-1*, 262
Miletus, *85*, *88*, *94*
Miltiades (c. 540-489 B.C.), 89, *90*, 115
Ming dynasty, 33
Minos, of Crete, 80, 81
Mohammed (570?-632), 198, 237-9
Mohenjo-Daro, *15*, 33
Monasteries
   contributions of, 227-8
   decline of, 229
   life in, 226-9
   reform of, 229-30
   revival of, 224-5
Money, effects of, 271-2, 274
Mongols, *31*, 32-3, 40, 55, *270*, 271
Moses, 23, 24, 26
Moslem Empire
   agriculture, 239
   art and architecture, 239
   and Crusades, 240, 243-9 *passim*, 271
   expansion of, 198, 200, 202, 204, 205, 229, 232, 239, 240
   Islam in, 198, 238-9
   legacy of, 239
   literature and learning, 239
   Mohammed, 198, 237-9
   science and technology, 239
   under Seljuk Turks, 240-7
   slavery in, *238*
   trade, 239, 243
   treatment of conquered lands, *238*, 239, 240, 247
Moslem invasions, 198, 200, 202, 204, 205, 229, 232, 239, 240
      Mount Sinai, *16-17*, 23, 24, 26, *57*
Mount Vesuvius, 170, **270**
Mulvian, battle of (312), 192
Mycale, battle of (479 B.C.), 89, *91*, *116*
Mycenae, 81, 82-3, 84, *85*, *88*

Naples, *88*, *201*, 225, *260-1*
Naxos, *85*
Nazareth, *148-9*, 185, *202-3*, 248
Neanderthal Man, 6, *8*, *15*
Near East, 15-29, 81, 82, 98, 183, 196. *See also* under individual countries
   agriculture, 16, 19, 28, 59
   art and architecture, 19, 20, 28, 29, 56, 60-2, 71-5, 183
   economy, 29, 60, 63
   government, 16, 18, 20, 28, 29, 58
   law, *22*, 24
   literature and learning, 19, 76-7
   religion, *18*, 19, 29, 58, 66-70, 71
   science and technology, 29, *29*, 77
   slavery in, 14, 19, 63, 64, 71
   social organization, 19, 58, 59, 63-5
   trade, 19, 22, 28, 29, 63
   writing, 16, 19, 22, 27, 28, 29, 76
Nebuchadnezzar (c. 605-563 B.C.), 20-2, 23, 25
Nefertiti (c. 1375-1358 B.C.), 70, 73

Neolithic Age, 10-16, 28, 81
   agriculture, 10-12, 13, 15-16, 28
   economy, 10-13
   government, 13
   population, 12, 15-16
   religion, 13
   science and technology, 12
   social organization, 12-13
   trade, 12
Nero, Emperor (54-68), 155, 168, 177, 191
New Kingdom, Egyptian, *27*, 28, 29, 58, 63, 74
New Stone Age. *See* Neolithic Age
New Testament, 184, 190
Nicaea, *202-3*, 243, *247*
Nile River, 33, 56, *57*, 59, 63, 74, 77, 78, *148-9*, 166, *202-3*
   gift of, 27-9, 60, 66, 68
   Neolithic civilization on, 15, 16, *16-17*
Nimrud, *16-17*
Ninevah, *16-17*, 20
Nirvana. *See* Buddhism
Nofretari (c. 1292-1225 B.C.), 74
Norman Conquest, 211, 212-13, 279
Normandy, *202-3*, 203, *210*
Norsemen, 203
Nubia, 29
Nuremberg, *260-1*, 263

Octavian. *See* Augustus
Oder R., *198-9*, 201, *202-3*
Odoacer, Emperor (476-493), 197
Old Kingdom, Egyptian, 28, 71
Old Stone Age. *See* Paleolithic Age
Old Testament, 23, 26, 77
Oligarchy, 88, 113
Olympus, Mount, *85*, *116*
Orléans, *210*, 219
Ostrogoths, 197
Otto, the Great (936-973), 203

Paleolithic Age, 8-10
Palestine, *16-17*, 23, 29, *57*, *94*, *148-9*, *202-3*
   and Christianity, 177, 184, 186, 187
   and Crusades, 248, 249
   and Moslems, 239, 240
Paris, *198-9*, *210*, *260-1*, 262, 264, 274
Paris, Treaty of (1259), 218, 220
Parliament, 214-15, 216
Parthenon, *78*, *91*, 125
Parthia, *148-9*, 155
Patricians, 144, 145-6
Patrick, St. (c. 385-461), 228
Paul, St. (d. 67?), 190-1, 193
Pax Romana (27 B.C.-A.D. 180), *148-9*, 159, 167
Peasant Crusade, *243*
Peasant rebellions, 274
Peisistratus (c. 605-527 B.C.), 110-11
Pella, *94*
Peloponnesian Wars, 90-1, 92, 95, 109
Peloponnesus, *85*
Pepin I (817-838), 200
Pericles (c. 495-429 B.C.), *91*, 96, 98, 100, 107, 109, 110
Persepolis, *16-17*, 20, *94*, 119
Persia, *16-17*, 20, 22, 23, 29, 32, 93-4, *116*, *148-9*, 167, *202-3*, 239. *See also* Persian Wars

Persian Wars (500-449 B.C.), 88-90, 98, 114-19, 121, 126
Peter, St. (d. 67?), 188, 190, 191, 193, 275
Petrarch, Francesco (1304-1374), 278, 279
Pharaohs, 28, 58, 59, 63, 65, 71-6 *passim*, 79, *154*
Pharsalus, battle of (48 B.C.), *148-9, 153*
Philip Augustus (1180-1223), 216, 247
Philip, of Macedon (359-336 B.C.), 92
Philistines, 23
Phillip the Fair (1285-1314), 275
Philosophy
    Chinese, 35-7
    Greek, 79, 134-6
    Roman Empire, 18, 139
    Roman Republic, 139, 143
Phoenicia, *16-17, 22, 88*
Pindar (c. 518-438 B.C.), 131
Piraeus, *85*, 98
Pisa, *202-3*, 243, *260-1*
Plague, 272-4, *275*
Plataea, battle of (479 B.C.), 89, *116*, 119, 126
Plato (429-347 B.C.), 103, 134
Plautus (c. 254-184 B.C.), *166*
Plebians, 144, 145-6
Poitiers, battle of (1356), *210*
Polis, rise of, 84, 87, 110
Pompeii, 170-1, *175*, 270
Pompey (106-48 B.C.), 152, 153-4
Pontius Pilate, 188, 189
Pontus, *148-9*, 152, *154*
Population
    Chinese, 38
    Greek, 84, 87, 98
    Medieval Europe, 251, 260, 262, 264, 270-1, 272
    Neolithic, 12, 15-16
    Roman Empire, 139, 159, 163, 166, 173
    Roman Republic, 143
Porus, of India (c. 325 B.C.), 94
Praetorian Guard, *161*
Pre-history, 3-13, 15, 49. *See also* Neolithic Age; Paleolithic Age
Prophets, Hebrew, 24, 26
Prussia, 211
Ptolemy I (304-283 B.C.), 95
Ptolemy XII (51-47 B.C.), *153*
Punic War, First (264-241 B.C.), 146-7
Punic War, Second (218-201 B.C.), 147-8, 149
Pyramids, 28, *29*, 56, 59, 60, 66, 71-3, 74
Pyrenees, Mts., *148-9, 202-3*, 239
Pythagoras (c. 582-507 B.C.), 137

Ramses (d. 1314 B.C.), 27
Ramses II (1292-1225 B.C.), 74
Realism. *See* Legalism
Red Sea, *15*, 63, *94, 148-9*
Religion. *See also* Christianity; Church, the; Eastern Church
    Chinese, 43-6
    Egyptian, 28, 58, 66-70, 71
    Greek, 86, 120-4, 125, 131
    Hebrew, 23-6
    Medieval Europe, *202*, 273, 279. *See also* Church, the
    Near Eastern, *18*, 19
    Neolithic, 13
    Persian, 22
    Roman Empire, 155, *166*, 183, 191. *See also* Christianity

Rhine R., 6, *148-9, 154, 164*, 196, *198-9, 201, 202-3, 260-1*
Rhodes, 83, *85*, 86, *88, 116*
Rhone R., *88*, 148, *148-9, 198-9, 201, 202-3 260-1*
Richard I, the Lionhearted, of England (1189-1199), 218
Richard II, of England (1377-1399), 274
River Valley Civilizations, 15-33
Roman Empire, 23, 35, 139, 154-83. *See also* Byzantine Empire; Rome, Decline and Fall of
    agriculture, 156, 163-4, 166
    art and architecture, 155, 166, 168, 178, 180, 181-3
    and Christians, 155, 158, 177, 183, 190, 191-2, 224
    economy, 156, 163, 164, 167, 170, 174-5
    education, 179-80
    entertainment, 168, 173-9
    expansion of, 139, *154, 161, 162*
    government, 154-5, 159-61, 163, 164, *166*, 180, 200
    and Greeks, 95, *143*, 149, 180, 181-3
    law, 139, 159, 160, 161-3, 188, 189
    legacy of, 139, 161-2, 163, 165, 196, 221, 278
    literature and learning, 139, 164-5, 180-1
    Pax Romana (A.D. 96-180), *148-9*, 159, 167
    philosophy, 139, 180
    policy towards colonies, 155, 160, 161, 162
    religion, 155, *166*, 183, 191
    roads and communications, 159, *164*, 165, 166, 172
    role of army, *154*, 155, 156-7, 158, 159, 160, *161*, 165
    science and technology, 139, 163, 165, 172, 180, 183
    slaves in, 166, 175, 177, 179
    social organization, 173-9, 180
    trade, 32, 156, 164-7, 251
Rome, *148-9, 198-9, 201, 202-3*, 225, *260-1*
Rome, Decline and Fall of
    barbarian invasions, 157, 158, 163, 193, 197-9, 260
    division of empire, 158
    Odoacer, Emperor (476), 158, 197, 198
    reasons for, 156-7, 158, *161*, 196-7
Rome and Roman Republic, 139-54. *See also* Roman Empire
    agriculture, 141, 150, 151
    art and architecture, 141
    economy, 141, 149-50
    under Etruscans, 141
    expansion of, 141-4, 145, 146-9, 151, 152-4
        effects of, 149-50
        First Punic War, 146-7
        reasons for, 141-3, 146, 149
        reasons for success of, 143-4, *148*
        Second Punic War, 147-8
    government, 144-6, *148*, 149-54, 159-60
        First Triumvirate, *152*, 153
        Second Triumvirate, 154, 181
    law, 146, 162
    literature and learning, 141
    philosophy, 139, 141
    policy towards conquered people, 144, 149
    struggle for reforms, 144-6, 149-52, 162
        Gracchi brothers, 151-2
    role of army, *142*, 143-44, 146, *147, 148*

science and technology, 139
slaves in, 149, 150, 153, 179
social organization, 143, 144-6, 149, *150*
trade, 141, 152
Rouen, 210, 219
Rubicon R., *148-9*, 154
Russia, *202-3*, 203, 239

Sahara Desert, 56, *148-9*
Saladin (1169-1193), 247
Salamis, battle of (480 B.C.), *85*, 89, 98, *116*, 118
Samos, *85, 116*
Sardinia, *88*, 146, *148-9*, 149, *198-9, 201, 202-3*, 243, 247
Sardis, *16-17, 94, 116*
Sargon, of Akkadia (c. 2400 B.C.), 20
Sargon II (722-705 B.C.), 24
Saul (c. 1025 B.C.), 23, 26
Saul of Tarsus. *See* Paul
Saxons, 196, 204. *See also* Anglo-Saxons
Saxony, 205
Scandinavia, *201, 202-3*, 203
Schliemann, Heinrich (1822-1890), 81
Science and Technology
    Chinese, 49-50
    Egyptian, 29, 77
    Greek, 78, 137
    Indian, 33
    Medieval Europe, 196, 232
    Moslem Empire, 239
    Near Eastern, 20
    Neolithic, 12
    Roman Empire, 139, 163, 165, 172, 180, 183
Scipio (234?-183 B.C.), 148
Sculpture. *See* Art and Architecture
Second Crusade, 247
Seine R., *198-9, 202-3, 260-1*
Segovia, *148-9*
Seleucid Empire, 94
Seleucus, of Persia (c. 312-280 B.C.), 94
Seljuk Turks, 94, 240-7
Serfs, 251, 274
Shang dynasty, 30, *31*, 48, 49
Sicily, 87, *88*, 146, 147, 148, 149, *198-9*, 200, *202-3*
Siddhartha Gautama (c. 563-483 B.C.), *44*. *See also* Buddhism
Sidon, *16-17, 57*
Silesia, *201, 270*
Sixth Crusade, 248
Slavery
    Egyptian, 63, 64, 71, 251
    Greek, 100, 101, 103, 251
    Medieval Europe, 196, 251
    Moslem Empire, *238*
    Near Eastern, 14, 19
    Roman Empire, 166, 175, 177, 179, 251
    Roman Republic, 149, 150, 153, 179
Sluys, battle of (1340), 210, 220
Social Organization
    Chinese, 40-3
    Egyptian, 58, 59, 63-5
    Greek, 84, 87, 96-7, 100-5, 111, 112-13
    Near Eastern, 19
    Neolithic, 12-13
    Roman Empire, 173-9, 180
    Roman Republic, 143, 144-6, 149, *150*
Socrates (469-399 B.C.), 109, 111, 134, 135
Solomon (c. 970-932 B.C.), 23, 26

…on (c. 639-599 B.C.), 110, 111
…hocles (496-406 B.C.), 79, 132
…in, *148-9, 198-9, 201, 202-3*
   barbarian invaders in, 157, 158, 197, 198, *238*
   and Moslems, 200, 232, 239
   and Rome, *143*, 147, 148, 149, 152, *153*, 159, 162, *164*, 165, 196
…arta, *85, 88, 94*, 111-13, *116*
   culture, 112
   education, 113
   expansion of, 112
   government, 88, 113
   social organization, 111-13
   wars with Athens, 90-1, 92, 109
…artacus (?-c. 71 B.C.), 153
… Han-Ch'en (c. 1300), 54
…lla (138-78 B.C.), 152
…mer, *16-17*
…ng dynasty, 32, *48*
…sa, *16-17*, 94
…zerain. *See* Feudalism, relationships of
…racuse, 87, *88*, 146, 148, *148-9*
…ria, *16-17*, 20, 29, 57, *94*, 95, 146, 148, *148-9*, 152, 167, 184, *202-3*, 239

…'ai Tsung, Emperor, 46
…agus R., *198-9*
…'ang dynasty, *31*, 32, *38*
…aoism, 37, 44, *48*
…arentum, *88*
…aygetus Mts., *85*
…hales, 137
…hames R., 6
…hebes, 29, 57, 68, 74, *116*
…hemistocles (c. 525-460 B.C.), 116, 118
…heodosius, Emperor (379-395), 192
…hermopylae, battle of (480 B.C.), 89, *116*, 117
…heseus, 110, 115
…hessaly, *85*
…hird Crusade, 247
…hrace, *85*, 89, 92, *94, 116, 148-9*, 152
…hucydides (c. 460-c. 400 B.C.), 133
…iber R., *141, 148-9*
…ibet, *31*

Tiglathpileser III, of Assyria (745-727 B.C.), 24
Tigris R., 15, 16, *16-17*, 19, 33, *94, 148-9*, 165 *202-3*
Tiryns, *85*
Titus, Emperor (79-81), 168, 182
Torah, the, *26*
Totila, of the Goths (d. 552), 225
Toulouse, *198-9, 210*
Tours, battle of (732), *202-3*, 239, 240
Town, medieval, *198-9*, 259-69, 272-4
   effects of, 268-9
   life in, 262-3, 264-9
   and trade, 260-2, 263-4
Trade
   Chinese, 32, 52, 167, 239, 261, 272
   Egyptian, 28, 29, 63
   Greek, 81-2, 83, 84, 98, 100
   Medieval Europe, 216, 229, 250, 251, 259-64, 268, 270, 271, 272
   Moslem Empire, 239, 243
   Near Eastern, 19, 22
   Neolithic, 12
   Roman Empire, 156, 164-6, 251
   Roman Republic, 141, 152
Trajan, Emperor (98-117), *141, 155, 156, 177, 191*
Trappist Monks, 226
Trasimeno, Lake, 148, *148-9*
Trojan War, 80, *82*, 83, *128-9*
Troy, 80, 81, 83, *85*, 128, 129, 141
Troyes, battle of (451), 197, *198-9*
Ts'ao Ts'ao (c. 221), *47*
Tunisia, *163*, 249
Turks. *See* Moslem Empire; Seljuk Turks
Tutankhamen, Pharaoh, (c. 1366-1357 B.C.), 66-7, 70, 73
Twelve Tables, the, 146, 162
Tyler, Wat (d. 1381), 274
Tyre, *16-17*, 57, *94, 260-1*
Tyrrhenian Sea, *148-9*

Ur, *16-17, 18*, 19
Ural R., *202-3*
Urban II, Pope (1088-1099), 240, 242, 243

Vandals, 196, 197, 198
Varro (? -216 B.C.), 148
Vassal. *See* Feudalism, relationships of
Venice, *201, 202-3*, 211, 249, *260-1*, 262, 277
Vespasian, Emperor (69-79), 168
Viking invasions, 203-4, 205, 229, 240
Village, medieval, 250-7, 271
Virgil (70?-19 B.C.), 180-1
Visigoths, 158, 197, *238*
Vistula R., *198-9, 202-3*
Volga R., *202-3*

Warfare. *See* individual countries; individual wars; weapons
Weapons, 10, 12, *32*
   Greek, 81, *83*, 87-8, *89, 90, 91*, 105, *112*, 115-19 *passim*, 128-30 *passim, 143*
   Medieval, 204-5, 208, 209, 212-13, 215, *243*, 245, 271, 272
   Near Eastern, *18, 20, 27, 29*, 60
   Roman, 142, 143, *147, 148, 151, 154, 155, 161*
Wen'Ti, Emperor of China (559-566), 34
West Goths, 197
Western Roman Empire. *See* Roman Empire
William the Conqueror, 211, 212, 216
Writing
   Chinese, 31, 46
   Egyptian, *27, 28, 29*, 76
   Greek, 80-1
   Near Eastern, 16, 19, 22, 76
Wycliffe, John (1328-1384), 276

Xanthippus (c. 400 B.C.), *91*
Xerxes, of Persia (485-465 B.C.), 89, 90, 98, 116-17

Yangtze R., 30, *31*, 36
Yellow R., 15, 30, *31*, 33
Yen Li-pen, 34, 36
Yorkists, 216

Zalla, of Goths, 225
Zama, battle of (202 B.C.), 148, *148-9*